The University of Michigan
Center for South and Southeast Asian Studies

MICHIGAN PAPERS ON SOUTH AND SOUTHEAST ASIA

Ann Arbor, Michigan

PĀṆINIAN STUDIES

Professor S. D. Joshi Felicitation Volume

edited by
Madhav M. Deshpande
Saroja Bhate

CENTER FOR SOUTH AND SOUTHEAST ASIAN STUDIES
UNIVERSITY OF MICHIGAN
Number 37

Open access edition funded by the National Endowment for the Humanities/ Andrew W. Mellon Foundation Humanities Open Book Program.

Library of Congress catalog card number: 90-86276
ISBN: 0-89148-064-1 (cloth)
ISBN: 0-89148-065-X (paper)

Center for South and Southeast Asian Studies
The University of Michigan

ISBN 978-0-89148-064-8 (hardcover)
ISBN 978-0-89148-065-5 (paper)
ISBN 978-0-472-12773-3 (ebook)
ISBN 978-0-472-90169-2 (open access)

CONTENTS

Preface vii
Madhav M. Deshpande
Interpreting Vākyapadīya 2.486 Historically (Part 3) 1
Ashok Aklujkar
Viṃśati Padāni . . . Triṃśat . . . Catvāriṃśat 49
Pandit V. B. Bhagwat
Vyañjanā as Reflected in the Formal Structure of Language 55
Saroja Bhate
On Paśya Mṛgo Dhāvati 65
Gopikamohan Bhattacharya
Pāṇini and the Veda Reconsidered 75
Johannes Bronkhorst
On Pāṇini, Śākalya, Vedic Dialects and Vedic Exegetical Traditions 123
George Cardona
The Syntactic Role of Adhi- in the Pāṇinian Kāraka-System 135
Achyutananda Dash
Pāṇini 7.2.15 (Yasya Vibhāṣā): A Reconsideration 161
Madhav M. Deshpande
On Identifying the Conceptual Restructuring of Passive as Ergative in Indo-Aryan 177
Peter Edwin Hook

A Note on Pāṇini 3.1.26, Vārttika 8 201
Daniel H. H. Ingalls
On Ekārthībhāva and Vyapekṣā 209
V. N. Jha
Parts of Speech in Pāṇini 231
Dinabandhu Kar
Economy and the Construction of the Śivasūtras 239
Paul Kiparsky
Bhavānanda on "What is Kāraka?" 263
Bimal Krishna Matilal
A Glimpse Into a Pre-Pāṇinian View About Vikaraṇas 283
G. B. Palsule
On the Interpretation of Vā Padāntasya (8.4.57) 289
K. Kunjunni Raja
Time for a Little Something 293
J. A. F. Roodbergen
Bibliography of Shivram Dattatray Joshi 323

PREFACE

Madhav M. Deshpande

Professor Shivram Dattatray Joshi was born in Konkan in the town of Ratnāgiri on August 15, 1926. He was born into a family of Sanskrit Pandits. His father and his uncle were both Sanskrit Pandits dedicated to the tradition of Vyākaraṇa. His father died when Shivram was still a child, and he was sent to Pune to stay with his uncle, Maheshwar Shastri Joshi, who taught Sanskrit at the Poona Sanskrit College in Datewadi near the Bhikardas Maruti temple in Sadashiv Peth. Under the guidance of his uncle, Shivram became a master of Sanskrit Vyākaraṇa at a very early age. He passed the *Vyākaraṇa-Tīrtha* examination of the Bengal Sanskrit Association in 1941 at the age of fifteen. He passed the *Vyākaraṇottamā* examination from Baroda in 1942; the *Vyākaraṇa-Cūḍāmaṇi* examination of the Vedaśāstrottejaka Sabhā, Pune, in 1944; and the *Vyākaraṇācārya* examination of the Poona Sanskrit College in 1945. Having become a recognized teacher of Sanskrit in Pune before reaching the age of twenty, he began teaching at the Poona Sanskrit College. While he thus pursued the path of traditional Sanskrit scholarship, other boys of his age went to English schools and colleges. The financial rewards for teaching Sanskrit were meager at best, and the young scholar and his students followed the honorable Pune tradition of *Mādhukarī*.[1] During this period, S. D. Joshi became a well-known teacher of Sanskrit in Pune, and many college students and even college teachers began studying with him. He was the principal of the Poona Sanskrit College from 1947-1955.

This was the situation when Professor D. H. H. Ingalls of Harvard University came to Pune in the early fifties. He wished to read Sanskrit grammatical texts with a Pandit, and the young S. D. Joshi was recommended to him by Dr. V. G. Paranjpe and Mahamahopadhyaya Kashinath Shastri Abhyankar. S. D. Joshi, who had never studied English, read these texts with Ingalls using Sanskrit as the medium of conversation. Ingalls soon recognized a brilliant mind and could see that, if his traditional learning were augmented by western training in critical methods, Joshi would become a scholar of unequaled abilities. With this realization, Ingalls encouraged Joshi to get his B.A. in Sanskrit and then to apply for a scholarship to go to Harvard for a Ph.D.

At this stage Joshi decided to finish the high school matriculation examination. In 1955 he received his B.A. in Sanskrit from the University of Poona. Although he was officially a student in their classes, his professors of Sanskrit were well aware of Joshi's exceptional abilities and often modified their views in accordance with his suggestions. It was during his college days, that my father, Murlidhar Vasudeo Deshpande, became his classmate. Initially my father was unaware of the fact that S. D. Joshi was already an accomplished scholar and teacher. To him he was just a close friend. One day, Joshi took him to Poona

Sanskrit College. My father mentioned that there was said to be a very learned teacher, called Panditji, in that college and that he would very much like to meet him. After some time, Joshi revealed the fact that he was that Panditji. I was just a child at the time, yet I distinctly remember my father's excitement. Panditji has remained a close friend to my father and a dear uncle (*kākā*) to me. He took me to my first restaurant in Pune. This was before he went to America to do his Ph.D.

After getting his B.A. in Sanskrit, S. D. Joshi was awarded a fellowship to study at Harvard. He went that same year. I still remember the long conversations he and my father had before he left. After some time at Harvard, he returned to Pune and married one of his college classmates, Kalavati Bhagwat, on June 22, 1958. After the birth of his son, Anandavardhan, he returned to Harvard and in 1960 finished his doctoral dissertation on Kauṇḍabhaṭṭa's *Dhātvarthanirṇaya* under the guidance of Professor Ingalls.

After returning to Pune in 1960, S. D. Joshi joined the Department of Sanskrit Dictionary at the Deccan College. In 1964, he joined the Centre of Advanced Study in Sanskrit at the University of Poona as a Reader in Sanskrit. In 1970, he became Professor and Head of the Department of Sanskrit and Prakrit Languages. From 1974 to 1987, he served as Director of the Centre of Advanced Study in Sanskrit. Since 1987, he has been the General Editor of the Sanskrit Dictionary Project at the Deccan College. In 1971-72, he was a visiting professor at Harvard, and in 1976-77, a visiting professor at Nagoya University, Japan. He has visited and lectured at numerous universities in and out of

India. He is currently the General Secretary of the All India Oriental Conference. Among the numerous honors he has received, we would like to mention the most recent one. Professor Joshi received an award from the President of India on August 15, 1991, as a Rāṣṭrīya Paṇḍita (National Scholar).

It was S. D. Joshi who inspired and encouraged me to join the field of Sanskrit studies. He did this by both his advice and his example. But, beyond our personal relationship, I honor and respect him as a teacher. During the two years (1966-1968) when I was studying for my master's degree in Sanskrit at Pune, Professor Joshi taught me more than I could have learned in twelve years with another teacher. Besides the two scheduled hours per week, he invited his class to his home every evening. During these long sessions, he explained to us in meticulous detail the intricate arguments in the *Mahābhāṣya* and the *Paribhāṣenduśekhara*. It was an unparalleled saturation and transmission of knowledge, a gift from a teacher to his students, one that cannot be matched. Many generations of students have experienced this same generosity, which was complemented almost daily by the hospitality of Mrs. Joshi.

Saroja Bhate and I decided to jointly edit this felicitation volume because we feel great love, affection, and gratitude toward Professor Joshi. In the past, he has shunned most public displays of honor and tried his best to discourage us from going ahead with this work. We strongly believe, however, that the world of Sanskrit scholarship must have an opportunity to express its respect, gratitude, and admiration for his contributions as a teacher and a scholar. By serving as the coeditors of this volume, we have merely provided an opportunity for that expression.[2] Let me conclude this preface by quoting a verse from the *Śataślokī of* Śaṅkarācārya.

दृष्टान्तो नैव दृष्टस्त्रिभुवनजठरे सद्गुरोर्ज्ञानदातुः
स्पर्शश्चेत्तत्र कल्प्यः स नयति यदहो स्वर्णतामश्मसारम् ।
न स्पर्शत्वं तथापि श्रितचरणयुगे सद्गुरुः स्वीयशिष्ये
स्वीयं साम्यं विधत्ते भवति निरुपमस्तेन वालौकिकोऽपि ॥

There is no comparison known in the world to describe a great teacher, the transmitter of knowledge. Perhaps one may think of a touchstone, which turns iron into gold. However, it does not turn iron into another touchstone. A great teacher transmits his own identity to the disciple who studies at his feet. This is what makes him incomparable and extraordinary indeed!

Notes

1. This refers to the practice of Brahman families supporting students by offering them meals. Sometimes a student would go to one or more families to get his food, and eat it at his own residence, or he might have meals with different families according to a schedule. Many generations of students residing in Pune were supported in this way.
2. We would like to thank all the contributors to this volume for their assistance, and especially for their

patience. Due to circumstances beyond our control, it has taken an unusually long time for this volume to be published. We would like to apologize for this delay. We also note with sorrow the deaths of Professor Gopikamohan Bhattacharya, who passed away in 1986 during a visit to Vienna, Austria, and Professor Bimal K. Matilal, who passed away at Oxford, U.K., on July 8, 1991.

INTERPRETING VĀKYAPADĪYA 2.486 HISTORICALLY (PART 3)*

Ashok Aklujkar

1.1 The first two parts of this study were published in the *Adyar Library Bulletin* (1981:581-601, Dr. K. Kunjunni Raja Felicitation Volume) and in *Indological and Buddhist Studies: Volume in Honour of Professor J. W. de Jong on his Sixtieth Birthday* (Canberra: Australian National University, Faculty of Asian Studies, 1982, pp. 1-10). I am happy that this third part is also appearing in a volume dedicated to a scholar who has contributed substantially to our understanding of Sanskrit *śāstras*.

1.2 *Vākyapadīya* (VP in abbreviation) 2.486, the first word of which I intend to discuss here, runs thus: *parvatād āgamaṃ labdhvā bhāṣya-bījānusāribhiḥ / sa nīto bahu-śākhatvāṃ candrācāryādibhiḥ punaḥ //* The question of the precise import of this verse has given rise to a substantial body of literature extending over 125 years (Aklujkar 1978:9). As I have already examined this literature directly and indirectly in the publications mentioned above, I shall merely state here that I prefer to translate the verse along the following lines: 'Having acquired the traditional knowledge from parvata, Candrācārya and others, who followed the indications in the *Bhāṣya*, again made it (i.e., the traditional knowledge) many-branched'. I should also clarify that in my view, as argued in the 1978 article, the verse was probably authored by a student of Bhartṛ-hari (B in abbreviation) and not by B as has been commonly supposed.

1.3 Although parvata is a common Sanskrit word with 'mountain, mountain range' as its definite meaning and it would not be incompatible in that meaning with the other words of VP 2.486, it has caused much reflection on the part of scholars. Goldstücker (1861:258), Weber (1862:161), Kielhorn (1874b:285-86; 1876c:244-45), and Bhandarkar (1883-85a/1933:184) refrain from translating it as 'mountain', although they must have known its most frequently attested meaning. Instead, they leave it untranslated as "Parvata" (note the capitalized initial) in their translations or paraphrases of the verse, giving the impression that they take it as a proper name, most probably that of a person. Nearer to our time, Joshi and Roodbergen (1976:xxxiii) and Joshi (1976:138) do the same,[1] while Varma (1971a:206) and Laddu (1981:193-94) explicitly take parvata as a reference to a particular person.[2] Then there are scholars who, while not giving up the common meaning of the word, pay special attention to it in order to identify the mountain intended by the author of the verse. These are: Tārā-nātha Tarka-vācaspati (1864: [introduction], p. 2; 1902: [introduction], p. 2), Peterson (1883-85:183), Ramakrishna Kavi (1930:239), Thieme (1956:20), Scharfe (1976:276), Cardona (1978:97, n. 36), and Bronkhorst (1983:393-97).

2.1 On the basis of *Rāja-taraṅgiṇī* (RT in abbreviation) verse 1.176, which is related in content to the VP verse we are discussing, Varma identifies parvata with King

Abhimanyu of Kashmir (and also with the land of Kashmir; see note 2). This is patently absurd. According to the context of 486, *vyākaraṇāgamaḥ . . . dākṣiṇātyeṣu vyavasthitaḥ*, parvata must be in the South (**3.3**). A king of Kashmir (or the Kashmir country) is hardly likely to have been viewed as Southern.[3] Secondly, regardless of the reading one accepts of the RT verse, Abhimanyu cannot rightly be viewed as the giver or source of the *āgama* in the case of Candrācārya and others (Aklujkar 1987:228).

2.2 Laddu, too, takes parvata as a reference to an individual, but this individual is the Vedic, and to some extent Epic and Purāṇic, seer whose only distinction seems to be that he is always found in the company of Nārada; otherwise, he is singularly characterized by a lack of individuality. The Classical authors, as far as I know, do not refer to him. He is not even remotely connected with grammatical studies.

3.1 Among those who prefer to take parvata as standing for a mountain, we find (a) the author of the *Ṭīkā*, Puṇya-rāja or Helā-rāja (Aklujkar 1974);[4] (b) modern scholars like Raghunātha Sharmā (1968:574), Raghavan Pillai (1971:146), and Subramania Iyer (1969:3; 1977:204) who reproduce the *Ṭīkā* explanation; and (c) other modern scholars such as Ramakrishna Kavi, Peterson, Thieme, Tārā-nātha Tarka-vācaspati, Scharfe, Cardona, and Bronkhorst (precise references in **1.3**) who either add to the *Ṭīkā* explanation or differ from it in the identification of the mountain.

3.2 Peterson, apparently following Müller,[5] accepts the view that the parvata involved is "the hill of Chittore" in modern Rajasthan. The reason he gives in support of this identification is that the hill of Chittore "was a centre of learning for the southern country." However, the reason is hardly adequate. Peterson did not prove, and in fact could not have proved, that there were no other centers of learning for the southern country, irrespective of what he means by "centre of learning" and "southern country" (see note 3). Nor did he prove that there was something so special about the center of learning at Chittore that only it could have preserved the *āgama* in question. He did not even attempt to answer preliminary questions such as: Is it known that Chittore specialized in the study of grammar or of Patañjali's *Mahā-bhāṣya* (MB in abbreviation) in the early centuries of the Christian era? Was it considered or likely to be considered 'southern' by B or his students (**1.2**)? Was it, or was it at least believed to be, a repository of manuscripts of rare works? Is Candrācārya said to have visited it? To propose an identification without raising even a few of these questions is to show disregard for the context of *parvatāt* (see also the point I make in note 13).

3.3 The more elaborate statement made by Scharfe is open to the same charge. In suggesting that parvata should be identified with Citra-kūṭa,[6] he asks none of the above questions. In addition, he makes a series of unproved assumptions. Why identify parvata with Citra-kūṭa? Because, he tells us, the oral tradition of the MB was alive there. How do we know that the oral tradition was alive there when verse 485 says *vyākaraṇāgamaḥ dākṣiṇātyeṣu grantha-mātre vyavasthitaḥ* 'The traditional knowledge (which would include the oral tradition) of grammar remained among the Southerners only in book form'? Because, according to

Scharfe, "the verse speaks only about the South Indian *Mahābhāṣya* tradition which had withered to the point that oral instruction had ceased." Now, how can one assert this when there is no indication in the preceding verses 481-84 that their author intends to speak of Southern Vaiyākaraṇas and Northern Vaiyākaraṇas separately? Are we going to say that *saṃkṣepa-ruci*, *alpa-vidyā-parigraha*, and *akṛta-buddhi* grammarians existed only in the South or that the confusion Baiji and others caused in MB studies was confined to the South? In the latter case, how do we account for the fact that the names Baiji, Saubhava, and Haryakṣa, although unusual, have nothing south Indian about them? In any case, why would the author of verses 481-86 be concerned with making a statement that applied only to south India? If he spoke of disintegration of MB studies only in the South, would it not follow that the state of these studies was satisfactory in the North (cf. Bronkhorst 1983:395)? Why, in that case, would he mention a single location in the North as the place where the *āgama* was recovered?[7] How would his assertion accord with the commonly noticed state of affairs that South India in general managed to preserve transmission lines for a longer period (Aklujkar 1981:599-600)? If the Northern tradition had not been disrupted, would Candrācārya's acquisition of the *āgama* be an achievement so remarkable as to deserve special mention? Why would Candrācārya try to improve the state of MB studies in the South? Was he a Southerner? If he was, how would one account for the traditions that connect him with either Kashmir or Bengal?[8]

3.4 Even if Scharfe's contextually improbable interpretation of *vyākaraṇāgamaḥ dākṣiṇātyeṣu grantha-mātre vyavasthitaḥ* is accepted, how would it imply that Citra-kūṭa was *the* place where the *āgama* was preserved? At most, the implication would be that the study of the MB did not suffer as much in the North as in the South. Furthermore, how does Scharfe establish Candrācārya's association with Citra-kūṭa? He does so on the basis of examples in the *Cāndra Vṛtti* pertaining to *sūtras* 1.3.106-7.[9] Therefore, the further assumptions are that: (a) Candrācārya of VP 2.486 is identical with Candra-gomin; (b) the *Cāndra Vṛtti* was in fact written by Candra-gomin;[10] (c) the sentence "we shall eat rice," given as an example in the above-mentioned part of the *Cāndra Vṛtti*, means 'we shall eat rice only once'; (d) if rice was eaten only once before reaching Kauśāmbī, the journey to Kauśāmbī could not have taken more than a day;[11] (e) if Candra-gomin thought the journey to Kauśāmbī required only a day's travel in the direction of the eastern city of Pāṭaliputra, his place of residence could have been anywhere up to fifty miles west of Kauśāmbī;[12] and (f) since Citra-kūṭa is about fifty miles west of Kauśāmbī, it must be the place where Candra-gomin resided.

3.5 Of the six assumptions outlined above, (a) and (b) are open to doubt, and those remaining, the ones that are crucial to establishing Candra-gomin's/Candrācārya's presence at Citra-kūṭa, do not form a logically tight series of propositions. They constitute a novel, and for that reason commendable, attempt to determine a location, but one that is far from definitive. Assumption (c) forms their basis, and once its validity is called into question, the others no longer remain tenable. Now, from my notes 11 and 12 here and from Bronkhorst 1983:397, it is evident that there are serious problems in relying on assumption (c).

3.6 To sum up, the impression I get from Scharfe's discussion of VP 2.486 and *Cāndra Vṛtti* 1.3.106-7 is that the possibility of connecting the two occurred to him and the force of that new idea made him overlook many indications to the contrary. He has proved nothing more than the likelihood that the author of the *Cāndra Vṛtti* was, at the time of writing his *Vṛtti*, in an area which lay to the west of Kauśāmbī and from which a journey to Kauśāmbī and Pāṭaliputra could be foreseen.[13]

4.1 The *Ṭīkā* provides a specification of *parvatāt* with the expression *tri-kūṭaika-deśa-varti-tiliṅgaika-deśāt.* This expression is printed as °*vartti-tri-liṅgai*° in Mānavallī's (1887:285) and Raghunātha Sharmā's (1968:574) editions and as °*vartino liṅgai*° in Kielhorn's (1874:286) article.[14] An examination of the manuscripts of the *Ṭīkā* reveals that the second variant reading is found only in a few inferior manuscripts[15] and the first variant reading is not found in any manuscript accessible at present.[16] Since this is the situation, an attempt like Thieme's (1956:20), which follows Kielhorn's reading and gives a *śiva-liṅga* in the Tri-kūṭa region as the location of Candrācārya's acquisition of the *āgama*, must be set aside.[17]

4.2 Besides, the word *eka-deśa* does not really compound well with *liṅga* (=*śiva-liṅga*) in the present context. A statement to the effect that 'the *āgama* was acquired from a part of the *śiva-liṅga* which stands on a part of the (mountain) Tri-kūṭa' is not likely to be intended, for there is no propriety in relating the acquisition to a *part* of the *śiva-liṅga*. Thieme realizes this and remarks: "*liṅgaika-deśāt* is perhaps a mistake for simply: *liṅgāt*, or, else, for *liṅgaviśeṣāt* 'from a particular liṅga,' the *ekadeśa*-part having been nonsensically repeated, or put in place of *-viśeṣāt*, from the preceding compound by a copyist." However, since the reading *liṅgai°* is objectively weaker than *tiliṅgai°*, there is no need to indulge in the kind of speculation that Thieme's statement contains. Besides, a corruption of *liṅga-viśeṣād* into *liṅgaika-deśād* is transcriptionally improbable. The available manuscripts do not even indirectly indicate that *°gaika-deśād* could have resulted from anything like *°ga-viśeṣād* (see note 15).

4.3 Explaining the *Ṭīkā* identification is partly easy and partly difficult. The easy part comes later, viz., *tiliṅgaika-deśāt*. Undoubtedly, *tiliṅga* is an earlier form of the modern name Telaṅgaṇā and refers to a part of Andhra Pradesh having approximately the same boundaries as modern Telangana.[18] An element of convenience in this fact is that the identification of parvata as a mountain in Telangana will stand even if no agreement is reached on the identification of Tri-kūṭa (**4.7**) and on the connection of the expression *tri-kūṭaika-deśa-varti* with the expression *tiliṅgaika-deśāt* (see note 24). I shall, therefore, postpone the consideration of *tri-kūṭaika-deśa-varti* and turn first to determining the specific area of Telangana that the *Ṭīkā* author and, if the *Ṭīkā* author has accurately preserved the tradition, the author of 486 are likely to have had in mind.

4.4 It is indeed strange that the author of 486 should give the location of a major achievement by using a general term like parvata. There are two possibilities under which such use seems sensible. Either the author does not know the precise location or parvata does not carry for him in this instance the general meaning it usually conveys.

The first possibility can be entertained in two ways: (a) The author is uncertain about the location beyond the fact that it was a mountain; or (b) the author cannot make up his mind as to which of the two or more mountains identified as the site of Candrācārya's achievement was the true location.

If (a) were the case, a form like *kasmād api*, indicating indefiniteness, would probably have accompanied the expression *parvatāt*. Besides, a tradition identifying the parvata rather precisely would not, in all probability, have arisen. It seems proper, therefore, to entertain the first possibility only in the form of alternative (b). This I shall do in a later section (**5.1**). It is more convenient at the present stage of our discussion to explore the second possibility.

4.5 Let us assume for a moment that the ordinarily general term parvata could have been used in 486 as a singular term referring to a mountain.[19] In other words, the question to be asked is: Is there a specific mountain in the South that could be referred to simply as parvata? I think Śrī-parvata[20] is the only mountain that meets the conditions contained in this question because (a) the stem parvata is more closely associated with it than with any other mountain frequently mentioned in the ancient and medieval literature of India. The other prominent mountains are quite freely referred to with compound names that contain one of the synonyms of parvata such as *adri, giri, śaila,* or *acala.* Śrī-parvata, on the other hand, does not commonly attract designations like *śrī-giri* (see note 20c). In addition, (b) if a mountain is to be referred to by dropping a part of its name for the sake of brevity or for the sake of preserving the meter, the part to be dropped should be dispensable from some point of view. The stem *śrī,* figuring in the name Śrī-parvata, is so commonly employed as an honorific before names (including the names of other prominent mountains) that we should not be surprised if it was occasionally looked upon as an honorific even in the name Śrī-parvata and thus thought to be dispensable.

The thoughts expressed in the preceding paragraph are not mere speculation. There is in fact a tradition of referring to Śrī-parvata simply as parvata (Ḍhere 1977:106, 121-23, 135). It may not have arisen for the reasons alluded to above and may be due to the importance of Śrī-parvata as perceived by the people of India, particularly of south India ('Śrī-parvata is *the* mountain; when someone uses the word parvata, it is Śrī-parvata that first comes to mind'). However, what matters for us is that it is clearly there and that even the interpretation 'mountain of Śrī' of the name Śrī-parvata did not preclude occasional dropping of the component *śrī.*

4.6 It will thus be seen that the second possibility (general term used particularistically) need not be viewed as a possibility in theory only. Besides explaining what looks like a lack of precision (it is not that an ancient author's usage is imprecise; it is our understanding of his usage that is deficient), it leads us to an identification that ties in well with *tiliṅgaika-deśāt* of the *Ṭīkā*, for Śrī-parvata is a part of Tiliṅga or Telangana (see notes 18 and 20). Furthermore, the identification agrees with indications in the Tibetan tradition and can be said to receive confirmation in the accounts of Chinese travellers.[21] According to the Tibetan tradition, Candra-gomin[22] encountered the MB exposition when he returned from Siṃhala (Ceylon) to southern Jambu-dvīpa (India). For the travellers from Ceylon to northern India, Śrī-parvata was not only a natural, well-trodden, and time-honored region to pass through (Moticandra 1953, map preceding index), but it was also a holy and fascinating place on account of its association with *siddha*s and *siddhi*s (Aklujkar 1982:6-7). In fact, there was a regular provision at Śrī-parvata in the early centuries of the Christian era for receiving travellers (particularly Buddhist travellers from Ceylon) as we learn from an inscription of Vīra-puruṣa-datta dated in the third century A.D. (Sircar 1965:235).[23]

4.7 Now, to turn to the first half, *tri-kūṭaika-deśa-varti*, of the identification in the *Ṭīkā*, Tri-kūṭa is said to be the name of at least four mountains in Sanskrit literature and Indian inscriptions:[24]

(a) A mythical mountain in the North that forms the southern ridge of the Meru, bears the Tri-pathagā Gaṅgā, is surrounded by the Milky Ocean, and has peaks made of iron, silver, and gold; cf. *Mahā-bhārata* 2.39.11, 2.82.11; *Mārkaṇḍeya-purāṇa* 55.6; *Bhāgavata-purāṇa* 8.2.1ff; *Śabda-*

kalpa-druma pt. III, p. 74; Wilson 1894:141, n. 2; Kirfel 1954:10.

(b) A mythical or semimythical mountain beyond the ocean in which Rāvaṇa's Laṅkā is situated; cf. *Mahā-bhārata* 3.261.53, 3.266.54-55; *Rāmāyaṇa* 5.2.1, 6.30.18 (and passage 18 on p. 950 of Appendix 1), 7.5.21-22, 7.11.20; *Vāyu-purāṇa* 1.48.26-29; *Pañca-tantra*, book 5, story 11 (Bühler's fourth ed., p. 63); Rudraṭa's *Kāvyālaṃkāra* 7.20; Bhoja's *Śṛṇgāra-prakāśa*, p. 419.

(c) A range of hills near the west coast of India which extends from northern Konkan to the west of the present district of Nasik; cf. Mirashi 1955:xl-xli, 1963: 106-7; Gupta 1973:45, 246. Probably the same as the Tri-kūṭa mentioned by Saida Mahaṃmada in his Kalpa-samūha (Ḍhere 1977:201).

(d) A mountain in the eastern part of the Deccan (Mirashi 1975:186), probably the same as the one which B. V. Krishna Rao (*Journal of the Andhra Historical Research Society* 10:191; reference according to Gupta 1973:246) specifies as Kotappakonda near Kavur in the Narasaraopeta taluq of the Guntur district.[25]

4.8 Of these four mountains bearing the name Tri-kūṭa, the one described in (a) is clearly alien to the spirit of this inquiry and can safely be ignored for that reason as well as for its uniform association with the North (**3.3**).

Mountain (b), too, ceases to be historical if Rāvaṇa's Laṅkā is identified, as is generally the case,[26] with the island of Ceylon (Sri Lanka) or some part thereof. As far as I can ascertain, no mountain in Ceylon was or is called Tri-kūṭa. Secondly, not only is there no corroboration of discovery in Ceylon in the other accounts of Candra's achievement, but the Tibetan accounts specifically state that Candra found the equivalent of the VP *āgama* after he left Siṃhala or Ceylon (**4.6**).

However, while we can dismiss the idea of a Tri-kūṭa understood to be associated with Ceylon, we cannot easily dismiss the Tri-kūṭa associated with Rāvaṇa's Laṅkā. The *Ṭīkā* author mentions Rāvaṇa and *rakṣas* immediately after the statement of identification we are discussing. It is probable, therefore, that the Tri-kūṭa he had in mind was the one that figured in the descriptions of Rāvaṇa's kingdom. This observation leaves only two alternatives open to us: (a) that the *Ṭīkā* author is correct in his statement of identification about parvata, but wrong in connecting the identified (Tri-kūṭa) parvata with Rāvaṇa; and (b) the *Ṭīkā* author does not understand Rāvaṇa's Laṅkā to be Ceylon but a region near an historical Tri-kūṭa.[27] Both these alternatives dictate that we determine independently which mountain or mountains can historically claim the name Tri-kūṭa.

4.9 Our attempt to determine this will of course be confined to mountains (c) and (d) of the list given in **4.7**, for the available evidence does not lead us in any other direction. Of them, (d) is a suspect candidate for its claim to the name Tri-kūṭa has not generally been accepted by specialists of ancient and medieval Indian geography. Gupta (1973:246-47), agreeing with V. S. Ramachandra Murty's article in volume II (p. 45) of the *Journal of the Andhra Historical Research Society*, concludes that there is little evidence to support the identification of Kotappakonda with the Tri-kūṭa mentioned in historical records.[28]

4.10 Mountain (c) was known as Tri-kūṭa from at least the third century A.D., as the evidence collected by Mirashi and others establishes (**4.7**c). Our acceptance of it as the mountain intended, or originally intended, in the tradition preserved by the *Ṭīkā* will not, therefore, be incompatible with the date of the *Ṭīkā* (Aklujkar 1982:3, 6, n. 4). It is also a mountain of the Dakṣiṇā-patha, so its acceptance will not go against the expression *dākṣiṇātyeṣu* of verse 485 (see note 3). We know that Northern scholars, *litterateurs*, and their works reached the southern part of India through the territory adjacent to this mountain.[29] Also, if we assume that in the *Ṭīkā* author's perception Laṅkā was situated near this mountain (**4.8**, note 27), we will have accounted not only for the presence of Rāvaṇa by the side of Tri-kūṭa in his statement but we will also have arrived at a hypothesis that scholars such as Shah and Sankalia, interested in determining the location of Vālmīki's Laṅkā, have independently developed (cf. Cardona 1978:97).

5.1 Taking parvata in its usual sense of 'mountain', we thus arrive at two likely locations for the retrieval of *vyākaraṇāgama*: Śrī-parvata and Tri-kūṭa. Both of these agree with contextual indications such as *dākṣiṇātyeṣu*; were well known in the period (the early centuries of the Christian era) to which the concluding verses of the *Vākya-kāṇḍa* belong; are likely to have been visited by Candra whether he started from Kashmir (as in the RT account) or returned from Siṃhala (as in the Tibetan accounts); had excellent potential for preserving the *vyākaraṇāgama* manuscripts as areas of pilgrimage (Katre 1954:25-26); and were frequented by followers of both Brahmanism and Buddhism, which jointly preserve Candra's memory.[30] Besides, both are supported by a piece of information recorded as early as the *Ṭīkā* (see note 13 for the value of this piece as evidence).

5.2 We have now reached a point in our discussion at which we can choose between the following positions: (a) The uncertainty regarding which of the two locations was actually the place of Candrācārya's discovery belongs to the period of the *Ṭīkā*; and (b) The uncertainty goes back to the period of the author of 486 (**4.4**). If we accept (b), it would be pointless to press this discussion further in the hope of being able to determine one location exclusively, for the author of 486 is our earliest source on what Candrācārya achieved. If he is deemed to be undecided, there is practically no hope of our being able to decide what the location of the recovery of *vyākaraṇāgama* was in the original account. However, before we accept alternative (b), let us remind ourselves that we have thus far proceeded on the basis of two assumptions: that *tri-kūṭaika-deśa* and *tiliṅgaika-deśa* are separable parts of the *Ṭīkā* phrase, and that the word *tri-kūṭa* can stand only for a mountain (see note 24). Both of these assumptions deserve further examination.

5.3 As is well known, readings in manuscripts should, as far as possible, be interpreted as they are. Assumption of loss or change of text matter should be resorted to only if the available reading cannot make contextually acceptable sense without such an assumption. Such is not the case with the *Ṭīkā* phrase. It can be understood to mean 'from a part of Tiliṅga which (in turn) exists in a part of Tri-kūṭa'.[31] There is nothing contextually incompatible in this meaning.

Mere repetition of *eka-deśa* would not be adequate justification for imagining a gap in the *Ṭīkā* phrase or for emending it. If Tri-kūṭa refers to a mountain, it is not at all improbable that it would refer also to the region around that mountain.[32] In fact, as Mirashi (1955:xli-xliv) notes, a name like Pūrva-tri-kūṭa-viṣaya 'East Tri-kūṭa district' is found in the Anjaneri plates of Bhoga-śakti, and Tri-kūṭa is mentioned in a list of countries in the Ajanta inscription concerning Hariṣeṇa (475-510 A.D.). A dynasty of Traikūṭakas, who most probably derived their name from association with the Tri-kūṭa region,[33] is also clearly attested in historical records (Mirashi 1955:xli-xliv; Mulay 1972:16, 29; Gupta 1973:246). True, Mirashi observes that "The Traikūṭaka kingdom at its largest extent seems to have extended from the Kīm in the north to the Krishṇā in the south, and to have comprised South Gujarat, North Konkan, and the Nasik, Poona and Satara Districts of Maharashtra," and thus it is not certain that the Traikūṭaka country included Tiliṅga. However, as the word "seems" in Mirashi's statement indicates, one cannot rule out the possibility that the borders of the Traikūṭaka country could have at times been different.[34] Evidence available for determining boundaries of political units in as early a period as the second to the sixth centuries A.D. rarely allows one to draw precise and final conclusions. As the Traikūṭakas emerged after the decline of the Sātavāhana empire, which included Tiliṅga, it is not unlikely that Tri-kūṭa, as the region of the Traikūṭakas, included or was thought to include Tiliṅga. Such a situation is especially likely to have prevailed in the early period of the Traikūṭaka dynasty, for which, as Mirashi observes, we have no records.

5.4 Thus, whether we accept a tradition of two locations for Candrācārya's achievement or a tradition of one location would depend on whether we are willing to concede the possibility of the inclusion of Tiliṅga in Tri-kūṭa and on how natural we find the repetition of *eka-deśa* in the *Ṭīkā* statement of identification. Acceptance of a tradition of one location does not involve assumption of textual corruption in the *Ṭīkā* but it does involve the assumption that Tri-kūṭa, as a region, at one time included Tiliṅga. As such an acceptance leads us to Śrī-parvata, it would better explain why the author of 486 used a general expression like parvata (**4.5**) in the singular number. But it would also enhance the possibility that even the author of 486 viewed Candrācārya's achievement as a miracle[35] and that the story of the recovery of *vyākaraṇāgama* is simply one of the myths associated with Śrī-parvata (Aklujkar 1982:6-7), thus having no specific historical value. Acceptance of a tradition of two locations, on the other hand, allows us to take Tri-kūṭa, in conformity with the indisputable part of the available evidence, as a region contiguous to the mountain range Tri-kūṭa. Such an acceptance leaves room for one further interesting connection. If B was a Maitrāyaṇīya and if the Maitrāyaṇīyas enjoyed a prominent presence in the Nasik area (see references collected in Bronkhorst 1983:396), the author of 486 probably belonged to the Nasik (i.e., the Tri-kūṭa) area. He could have then recorded in his composition a piece of local history and intended to refer to Tri-kūṭa by the word *parvatāt*.[36]

6.1 At this point, I would like to return to the possibility entertained at the beginning (**1.3**) of this exploration of parvata, the one in which parvata could be taken to refer to a person. Although the specific identifications proposed by Varma and Laddu are unacceptable (**2.1-2**), I do not consider the possibility itself a weak alternative. According to the *Bṛhacchaṅkara-vijaya* of Vidyāraṇya-svāmin, quoted by Rāma-toṣaṇa Bhaṭṭācārya in his *Prāṇa-toṣiṇī* (p. 956), parvata is employed in the sense of a certain type of ascetic.[37] Furthermore, Bhaṭṭoji Dīkṣita, in his *Siddhānta-kaumudī* on the Pāṇinian (2.2.34) rule *alpāctaram* and the vārttika *abhyarhitaṃ ca*, gives as an example the expression *tāpasa-parvatau*. This example is sensible only if parvata is comparable in some way to *tāpasa* 'ascetic'.[38] Thus, it is not improbable at all that parvata carried a meaning of the form 'an ascetic who is found in a mountain area, a wild ascetic, an ascetic given to extreme modes of ascetic conduct'.[39] If this meaning is assigned to parvata in 486, one can explain at least two things: the occurrence of the *brahma-rakṣas* 'brahmin ogre' element in the *Ṭīkā* and *Patañjali-carita* accounts of Candra's achievement (see note 21a), and the use of a very general term like parvata by the author of 486 when we expect him to tell us how or where the *vyākaraṇāgama* was recovered. If parvata is taken to be expressive of location, then the author has been unexpectedly imprecise; he has not specified anything beyond a mountain in the South. On the other hand, if parvata is viewed as a word used in the rather specific ascetic-directed sense, the author cannot be faulted for having used too general or too wide a term. It is not his expression that lacks precision; rather, it is our knowledge of the expression he uses that needs to be widened. Similarly, if parvata stands for an ascetic haunting mountains or caves and having a wild, frightening, or repulsive appearance, we can see how a *brahma-rakṣas* came to be associated with the verse as a benefactor of Candra. I should also point out that the use of the ablative *parvatāt* in 486 somehow seems more natural in the case of a sentient source of acquisition than in the case of a location. If the author of 486 intended to give us the location of the acquisition made by Candrācārya, would he not have used the locative form *parvate*?[40] These observations should explain why we cannot absolutely exclude the possibility of parvata being a reference to a person.

6.2 The word parvata in the sense elucidated just now could be a variant or a corrupt form of a secondary (*taddhita*) derivative *pārvata*. Indications available in the *Kāśikā*, *Nyāsa*, and *Pada-mañjarī* on Pāṇini 2.4.23, 3.2.53, and 4.2.144 suggest that there was an older commentarial tradition according to which the word *amanuṣya* occurring in Pāṇini did not convey a literal or etymological (*yaugika*) meaning of the form 'anything or anyone other than a human being' but a specific conventional (*rūḍha*) meaning like 'a *rakṣas*, *piśāca*, etc.', that is, 'a member of a species thought to be similar to humans, but having strange capacities'.[41] If this is so, one early, if not exclusive, understanding of *pārvata* (and *parvatīya*) derived by Pāṇini 4.2.144, *vibhāṣāmanuṣye*, must have been something like 'a person of extraordinary or miraculous capacities associated with a mountain'. The probability that the pre-*Kāśikā*

Pāṇinīyas such as B and his disciples were aware of this meaning of *pārvata/parvata* and used the word in that sense in their writings is thus strong.[42]

6.3 One consequence of attaching the meaning 'mountain ascetic' to the word parvata, as in the case of identifying parvata with Śrī-parvata (**5.4**), will be that the probability of tracing back the miraculous element in the accounts of Candra to B's time will be strengthened. This element is indeed widespread, as will incidentally become clear in part 4 (under preparation) of the present study. Moreover, since B or his students (**1.2**) were not totally against the possibility of knowledge through extraordinary means (Aklujkar 1970b:42-50), it is not incongruent to associate them with the miraculous. While this realization will deprive the *Vākya-kāṇḍa* verses of some of their value as a historical statement, it cannot be avoided by any historian who, rightly, evaluates his evidence before allowing it to lead him to definite conclusions.

7.1 There is a way in which both lines of interpretation, taking parvata as a reference to an individual and taking parvata as a reference to a mountain, come together. If Candrācārya and others recovered, in the eyes of the author of 486, the *āgama* from a *siddha*-like ascetic on a Southern mountain (most probably Śrī-parvata, which was famous for such ascetics), then, while the first-level or initial interpretation of parvata would differ as 'a mountain ascetic' and 'a mountain', the ultimate import will be the same. We will have satisfied both expectations to which the context of 486 gives rise: (a) Who among the *dākṣiṇātya*s had the *vyākaraṇāgama*? (b) Where in the South was the *vyākaraṇāgama* found? The *Ṭīkā* explanation, *in effect*, accomplishes this, although it speaks of a *brahma-rakṣas* in the place of a parvata ascetic.

7.2 *Parvatāt* is the only "down-to-earth" detail in VP 2.486. It is unfortunate that we are required to keep two lines of interpretation (mountain and person) open and to entertain two possible identifications (Śrī-parvata and Tri-kūṭa) in the first line of interpretation. However, I believe such a course will serve the interests of future research better than a rushed, precise identification. Our ignorance of what actually happened may be disturbing but now it will at least have well-defined boundaries.

If a preference must be indicated, I would rank as follows the identifications defended above. In the present state of our knowledge, the strongest identification appears to be 'parvata = an ascetic or *brahma-rakṣas* belonging to Śrī-parvata'. Next in strength seems to be 'parvata = Śrī-parvata', with the attendant assumption that some scholar, or scholarly community, on Śrī-parvata had in his, or its, possession the manuscripts in which the *āgama* of the MB was preserved. Last in terms of acceptability is the equation 'parvata = Tri-kūṭa (as mountain or region)'.

This rank-ordering is based (a) on a consideration of how many independent lines of evidence point in the same direction, and (b) on whether an identification forces us to assume something which is not in the evidence and thus to sacrifice economy of explanation.

The elements of what I consider to be the strongest identification can be related to the evidence as shown in table 1.

a person,	<--	grammatical considerations
who is associated with parvata,	<--	*Kāśikā* (*Nyāsa*, Pada-mañjarī), Siddhānta-kaumudī
i.e., a mountain or its equivalent:	<--	*Ṭīkā*, (possibly also the) Chinese travelogues
a tall structure/ temple,	<--	Chinese travelogues, Tibetan legends
strongly associated with the word parvata, and	<--	*Ṭīkā*, Chinese travelogues, Ḍhere
well inside South India	<--	*Ṭīkā*, Tibetan legends, Chinese travelogues
who is seen as transcending the ordinary human condition, and	<--	*Kāśikā* (*Nyāsa*, Pada-mañjarī), Siddhānta-kaumudī, *Ṭīkā*, Tibetan legends, Patañjali-carita
who serves as a source well inside South India	<--	*Ṭīkā*, Tibetan legends, Patañjali-carita

Table 1

It can be seen from this table how almost all the relevant evidence converges in the case of, or can be accommodated in the frame of, the first identification. For what I consider to be the next best identification, only the boxed part of the convergence holds good. On the other hand, the 'parvata = Tri-kūṭa' identification rests only on the statement in the *Ṭīkā* and this, too, when the original form of that statement is assumed to be different from what it is now.

Notes

* Conclusions reached in this part were reported in the form of a short paper on 21 March 1983 at the 193rd meeting of the American Oriental Society held at Baltimore. The author was able to study many of the sources used in the article because of financial assistance provided at various times since 1969 by the University of B.C. Humanities and Social Sciences Research Committee, the Social Sciences and Humanities Research Council of Canada, the Shastri Indo-Canadian Institute, the American Council of Learned Societies, and the Alexander von Humboldt Stiftung of the Federal Republic of Germany. I also wish to acknowledge the dispassionate response to my criticism of his position that Professor Hartmut Scharfe gave in his letter of 6 November 1987. The response based on the 26 October 1987 version of the paper helped me in clarifying some points and correcting a few errors.

1. The implicit refusal to take parvata as 'mountain' is especially remarkable in the case of Weber and later researchers mentioned here. Weber (1862:161n) and Kielhorn (1974b) knew at the time of their relevant writings that Tārā-nātha Tarka-vācaspati had given a specification of parvata as Citra-kūṭa or Tri-kūṭa. An earlier edition of Tārā-nātha's *Śabdārtha-ratna* (the reference according to the third edition available to me is 1902:2) is mentioned by Weber, and Tārā-nātha's edition of the *Siddhānta-kaumudī* (1864:2) and Weber's article are mentioned by Kielhorn. Kielhorn also knew that Puṇya-rāja, an ancient commentator of VP 2.486, had understood *parvatāt* to be a reference to a region. Finally, it is beyond doubt that Bhandarkar and most of the later scholars mentioned here exhibit an awareness of Kielhorn's writings.
2. Varma (1971a:350) contradicts himself when he also takes parvata in its sense of 'mountain' and identifies it with Kashmir (as mountainous country) of King Abhimanyu's time.
3. (a) Any directional adjective like *dākṣiṇātya* 'southern' is relative in its application, for what is southern to one user can very well be northern to another. However, it is reasonable to assume that in most Classical Indian uses of *dākṣiṇātya* the reference would be to persons or objects of the Dakṣiṇā-patha unless a further specification is available in the context (Sircar 1960:172, n. 2). Another consideration one should keep in mind in the case of VP 2.486 is that, as its author belonged to the Pāṇinian tradition of Sanskrit grammar, his under-

standing of *dākṣiṇātya* is not likely to be very different from that of Patañjali (Kielhorn's ed., vol. 1, p. 8), who indicates that the author of the *vārttika yathā laukika-vaidikeṣu* was a *dākṣiṇātya* (Cardona 1976: 268-69). The third helpful consideration in ascertaining the common meaning of *dākṣiṇātya* in the Classical period is the remark by several authors to the effect that the word *cora/caura* in the language of the *dākṣiṇātya*s means *odana* 'cooked rice' not 'thief'; cf. Prabhā-candra, *Nyāya-kumuda-candra*, p. 547; Jayanta-bhaṭṭa, *Nyāya-mañjarī*, p. 242; and Abhinava-gupta, *Tattva-viveka* on *Parā-triṃśikā* 5-9ab, p. 125, who distinguishes between *saindhava*s and *dākṣiṇātya*s. With reference to the meaning of the same *cora*, Vādi-deva-sūri (*Syād-vāda-ratnākara*, p. 703) distinguishes between *gurjara*s and *drāviḍa*s; the latter must obviously be *dākṣiṇātya*s in his view. Probably Śrīdhara (*Nyāya-kandalī*, p. 215) also has a relevant observation to offer in this case, although I cannot verify the reference at present.

(b) For a determination of the reference of Dakṣiṇā-patha, see Law 1932/1979:xv, xix, 3-4, 44, 48, 60, 66; Raychaudhuri in Yazdani 1960:3-4; Sircar 1960: 14-15, 52, 57, 73, 172-73, 178, 242; Gupta 1973:8-9; and Siṃha 1974:85.

4. (a) *parvatāt tri-kūṭaika-deśa-varti-tiliṅgaika-deśād iti.*

(b) Variant readings available for the *Ṭīkā* phrase in (a) are given in note 15. The possibility of its having suffered some damage in manuscript transmission will be discussed in **4.2**, note 24, and **5.3**.

5. Peterson does not specify how, when, or where Müller's suggestion about parvata was made.

6. (a) Tārā-nātha Tarka-vācaspati offers the same identification as Scharfe's without giving any reasons to support it, as if he was simply explaining or replacing the reading *tri-kūṭa* of the *Ṭīkā* with *citra-kūṭa.*

   (b) Scharfe does not indicate awareness of the information given in (a), which, one expects, would have been known to him through Weber 1862.

   (c) Scharfe's presentation differs also in that he further identifies Citra-kūṭa with Rāma-giri, presumably the same Rāma-giri as the one mentioned by Kālidāsa in his *Megha-dūta.* It should, therefore, be noted that the identification of Citra-kūṭa with Rāma-giri is not universally accepted (cf. Gupta 1973:101-3) as Scharfe seems to have thought.

   (d) Bronkhorst (1983), who also does not indicate awareness of the information in (a), follows Scharfe in a strange way. On pages 393 and 395, he has Candra going to the Himālaya to acquire "[correct] traditional knowledge" or "The Patañjalian oral tradition." On the other hand, on page 397, he has Candra at least contemplating a journey through Kauśāmbī, as in Scharfe's view, but not necessarily residing at Citra-kūṭa, as is Scharfe's view. In other words, Bronkhorst uses Scharfe's discussion to assign Candra to Gujarat or north Maharashtra but not to explain Candra's retrieval of the *āgama.* In so doing, he severs the direct connection between VP 2.486 and *Cāndra Vṛtti* 1.3.106-7 that Scharfe seeks to establish. Thus, his view is similar to Varma's (**2.1**) and is partly based on what Scharfe thought to be justified. As my discussion shows, both Varma and Scharfe have put forward views that violate contextual considerations and go against the available evidence about Candra's achievement. Bronkhorst's composite view, therefore, stands doubly refuted and need not be discussed separately.

7. (a) Note that the option of considering Citra-kūṭa as relatively southern is not open to Scharfe because in his view the verses deal with the withering of the MB tradition in the South and hence the location of *āgama* retrieval must be in the North; cf. Bronkhorst 1983:395.

(b) In his letter of 6 November 1987, Scharfe makes the following remarks, which serve to clarify his 1976 interpretation of verse 485: ". . . the VP stanza says that the southern tradition existed only in manuscripts; that implies that it existed in the north also orally, and that would be the place to get this tradition. If B had wanted to say that these manuscripts were all that existed of the Mbh [= Mahā-bhāṣya] tradition, it would be odd to refer to South India at all. He would rather have said: "The tradition existed only in manuscripts." My preceding remarks should suffice to establish that this interpretation is contextually improbable. It is also flawed by lack of logical implication. There is no incompatibility between (i) saying that the MB tradition existed only in the form of manuscripts, and (ii) saying that the MB tradition existed only in the South. Third, there is no justification for taking *āgamaḥ dākṣiṇātyeṣu grantha-mātre vyavasthitaḥ* as synonymous with *dākṣiṇātyaḥ āgamaḥ grantha-mātre vyavasthitaḥ*, as Scharfe does.

8. (a) See S. K. De 1938:258-59, and Siṃha 1969:242-43, for a discussion of Candra's/Candra-gomin's province of birth.

   (b) The presence of Gauḍas in early Kashmir is proved by RT 4.323-35 and Kṣemendra, *Deśopadeśa*, *adhyāya* 6. The latter refers to students from Bengal who had come to Kashmir to study Sanskrit and Sanskritic branches of knowledge. The grandfather of the remarkable author Jayanta-bhaṭṭa was also a Gauḍa who migrated to Kashmir.

   (c) Bronkhorst (1983:396-97) actually accepts Candra's residence in the South, i.e., in Gujarat or north Maharashtra. His discussion of Candra's locality shows no awareness of the literature referred to in (a). He obviously assumes that Candrācārya is definitely the same as Candra-gomin, that a Buddhist like Candra-gomin must have lived in an area inhabited by followers of the Maitrāyaṇīya recension of the Veda, and that the possibility of the localities of Candrācārya and Candra-gomin being different need not be entertained!

9. There are some minor but complex problems, in addition to the major problems indicated here, associated with Scharfe's use of the examples in the *Cāndra Vṛtti* and other related texts. It would be better to take them up for discussion in a separate publication.

10. The problems connected with the acceptance of Candragomin's authorship of the available *Cāndra Vṛtti* are discussed in Birwé 1968.

11. It is not clear to me exactly how Scharfe deduces from "We shall eat (*bhokṣyāmahe*) rice" that Candra-gomin's was a one-day journey to Kauśāmbī. Since Scharfe contrasts this example with others meaning "We shall eat twice," I have assumed that in his view "We shall eat rice" implies 'We shall eat rice once' and one rice meal implies one day's journey. However, who is likely to eat only one rice meal or only one meal per day? Does the example presuppose a Buddhist monk as the speaker of the sentence? In that case, why is there nothing in the context of the example that would suggest restriction of the example to a monk's situation? If, on the other hand, the inference that the distance was to be covered in one day is to be drawn only from the grammatical form *bhokṣyāmahe*, why do other grammarians specify the number of times they would carry out a particular act in a similar situation? Why does the *Kāśikā* (3.3.136, 138) see nothing wrong in changing *odanaṃ bhokṣyāmahe/bhoktāsmahe* to *dvir odanaṃ bhokṣyāmahe/bhoktāsmahe*, although it, too, speaks of a journey through Kauśāmbī to Pāṭaliputra? Scharfe (1976:275) glosses over the problem the *Kāśikā* examples pose by stating that they "appear to be compounded renderings of the sentences found in the *Candra-vṛtti* and Abhaya-nandin's *Mahāvṛtti* . . . the example must be regarded as one of those standard examples handed down through the times and used without respect for its actual [factual?] accuracy." Before

blaming the evidence that inconveniences his speculation, however, Scharfe should have asked himself: Why would the *Kāśikā* opt for compounded renderings? Is it certain that the *Kāśikā* was written later than the *Cāndra Vr̥tti* and the *Mahā-vr̥tti*? I am aware that, since Kielhorn's 1886 article, it has generally been held that the *Kāśikā* is influenced by the Cāndra *vyākaraṇa*. However, as I pointed out at the time of the 192d meeting of the American Oriental Society in 1982, this view may not be valid. Recently, Bronkhorst (1983:368) has argued that there is no Cāndra influence on at least the *sūtra* text in the *Kāśikā*. As for Abhaya-nandin, he has been placed in the post-*Kāśikā* period by the historians of Sanskrit grammar on very good grounds (Yudhiṣṭhira Mīmāṃsaka, 1973/*saṃvat* 2030, vol. 1, 3d ed., pp. 458-71, 584-86; also pp. 9, 24, and 51-52 of the introductions contributed by Vāsudeva-śaraṇa Agravāla, Nāthū-rāmajī Premī, and Yudhiṣṭhira Mīmāṃsaka to Śambhu-nātha Tripāṭhī's edition of Abhaya-nandin's *Mahā-vr̥tti*, Kashi: Bhāratīya Jñāna-pīṭha, 1956). Moreover, two of the *Kāśikā* phrases that could be said to have been inspired by the *Mahā-vr̥tti* are not as precise as their counterparts (compare *tatra saktūn pāsyāmaḥ* and *yuktā adhyaimahi* with *tatra . . . dviḥ saktūn pāsyāmaḥ* and *yuktā dvir adhyaimahi*). If the *Kāśikā* were at the borrowing end, why would it sacrifice the existing precision? That the *Kāśikā* elsewhere copies examples from such works as the MB hardly constitutes sufficient proof for the present purpose.

12. The questions I have about this particular assumption are: Was travel in the range of fifty miles generally viewed by Candra's contemporaries as possible in one day? Would an ordinary man eat only once during a fifty-mile journey when the journey is to be completed with ancient means? Would it be correct to hold that the *Cāndra Vṛtti* example is from the perspective of a monk who eats only one meal per day?

13. The attitude that may be implicit in Peterson's and Scharfe's attempts at identification also needs comment. Both these scholars write as if the *Ṭīkā* identification does not exist or need not be taken seriously. This is hardly a justifiable view to take of a piece of information that is about one thousand years old; that is unlikely to have been given unless it was known to earlier students and commentators of the VP (cf. *anuśrūyate* in the *Ṭīkā*); and that is in itself very plausible (especially because it contains the names Tri-kūṭa and Tiliṅga attested in a number of inscriptions, etc.). If Peterson or Scharfe had pointed out that the *Ṭīkā* detail offends common sense (has a mythic character like some other details in the *Ṭīkā*) or is contradicted by another equally old source, they would have been justified in setting it aside. By not following any such procedure they give the impression that information preserved by scholars directly in the line of transmission deserves little or no credence. This is an unwarranted and unprofitable position to take. Moreover, since their own views are based on the use of some indirectly related tradition, they are open to a charge

of self-serving eclecticism. The same comment can be extended to Bronkhorst's discussion.

14. Mirashi (1955:xl) follows a reading °*varti-tri-kaliṅgaika*° not found in Mānavallī's edition (1887), which Mirashi apparently used. As note 15 establishes, there is *some* trace of this reading in the generally inferior manuscript E7 and its transcript E14 but there is no clear support for it in any of the available manuscripts. Even in E7, the presence of *ka* is due to the copyist's inability to decide whether his exemplar reads *ta/ti* or *ka*. It would appear that Mirashi read the name Tri-kaliṅga in his source through an oversight caused by the memory of that name, which occurs in other historical records handled by him.

15. Following the designations given in Rau 1971, the deviations noticed in manuscripts from the *Ṭīkā* text accepted here can be specified as follows:

    (a) *trikūṭekadeśa*° E1, *trikūṭaideśa*° E25, *trikūṭaiddeśa*° E5, *trikūṭadeśa*° E7, *trikūṭe deśa*° E14.

    (b) °*varttinetiliṃgai* E8, °*varttinotiliṃgaika*° E1, °*vartinoliṃgaika*° E3, E9, E9a, E22, °*varttinoliṃgaika*° with *no* changed to *ti* in the margin E10, °*vartita-kaliṃgaika*° E7, E14, °*varttitaligauka*° E5, °*vartiti liṃgaika*° E20, °*varttine* [or *te*] *ligaika*° E23, °*varttiteliṃgaika*° E4, E21, E25, °*vavartitiliṃgaika*° E6.

    The difference of one *t* between *varti* and *vartti* is of no consequence, as anyone conversant with common features of Sanskrit orthography knows.

    The generally reliable manuscripts of the *Ṭīkā* are E4, E6, E11, E13, E15, E16, E21, E24, and E25, as my planned critical edition of the *Ṭīkā* will establish. They agree in reading the *Ṭīkā* phrase as I have accepted it in this study, except for the redundant writing of *va* in E6 and the presence of *te* in the place of *ti* in E4, E21, and E25. The last variation does not make any significant difference. Tiliṅga and Teliṅga are well-attested names of the same Telaṅgaṇā region.

The manuscripts designated E2, E17, E18, E19, and E26 by Rau do not contain the required portion. Rau's E12 is a modern transcript of E2. E9a did not somehow come to Rau's notice but was made available to me at the library of the Sanskrit College in Calcutta.

16. (a) I have not yet had time to determine which, if any, of the manuscripts accessible to me Mānavallī followed in his *editio princeps* of the *Vākya-kāṇḍa-ṭīkā*. It is possible that, as a nineteenth-century pandit, he showed preference for the Sanskrit-sounding form *triliṅga* over the Prakrit or *deśya*-sounding forms *tiliṅga* and *teliṅga*.

(b) *triliṅga* is noticed elsewhere as a variant of *tiliṅga* (see note 18cd). Its acceptance would not affect the subsequent discussion in this study.

17. For a critical examination of the other aspects of Thieme's view, see Aklujkar (1986).

18. (a) This spelling is according to the National Atlas of India. The spellings "Telingana," "Telengana," etc., are also noticed.

(b) For information on Tiliṅga or Telangana, see Raychaudhuri in Yazdani 1960:27-29; Sircar 1960:16, 71, 75-76, 88, 89; Gupta 1973:37; and Schwartzberg 1978:137, maps a and b; 38, map b; 39, map c; and 100, map a.

(c) *tri-liṅga, tiriliṅga*, etc., are attested as variants of *tiliṅga*. A secondary derivative *tailaṅga* is also found.

(d) "The name Tiriliṅga (Skt. Tri-liṅga) is traditionally derived from three shrines (*liṅgas*), namely, those at Kāleśvaram, Śrīśailam and Drākṣārāma . . .". (Gupta 1973:37). Bhīmeśvara in the place of Drākṣārāma is given as the third *liṅga* leading to the formation of Tri-liṅga by Lüders in ***Epigraphia Indica*** 6, no. 10 (1900-1): 93.

19. Parvata is also taken as a proper name of a region in northwestern India. According to Schwartzberg (1978: 184a), it refers to Jammu. It does not seem likely, however, that this reference was current in the days of B and his disciples. Besides, this Parvata was not likely to be thought of as southern in the period with which we are concerned (see note 3).

20. (a) For references to Śrī-parvata in Sanskrit literature, inscriptions, etc., see Aklujkar 1982:8. For the importance of Śrī-parvata in Indian religious history, see Ḍhere 1977:105-9, 179-80, 194-95.

(b) The geographical location of Śrī-parvata is shown in Schwartzberg 1978:22, map a; 27, map b; and 32, map a.

(c) Śrī-parvata and Śrī-śaila have been treated as practically identical in the publication mentioned in (b), as well as in some Sanskrit works and modern research publications. Śrī-parvata would seem to be the older of the two names and has a general as well as a specific reference. In its former role, it seems to stand for the mountain range toward the southwestern extremity of which the Brahmanical site of Śrī-śaila took shape (cf. Sircar 1965:235, n. 3; Schwartzberg 1978:27, map b). In the latter role, Śrī-parvata appears to be a predominantly Buddhist site near Nagarjunakonda in the northeastern part of the same Nallamala (alternative spellings "Nallamalur" and "Nalamalai") mountain range.

(d) The location of Śrī-śaila is shown in plate 35 of the *National Atlas of India* and in Schwartzberg 1978:21, map a; 25, map a; 26, map a; 27, map b; 31, map a; 34, maps a and b; 38, maps a and b; 41, map a; 47, map a; 99, map a; and 140, map a.

21. (a) Accounts of Candra's discovery, including those in Tibetan, will be compared in part 4 of this study.

(b) Fa-hsien's report of his travels in India between 399 and 414 A.D. contains a hearsay description of a five-tiered, or five-storied, mountain monastery (*Po-lo-yu* or *Po-lo-yue*) called approximately *pāravā* in the local language. At least some specialists of the travelogues of Chinese visitors to India have come to the conclusion that this monastery is identical with the one (*po-lo-mo-lo-ki-li*) which Yuan Chwang (=Hiuen Tsiang) visited about two hundred years later and which was on Śrī-parvata, associated with Nāgārjuna. Accordingly, Watters (1905:200-1; cf. Yazdani 1960:146-47) sees in Fa-hsien's *pāravā* the Sanskrit word parvata (not *pārāvata* 'pigeon' or 'columbarium' as Fa-hsien thought) standing for Śrī-parvata.

22. The tentative assumption here is that Candra-gomin is the same individual as Candrācārya or was confused with Candrācārya by this time.

23. Thus, Ramakrishna Kavi was on the right track when he included the guess "somewhere near Śrī Parvata, probably in the Andhra country" in his 1930 article (p. 239). However, he did not give any evidence or reasoning in support of his remark or provide a geographical specification of Śrī-parvata.

24. (a) Another possible identification of Tri-kūṭa, not as a mountain but as a region or country, will be taken up in **5.2**.

The assumption in my discussion at this point is that the *Ṭīkā* phrase *tri-kūṭaika-deśa-varti-tiliṅgaika-deśād* could originally have been different (a suspicion based on the repetition of *eka-deśa*, as on Thieme's part, but not resolved in the same way as Thieme proposes). The original form of the phrase was perhaps as follows: *tri-kūṭaika-deśa-[varti . . . ity eke. anye tv āhuḥ . . .-]varti-tiliṅgaika-deśād iti*, i.e., the text available at present could be a result of haplography caused by the recurrence of *varti*.

Resting on this assumption is the point of view that two possible lines of identification, one based on the name Tri-kūṭa and the other based on the name Tiliṅga, should be kept apart at this stage of the discussion.

(b) As the *Śabda-kalpa-druma* (p. 655) notes, Sanskrit lexicons give the names Tri-kakud, Suvela, Tri-mukuṭa, Tri-śṛṅga, and Citra-kūṭa in the same group as Tri-kūṭa. Except for Suvela, which may be helpful in determining the location of the Tri-kūṭa mentioned in Rāma narratives, the other mountains seem to have been grouped with Tri-kūṭa only on account of the structural similarity of the names.

25. This mountain would be very close to Śrī-parvata (see note 20) if not identical with a part of Śrī-parvata understood as a mountain range.
26. Mirashi (1975:205-19) establishes that, in the perception of many Classical authors, Laṅkā was located in Siṃhala.
27. (a) It would be simplistic to hold that only one tradition regarding the location of Laṅkā was current in as diverse and large a country as India and throughout as long a period as that of Classical Sanskrit literature.

    (b) The view that, in Vālmīki's perception, Rāvaṇa's Laṅkā was situated in a place other than Ceylon, probably near the Vindhyas, has been expressed for many years. Shah (1976) and Sankalia (1982) are the most recent exponents of that view known to me.
28. If, however, the identification is correct with reference to a part of the historical evidence available (see note 34) and we have in fact two Tri-kūṭas (approximately on the western and eastern borders of the Sātavāhana empire), then we will have open to us the alternative 'parvata = Tri-kūṭa = Kotappakonda', but it will not materially be very different from the alternative 'parvata = Śrī-parvata' (see note 25).
29. For understandable reasons, the ancient traveller in India had to move along those areas where the height of mountains like the Vindhyas was either not to be met

with or was negotiable. A sort of western corridor for the movement of men and goods, therefore, seems to have developed near the Nasik area.

30. (a) Tri-kūṭa is near such ancient Buddhist sites as Kanheri and Ajanta, and near Brahmin holy places like Tryambakeśvara. The appeal that Śrī-parvata had for Buddhists and Brahmins can be judged from the information and sources given in note 20.

    (b) I intend to discuss the problem of the religious affiliation of (B and) Candrācārya in a separate publication. One's conclusions in this regard will naturally depend on whether Candrācārya is held to be identical with Candra-gomin and, to some extent, on what view one takes of the religious affiliation of B and his disciples.

31. Subramania Iyer's (1977:li, 204) renderings of the *Ṭīkā* phrase, "Triliṅga country, near the Trikūṭa mountain" and "Trikūṭa," are not as precise as they should have been.

32. The *Ṭīkā* author could also be said to have a region rather than a mountain in mind. In the latter part of his identifying phrase, *eka-deśa* is compounded with *tiliṅga*, the name of a region. The same is, therefore, likely to be true of *eka-deśa* in *tri-kūṭaika-deśa*.

33. Thus, Schwartzberg (1978:137, map a) is right in showing Tri-kūṭa as a region.

34. As possible evidence to the effect that Tri-kūṭa could have at times denoted a larger area than the one determined by Mirashi, note the following:

(a) The word *tri-kūṭa*, probably referring to an area, occurs in a third-century A.D. plate discovered in the Vizagapatnam district; cf. Hultzch, *Epigraphia Indica* 3, no. 3 (1894-95):19-20.

(b) A temple of Tri-kūṭeśvara is said to be near the village Koṇḍakāvūru, which is eight miles south of Narasarāvupeṭā; cf. Lüders, *Epigraphia Indica* 6, no. 12 (1900-1):116, 127.

(c) In a Viṣṇukuṇḍin inscription, Prince Mādhava-varman II, whose headquarters were at Amara-pura (= Amarāvatī near Śrī-parvata?) has been called *tri-kūṭa-malayādhipati*; cf. Sircar 1960:189.

(d) If there were in fact two historical Tri-kūṭās, (c) and (d) of our list in **4.7**, it is possible that the area between them governed by rulers such as the Sātavāhanas was known as the country of the Tri-kūṭeśvaras or as Tri-kūṭa.

(f) There is a temple of Tri-kūṭeśvara existing from at least 1191 A.D. at Gadag in Dharwar district; cf. Kielhorn, *Epigraphia Indica* 3, no. 30 (1894):217-20.

(g) Mishra (1973:139), on the basis of Sumpa Mkhan-Po's *Pag-Sam-Jon-Zang* (p. lxvi) edited by S. C. Das, points out the probability that there once was a Traikūṭaka *vihāra* in West Bengal.

35. There are no expressions indicating a miracle in 486 (Aklujkar 1981:600), although a miracle is at least suggested in all the other known accounts except the one in the RT.

36. Under this possibility, what the author of 486 would, in effect, be saying would be this: 'Candrācarya and others

came from the North and acquired from the mountain the *āgama* that had survived only in a written form among the *dākṣiṇātyas*, that is, among us'. B, as the author's teacher, would then be the person who built on the foundation prepared by Candrācārya (verse 487) and revived the tradition, at least in the Nasik area.

37. (a) *'vaset parvata-mūleṣu prauḍho yo dhyāna-dhāraṇāt / sārāt sāraṃ vijānāti parvataḥ parikīrtitaḥ //* 'He who lives in the foot-areas of mountains, is advanced/ mature on account of practice of meditation, and knows the quintessence, is said to be parvata'.

(b) According to the *Hindī Śabda-sāgara* (vol. 6, p. 2883), parvata is a *saṃnyāsin* who belongs to the Daśanāmī sect and lives at the foot of a mountain, devoting himself to meditation. This information is corroborated by the *Bṛhacchaṅkara-vijaya* passage quoted in the *Prāṇa-toṣiṇī*. The names of the ten *saṃnyāsins* are given in that passage in this order: *tīrtha, āśrama, vana, araṇya, giri, parvata, sāgara, sarasvatī, bhāratī,* and *purī.*

(c) Prior to quoting the verse in (a) as a definition found in the Avadhūta chapter of the *Prāṇa-toṣiṇī*, the *Śabda-kalpa-druma* (III, pp. 77-78) informs us that parvata in this sense is "a specific kind of disciple/ follower of Maṇḍana-miśra, who was the disciple of Śaṃkarācārya." I do not know the basis for the specific association with Maṇḍana-miśra.

38. The author of the *Bāla-manoramā* commentary is puzzled by Bhaṭṭoji's example, as can be seen from his comment: *parvatasya sthāvara-janmatayā tāpasasya tad-apekṣayā-*

bhyarhitatvaṃ bodhyam. bhāṣye tu mātā-pitarāv ity udāhṛtam. 'Since a parvata is born of a stationary entity (or is stationary by birth), a *tāpasa* should be understood as worthy of respect in comparison to him. The example in the *Bhāṣya* is, however, *mātā-pitarau*'. The *Tattva-bodhinī* commentary does not even indicate awareness of the example *tāpasa-parvatau.*

39. (a) See note 37.

(b) It might be asked if this sense of parvata could be as old as the author of 486. I am not aware of any evidence that would conclusively prove this sense to be so old. However, since Vidyāraṇya's list of the ten classes of monks is not very logical (in the first seven location is the criterion, whereas in the last three it is not; there is also overlapping between *āśrama, vana,* and *araṇya,* and between *giri* and *parvata*), it may be inferred that it has old as well as new terms simply put together. See also **6.2**.

40. (a) Or has he used *parvatāt* for *parvate* simply because, in the phrase *parvate āgamaṃ labdhvā,* the word *parvate,* reduced to *parvata* by *saṃdhi,* would have disturbed the meter?

(b) Scharfe (1976:276, n. 21) simply dismisses the view of "an eminent Indian Sanskritist" that *parvate* would have been proper if a mountain was intended and that the use of *parvatāt* indicates that a person was probably intended. Scharfe does not point out, as he should have, any instances in which an 'ablative + *labh*' construction is used to give the location (as distinct from a conscious source) of an acquisition.

Note that, for the resolution of the grammatical point involved here, it is not necessary that the acquisition be that of an *āgama.* I am not making the unreasonable expectation that another occurrence strictly of the type 'ablative of location + *āgamaṃ* + *labdhvā*' be pointed out, for I do realize that there would be very few occasions requiring one to speak of the acquisition of an *āgama.* Similarly, any form of *labh* or a synonymous root would do. The point is that Scharfe should have cited at least one parallel instance favoring the 'location' interpretation before setting aside so casually the observation he attributes to an eminent Indian Sanskritist.

In his letter of 6 November 1987, Scharfe informs me that the observation was made by V. Raghavan at the time of the American Oriental Society meeting held at Santa Barbara.

(c) As the correct reading of RT 1.176 is *candrācāryādibhir labdhvādeśaṃ tasmāt* (Aklujkar 1986), the source in that 'ablative + *labh*' construction is King Abhimanyu, i.e., the source is sentient.

41. (a) Since the etymological or wider meaning of *amanuṣya* is something anyone knowing Sanskrit would think of right at the outset, it does not need a tradition to come into existence, but the narrow meaning is so specific and unexpected that it is not likely to be found in commentaries like the *Kāśikā* unless a tradition to the effect that it was intended by Pāṇini existed.

(b) From Patañjali's comments on 3.2.52-3, it seems that commentators of Pāṇini had begun by Patañjali's time to entertain the possibility of taking *amanuṣya* in a literal sense. The *Kāśikā* does not appear to be the first commentary to do so.

42. As the secondary derivatives tend to acquire a general meaning (such as 'belonging to, pertaining to, associated with') in the history of Sanskrit, *pārvata* (and *parvatīya*) probably expanded beyond the sense 'a parvata-dwelling ogre/ghost/ascetic' to include items associated with mountains in general; i.e., *pārvata* (and *parvatīya*) could also be used as adjectives of things such as water and fruit found on a mountain. It is likely that because of this semantic development the *Kāśikā* decided not to follow consistently the narrow meaning of *amanuṣya* it advocated in the case of Pāṇini 2.4.23.

Select Bibliography

Items for which publication details have been specified in the earlier parts of this study or can be gathered from Cardona (1976) have not been included here. The same applies to well-known works like the *Rāmāyaṇa* and well-known series such as *Epigraphia Indica.*

Aklujkar, Ashok. 1987. "Rāja-taraṅgiṇī 1.176." In *Ancient Indian History, Philosophy and Culture, Essays in Memory of Professor Radhagovinda Basak Vidyavacaspati.*

(Eds.) Pratap Bandyopadyay and Manabendu Banerjee, 224-45. Calcutta: Sanskrit Pustak Bhandar.

Bronkhorst, Johannes. 1983. "On the History of Pāṇinian Grammar in the Early Centuries Following Patañjali." *Journal of Indian Philosophy* 11:357-412.

Cardona, George. 1976. *Pāṇini: a Survey of Research.* The Hague, Paris: Mouton. Indian edition. Delhi: Motilal Banarsidass.

De, S. K. 1938. "Candra-Gomin." *Indian Historical Quarterly* 14:256-60.

Ḍhere, Rāma-candra Cintāmaṇa. 1977. *Cakra-pāṇi (ādya marāṭhī vāṅmayācī sāṃskr̥tika pārśva-bhūmī).* Poona: Viśva-karmā Sāhityālaya. In Marathi.

Gupta, Parmanand. 1973. *Geography in Ancient Indian Inscriptions (up to 650 A.D.).* Delhi: D. K. Publishing House.

Hindī Śabda-sāgara. Revised ed. 1969. Kāśī Nāgarī Pracāriṇī Sabhā. Prayag: India Press, Ltd. In Hindi.

Joshi, S. D. 1976. "Sanskrit Grammar." In *Ramakrishna Gopal Bhandarkar as an Indologist, a Symposium.* (Ed.) Dandekar, R. N., 113-42. Poona: Bhandarkar Oriental Research Institute.

Joshi, S. D., and Roodbergen, J. A. F. 1976. *Patañjali's Vyākaraṇa-Mahābhāṣya Anabhihitāhnika (P. 2.3.1-2.3.17).* Poona: University of Poona. Publications of the Centre of Advanced Study in Sanskrit, class C, no. 11.

Katre, S. M. 1954. *Introduction to Indian Textual Criticism.* Poona: Deccan College Post-graduate and Research Institute. Deccan College Handbook Series, no. 5.

Kirfel, Willibald. 1954. *Das Purāṇa vom Weltgebaude.* Bonn: Selbstverlag des Orientalischen Seminars der Universität Bonn.

Laddu, S. D. 1981. "A Reconsideration of the History of the Mahābhāṣya." In *C.A.S.S.* [Centre of Advanced Study in Sanskrit] *Studies*, no. 6, pp. 187-97. Poona: University of Poona.

Law, Bimala Churn. 1932. *Geography of Early Buddhism.* London: Kegan Paul, Trench, Trubner & Co. Reprint 1979. New Delhi: Oriental Books Reprint Corp.

Mānavallī, Gaṅgādhara Śāstrī (Ed.). 1887. *Vākyapadīyaṃ . . . śrī-bhartṛhari- . . . viracitaṃ śrī-puṇya-rāja-kṛta- . . . ṭīkā-yutam.* Benares: Braj B. Das & Co. Benares Sanskrit Series, nos. 11, 19, 24.

Mirashi, Vasudev Vishnu. 1955. *Inscriptions of the Kalachuri-Chedi Era.* Corpus Inscriptionum Indicarum, vol. 4, pt. 1. Ootacamund: Government Epigraphist for India.

-------. 1963. *Inscriptions of the Vākāṭakas.* Corpus Inscriptionum Indicarum, vol. 5. Ootacamund: Government Epigraphist for India.

-------. 1975. *Literary and Historical Studies in Indology.* Delhi: Motilal Banarsidass.

Mishra, Vibhuti Bhushan. 1973. *Religious Beliefs and Practices of North India During the Early Mediaeval Period.* The Hague: E. J. Brill.

Moticandra. 1953/1966. *Sārthavāha.* Patna: Bihāra-rāṣṭra-bhāṣā-pariṣad. In Hindi.

Mulay, Sumati. 1972. *Studies in the Historical and Cultural Geography and Ethnography of the Deccan. . . .*

Poona: Deccan College Post-graduate and Research Institute. Deccan College Dissertation Series D, no. 68.

Rāma-toṣaṇa Bhaṭṭācārya. *Prāṇa-toṣiṇī.* (Ed.) Jīvānanda Vidyāsāgara Bhaṭṭācārya. 3d ed. Calcutta: n.p., 1898. Dates of earlier editions not known.

Sankalia, Hasmukhlal Dhirajlal. 1982. *The Rāmāyaṇa in the Historical Perspective.* Delhi: Macmillan.

Scharfe, Hartmut. 1976. "A Second 'Index Fossil' of Sanskrit Grammarians." *Journal of the American Oriental Society* 96:274-77.

Schwartzberg, Joseph E. (Ed.). 1978. *A Historical Atlas of South Asia.* Chicago, London: University of Chicago Press. Association for Asian Studies Reference Series, no. 2.

Shah, U. P. 1976. "The Sālakaṭaṅkaṭas and Laṅkā." *Journal of the American Oriental Society* 96:109-13.

Siṃha, Raghu-nātha (Ed., trans.). 1969. *Kalhaṇa's Rāja-taraṅgiṇī,* vol. 1. Varanasi: Hindī Pracāraka Saṃsthāna. In Hindi.

------- (Ed., trans.). 1974. *Kalhaṇa's Rājataraṅgiṇī,* vol. 2. Varanasi: Hindī Pracāraka Saṃsthāna. In Hindi.

Sircar, D. C. 1960. *Studies in the Geography of Ancient and Medieval India.* Delhi: Motilal Banarsidass.

Subramania Iyer, K. A. 1977. *The Vākyapadīya of Bhartṛhari, Chapter II, English Translation.* Delhi: Motilal Banarsidass.

Tārā-nātha Tarka-vācaspati (Ed., comment.). 1864 (*saṃvatsara* 1921). *Siddhānta-kaumudī, parārddham* [second half]. Calcutta: Saṃskṛta-yantra [press of the Sanskrit College?].

-------. 1902. *Śabdārtha-ratnam.* 3d ed. Calcutta: Dakṣiṇā-caraṇa Cakravartin at V. L. Press. Dates of the first two editions not known.

Watters, Thomas. 1905. *On Yuan Chwang's Travels in India (A.D. 629-645).* London: Royal Asiatic Society. First Indian ed./rpt. 1961, two vols. in one. Delhi: Munshi Ram Manohar Lal.

Wilson, H. H. 1894 (Trans., annot.). *The Viṣṇu Purāṇa. . . .* Edition with introduction by R. C. Hazra, 1972. Calcutta: Punthi Pustak.

Yazdani, G. (Ed.). 1960. *The Early History of the Deccan.* Parts 1-6 in one volume. London: Oxford University Press.

VIṂŚATI PADĀNI . . . TRIṂŚAT . . . CATVĀRIṂŚAT

Pandit V. B. Bhagwat

'तपरस्तत्कालस्य ' (पा. १.१.७०) इति सूत्रे महाभाष्यकारः ध्वनिवर्णयोः पृथग्भावं विशदीकर्तुं 'तद्यथा भेर्याघातः भेरीमाहत्य कश्चिद्विंशति पदानि गच्छति, कश्चित् त्रिंशत् कश्चित् चत्वारिंशत् । स्फोटस्तावानेव भवति, ध्वनिकृता वृद्धिः' इति दृष्टान्तं प्रस्तौति ।

अत्र दृष्टान्तप्रघट्टके शब्दसाधुत्वमर्थसंगतिश्च इत्युभयत्रापि महती विप्रतिपत्तिर्भवति प्रेक्षावताम् । तथार्थसंगतिं साधयितुं प्रदीपोद्योतयोः महाभाष्यप्रसिद्धटीकयोः बहुतरकं शब्दच्छलमाश्रित्य प्रयतितम् । शब्दसाधुत्वविषये न ताभ्यामीषदपि विप्रतिपत्तिराशङ्किता, नापि निराकृता । अत्र लघुप्रबन्धे सेयं शब्दसाधुत्वविषये विप्रतिपत्तिः विचार्यते ।

तत्र मुद्रितपुस्तकेषु त्रिषु[१] विंशति पदानि इति पृथक् पदे, पञ्चसु[२] विंशतिपदानि इति अविभक्तमेकं सामासिकं पदम्, एकस्मिन्[३] पुस्तके विंशतिं पदानि इति द्वितीयैकवचनान्तं विंशतिं पृथक्पदम् इति त्रयी विधा दृश्यते ।

तत्र यथाक्रममेकैका विमृश्यते ।

यदि पृथक् पदे तर्हि विंशति इति संख्येयपरे पदानीत्यस्य विशेषणे एकत्वं नपुंसकत्वं च व्यक्तमभ्युपेये । तत्र एकत्वं शास्त्रकोशव्यवहारसंमतम् । नपुंसकत्वं तावत्सर्वथा असंमतम् । विंशत्यादीनां संख्येयपराणामर्थात् विशेषणानामपि सर्वत्र नित्यस्त्रीत्वाभ्युपगमात्[४] । स्पष्टमभ्युपगतश्चायं समयविशेषः 'अन्ये च गुणवचनाः द्रव्यस्य लिङ्गसंख्ये अनुवर्तन्ते, ------ विंशत्यादयः पुनर्नानुवर्तन्ते' इति प्रघट्टके महाभाष्यकारेण (५.१.५९) । कोशैः[५] व्यवहारेण च स एव समयविशेषः नित्यमनुसृतोऽस्त्यव्यभिचारम् ।

अथ विंशतिपदानि इति एकमपृथक्सामासिकं पदम्, तदा पूर्वं निर्दिष्टः लिङ्गवचनदोषावकाशः नास्ति, तथापि तत्र समासानुशासनविरोधः शास्त्रानु-

सरणशीलानां मनांसि द्रढीयो दुनोति इति सर्पाद्रक्षितस्य व्याघ्रमुखे पातः । यतः 'दिक्संख्ये संज्ञायाम्' (पा. २.१.५०) इति नियमसूत्रं 'संज्ञायामेव' इति संख्यापूर्वपदं समासं नियमयति । न च विंशतिपदानि इति कस्यापि पदसमूहस्य भूखण्डस्य वा संज्ञास्ति, येन तत्र समासः शास्त्रेण सुसंपादः स्यात् ।

यद्यपि 'तद्धितार्थोत्तरपदसमाहारे च' (पा. २.१.५१) इति सूत्रं पूर्वसूत्रेण नियतं संख्यापूर्वपदं समासं प्रतिप्रसूते, तथापि तद्धितार्थे, उत्तरपदे, समाहारे इति त्रिष्वेव विषयेषु स प्रतिप्रसवः, 'विंशतिपदानि' इत्यत्र एतेषु त्रिष्वन्यतमः कोऽपि विषयो नास्ति ।

डॉ. किल्होर्नसंपादितमहाभाष्यस्य तृतीये संस्करणे (१९६२) अन्तिमटिप्पणीषु ५६८ तमे पृष्ठे 'विंशतिपदानि' इति समासाश्रयणम् अपृथङ्मुद्रणं च साधु इति अत्र समाहितम्, तथापि 'दिक्संख्ये संज्ञायाम्' इति नियमे ललाटंतपे कथं स समासः न दुष्येत, कथंकारं च व्याकरणाध्ययनं प्रशंसन् व्याकरणमहाभाष्यकारः स्वयमेव शास्त्रविरुद्धं प्रयुञ्जीत इति विमर्शनार्हं विपश्चिताम् ।

विंशतिं पदानि इति सर्वथा साधुः प्रयोगः, तथापि स पाठः केवलमेकस्मिन् काश्मीरहस्तलिखिते उपलभ्यते । यच्च अत्यन्तं लघु, मध्ये मध्ये भूयः खण्डितमतः न प्रमाणरूपेण स्वीकर्तुमलमिति भूयसां महाभाष्यसंपादकानां स्यादभिप्रायः, तेन स द्वितीयैकवचनान्तः पाठः एकेनैव समाश्रितो दृश्यते ।

अथ 'कश्चित्त्रिंशत् कश्चिच्चत्वारिंशत्' इति प्रयोगविषये साधुत्वासाधुत्वे विमृशामः । शास्त्रकोशव्यवहारान् अनुसृत्य 'कश्चित्त्रिंशतम् कश्चिच्चत्वारिंशतम्' इत्येव साधुः प्रयोगः, यतः त्रिंशत्-चत्वारिंशत्-शब्दौ पूर्वोक्तप्रमाणमनुसृत्य नित्यं स्त्रियामेकत्वे च वर्तेते । अत्रापि निर्दिष्टचरे काश्मीरहस्तलिखिते शुद्धः पाठः उपलभ्यते इति डॉ. किल्होर्नसंपादिते पाठभेदविभागे निर्दिष्टम्, तथापि तद् हस्तलिखितं प्रमाणमिति अवलम्बितुमनलम् इति अधुनैवोक्तम् । कदाचित् केनचित् सुज्ञतमेन लिपिकरेणापि तत्राशुद्धिं परिहर्तुं तथा शुद्धं लिखितं स्यात्, यतः अन्यत्र सर्वत्र हस्तलिखितेषु यः समानः पाठः उपलभ्यते स एव मूलभूतः प्रमाणपूतश्चापि स्यादिति संपादकमहाशयानामाशयः केवलं 'भूयस एव ग्रहणानि भविष्यन्ति' (म. भा. १.१.४८.४) संख्याधिक्यं प्रमाणाधिक्यं वा प्रामाण्यनिर्णये ऽलमिति वा न्यायमनुसरति ।

अथेदानीमिदमपि चिन्तनीयं यत् यदि 'विंशति पदानि . . . त्रिंशत् . . . चत्वारिंशत्' इत्येव मूलः प्रामाणिकः च पाठः, यदि च पाणिनीये

व्याकरणे कृतभूरिपरिश्रमाणां सूक्ष्मतमचक्षुषां कैयटभट्टोजीदीक्षितनागेशानां महाभाष्यटीकाकाराणां पुरतः अयमेव सर्वथा असाधुः पाठः अवर्तिष्यत, तर्हि कुतस्ते तस्यासाधुत्वे सर्वथा मौनमेवालम्बिष्यन्त, यतः अन्यत्र नैकत्र महाभाष्य-प्रयोगेषु भाष्यवचनानि शास्त्राननुसारमतः असाधूनीव प्रतीतानि, तदा यथाकथमपि साधुत्वं समर्थयितुं ते बहुतमकं प्रायतन्त[६]। यत्र च साधुत्वसमर्थनं सर्वथा अशक्यसंभवं तदा भाष्यकारवचनात्साधुत्वम्[७] इति धाष्टर्यमवलम्बितुमपि ते धृष्णुवन्ति । न केवलं शब्दसाधुत्वविषये एव , किंतु धर्मशास्त्रादिविषये अपि ते महाभाष्यस्याकुण्ठं प्रामाण्यमभ्युपगच्छन्ति ।

कदाचित्तथासमर्थने महिष्ठेन धाष्टर्येन द्रढिष्ठप्रामाण्याभ्युपगमे च तेषामयमभि-प्रायष्टीकाकृतां संभवति, यत् व्यवहारनीतिधर्मादीनि शास्त्रान्तराणि यद्यपि 'यान्यस्माकं सुचरितानि तानि त्वया सेव्यानि नो इतराणि' इत्युपनिषदुपदेशं[८] प्रमाणयन्ति, तथापि व्याकरणशास्त्रं प्रयोगविषये तानि सविशेषमतिशेते, यतः प्रयुक्तानामिदमन्वाख्यानमतः यान्यस्माकं प्रयुक्तानि असाधूनीति प्रतीतानि, तानि नासाधूनि किंतु साधूनि इति अभ्युपेयानि, समर्थनीयानि च ।

अपि च प्राचीनां श्रद्धाप्रणालीमनुसृत्य व्याकरणशास्त्रे पाणिनिः, कात्या-यनः, पतञ्जलिश्चेति त्रय एव लक्ष्यैकचक्षुष्काः, अन्ये भर्तृहरिप्रभृतयोऽपि सर्वे लक्षणैकचक्षुष्काः इति, अतः पाणिन्यादीनां त्रयाणां मुनीनां सर्वाणि लक्ष्याणि अर्थात्साधवः शब्दाः करबदरसदृक्षाः प्रत्यक्षा एव, एवं स्थिते ते कथंकारमसाधून् प्रयुञ्जीरन्, ये च तैः प्रयुक्ताः, ते सर्वे साधव एव, न जातुचित् कश्चिदप्यसाधुः स्यात् ।

श्रद्धायेमां परंपरां प्रस्तुतं प्रस्तुमः, यत् यदि च ते कैयटादयः एतादृशमसाधुं पाठमलप्स्यन्त तर्हि तत्रावश्यमसाधुत्वमशङ्किष्यन्त, अन्ते च कदाचिदेवमपि निरणेष्यन्त यत् महाभाष्यकारवचनात् विंशत्यादीनां संख्येयपराणां लिङ्गं क्वचन विशेष्यनिघ्नमपि, अथवा विंशति त्रिंशत् चत्वारिंशत् इति प्रातिपदिकनिर्देशो ऽयम्, प्रातिपदिकनिर्देशाश्चार्थतन्त्रा भवन्ति (म. भा. १.१.५६) इति ।

यतः तेषु प्रथितेषु टीकाकृत्सु नैकतमोऽपि अत्र साधुत्वे संशेते, न वा कथमपि समर्थयते, तेन मन्यामहे यत्सर्वेषु बहुसंख्याकेषु वा हस्तलिखितेषु समुपलब्धः प्रायः सर्वैरपि संपादकमहाशयैः भूयोऽनुग्रहबुद्ध्या प्रमाणमितिसमाश्रितः सर्वथा अशुद्धः पाठः न तैः कैयटादिभिः प्रमाणत्वेन स्वीकृते हस्तलिखिते स्यात् । किंतु ज्ञानलवदुर्विदग्धः पण्डितंमन्यः कश्चेल्लिपिकरः पदानीति विशेष्यस्य नपुंसकत्वं,

विंशत्यादीनां संख्येयवचनानां नित्यैकत्वमात्रं, न तु नित्यस्त्रीत्वमपि, कुतश्चिदधिगत्य तादृशमशुद्धं पाठं लिलेख, ततः अन्धपरंपरान्यायेन स एवाशुद्धः पाठः अन्यैर्लिपिकरैरनुसृतः स्यात् अथवान्येन केनापि कारणेनायं सांप्रतिकः अशुद्धः पाठः सर्वत्र प्रथितः बहुलीभूतश्च स्यात्, स एवाधुनिकैः संपादकैः दुराचारं स्वापत्यमिव क्रोडीकृतः स्याद्वात्सल्येन इत्येव तर्कयितुं प्रभवामो वयम् ।

विषयोऽयं निपुणमतिभिः संपादनशास्त्रनदीष्णैराधुनिकैरवश्यं विमर्शनीय इति उपन्यस्तोऽत्र ।

संदर्भाः

१. I. भांडारकरप्राच्यविद्यासंशोधनमंदिरप्रकाशितम् ।
II. हरयाणा जज्झरप्रकाशितम् ।
III. चारुदेवशास्त्रिकृतहिन्दीभाषान्तरसहितम् ।

२. I. विद्योदययंत्रालय शिलाप्रेसकाशी
II. निर्णयसागर मुंबई
III. प्रदीपोद्योततत्त्वालोकसहितम्
IV. तिरुचिरपल्लि, सुब्रह्मण्यशास्त्रिकृतम् आंग्लभाषानुवादसहितम्
V. गुरुप्रसादशास्त्रिसंपादितम् काशी

३. I. डेक्कनेज्युकेशनसोसायटी पुणे प्रकाशितं मराठीभाषान्तरसहितम्

४. I. विंशत्यादिरानवतेः, लिङ्गानुशासनम् १३
II. महाभाष्य ५.१.५९

५. विंशत्याद्याः सदैकत्वे ---- अमरकोश द्वितीयकाण्डं वैश्यवर्गः ॥८३॥

६. I. प्रदीपटीकायाम् -- मयूरव्यंसकादित्वाच्चात्र समासः । (१.१.२९)
मृदुश्चासौ विशदश्चेति कर्मधारयः (१.४.४९)
वैयधिकरण्येऽपि विस्पष्टपटुवत् (२.१.४७)
सुप्सुपेति समासः
II. उद्योतटीकायाम् -- मध्यमपदलोपी समासः ।. (१.१.४८)
पुकि अन्तः इति सुप्सुपेति समासः । (१.१.३)

७. I. प्रदीपटीकायाम् -- भाष्यकारवचनप्रामाण्यात् ह्रस्वः (१.४.१०९)

II. कौस्तुभे -- 'वस्तुतस्तु उक्तभाष्यानुरोधात् पुंस्त्वायोगमात्रं व्यवच्छेद्यम्' पस्पशा सक्तुमिव तितउना . . . ।
'ऋषिवचनत्वाविशेषात् भाष्यकारोक्तेर्मानवादेश्च व्रीहियववत् विकल्प एव' पस्पशा -- पुराकल्प एतदासीत् --- इति भाष्यविवरणे

III. उद्योते 'ईदृशप्रकारोऽपि भाष्यप्रामाण्याद्युक्त एव' १.२.४५.४

८. तैत्तिरीयोपनिषद् १.११.२

VYAÑJANĀ AS REFLECTED IN THE FORMAL STRUCTURE OF LANGUAGE

Saroja Bhate

The close relationship between poetics and grammar has often been articulated in Indian tradition. Ānandavardhana, the author of the *Dhvanyāloka*, the well-known treatise on poetics, remarks *prathame hi vidvāṃso vaiyākaraṇāḥ* 'The grammarians are the foremost scholars'.[1] The doctrine of *dhvani* owes its existence to the grammarians' doctrine of *sphoṭa* according to Abhinavagupta, the author of the commentary *Locana* on the *Dhvanyāloka*.[2] Since *śabda* 'word' is the nucleus in both these systems, they share some topics in common. For instance, the diverse types of meanings understood from a word are treated in both the grammar and the poetics. In addition to the two well-known functions of a word, namely, *abhidhā* 'expressive function' and *lakṣaṇā* 'secondary function', a third is added by rhetoricians like Ānandavardhana. This is known as *vyañjanā* 'suggestive function'. It is of the utmost significance and plays a vital role in poetics. It is introduced and established by Ānandavardhana and his followers who have further elaborated it by classifying it into several kinds. He says, "The language of the great poets is possessed of an extraordinary power of suggestion which pervades the whole poetry like the charm of a beautiful woman which is over and above her limbs and features."[3] The suggested meaning, which is understood through the function of *vyañjanā*, is known as *dhvani*. *Dhvani*, the soul of poetry, is, on the one hand, the manifestation of *pratibhā* 'intuition' of the poet. On the other, it is subject to the understanding of those listeners or readers who possess *pratibhā*.

It is generally believed that among the grammarians of Sanskrit it is Nāgeśa who first recommends acceptance of *vyañjanā* as a separate function of words. He not only describes the nature of *vyañjanā* following the rhetoricians but also refutes the claim of the Naiyāyikas, the logicians, that *vyañjanā* can be subsumed under *lakṣaṇā*.[4]

According to the exponents of the *dhvani* theory, the hidden beauty of poetry is understood only through the function of *vyañjanā*. Various kinds of *dhvani* as well as *vyañjanā* are described in different works on poetics.[5] It has been recognized by the *dhvanivādins* that the *dhvani* is communicated by both linguistic and extralinguistic factors. Among the extralinguistic factors are listed the specific character of the speaker as well as that of the listener, the presence of another person, the context, the situation, time, place, and gesture.[6] The linguistic factors that convey *dhvani* are sentence, compounds, words, word-parts, suffix, syntax, and the poetry as a whole.[7] Rhetoricians from Ānandavardhana to Jagannātha have supplied a number of illustrations to show how *dhvani* is understood from various linguistic elements. A few illustrations cited by the rhetoricians are given below to make the point clear.

In the *Sāhityadarpaṇa* a verse from the second act of the well-known drama of Kālidāsa, the *Abhijñāna-Śākuntalam*, is cited. The verse runs as follows: *Muhuraṅgulisaṃvṛtā-dharoṣṭhaṃ pratiṣedhākṣaraviklavābhirdāmam / Mukham aṃsavivarti pakṣmalākṣyāḥ katham apy unnamitaṃ na cumbitaṃ tu //*[8] 'Gently she covered her lower lip with her finger, [but] charmingly she could not say "no." [I] somehow lifted her face, [which she] turned [away from me] toward her shoulder, but I did not kiss it'. Viśvanātha remarks "*atra 'tu' iti nipātasya anutāpavyañjakatvam*" 'Here the particle *tu* suggests repentance'.[9]

A verse from the *Meghadūtam* of Kālidāsa is cited in the *Dhvanyāloka* as follows: *tālaiḥ śiñjadvalayasubhagaiḥ kāntayā nartito me / yām adhyāste divasavigame nīlakaṇṭhaḥ suhṛd vaḥ //* '[O cloud! It is the golden perch] on which sits the peacock, your friend who is made to dance every evening by my wife on the rhythm of the clappings of her hands making sweet sound of her tinkling bangles'.

Here the plural ending added after the word *tāla* implies the versatile character of the heroine and thereby suggests the intensity of the pangs of separation experienced by the hero.[10]

Many other citations may be found in different treatises on poetics. The two illustrations given above are enough to show how, according to the poeticians, various linguistic elements such as the indeclinable *tu* and the case-endings suggest certain feelings. The point to be noted in this connection is that it is implied by all the rhetoricians that the *dhvani* is purely subjective or intuitive. It flashes in the heart of the reader as soon as he reads a particular sentence, word, or word-element. The question that arises is, therefore, do all the readers comprehend the same *dhvani* from a certain linguistic expression? Or does it change from reader to reader? Even if it is admitted that only the *sahṛdayas*, the connoisseurs, have the ability to grasp the *dhvani*, do all the aesthetes agree in their understanding of the same *dhvani* from an expression?

Generally, they do not. The suggested meaning is thus a purely subjective matter. Two readers may not read the same meaning between the lines of poetry. And the more subjective is the appreciation of poetry, the less theoretical it turns out to be. This leads to the lack of uniformity, precision, and accuracy that are essential to make a system a formal science. It is precisely for this inconsistent and obscure character of the *dhvani* that the Naiyāyikas, Jayanta-bhaṭṭa in particular, vehemently attacked the *dhvani* theory and rejected *vyañjanā*, as a separate function.[11] This aspect of the doctrine of *dhvani* and *vyañjanā* seems to lead poetics away from a formal science. It tends to be more intuitive rather than theoretical. One therefore wonders if some kind of uniformity can be brought about in the literary evaluation, based on *dhvani*, of a piece of poetry. Apparently diverse emotive and attitudinal meanings cannot be tied down to any linguistic factors, although some of them have been found to be associated with accent and intonation.

It has already been pointed out that the concepts of *vyañjanā* and suggested meaning make their appearance in the domain of grammar in the seventeenth century. However, Pāṇini, the foremost grammarian of Sanskrit, had already assumed this kind of meaning as one of the meanings understood from a linguistic expression. Although Pāṇini never uses the term *vyañjanā* or any other similar terms, he has, while analyzing the Sanskrit language, successfully handled the suggested meaning at the level of the structure of language. In his *Aṣṭādhyāyī*, he showed in at least two hundred rules that a number of emotive and attitudinal meanings were relevant to the form of language. The attitudinal meaning is associated not only with intonation and accent but also with different linguistic elements such as suffixes, prefixes, and sometimes even augments.

Students of Pāṇini's grammar are quite familiar with the fact that some of the sets of verbal endings are directly connected with the feelings and attitudes of the speaker. The sets of verbal endings related to moods such as optative (*lIṄ*) and imperative (*lOṬ*) are, for instance, described as conveying various feelings like *vidhi* 'prompting', *nimantraṇa* 'invitation', *āmantraṇa* 'permission', etc.[12] For example, in the sentence *bhavān bhuñjīta* 'You may please take food', the verbal ending *ta* conveys request or wish in the mind of the speaker. More interesting cases treated by Pāṇini will be discussed in the following pages.

Pāṇini states that the preposition *api* is a *karmapravacanīya* when it conveys disgust in the mind of the speaker.[13] In the sentence *api stuyād vr̥ṣalam* 'One may praise even an outcaste', *api* conveys disgust. Elsewhere it is an *upasarga*. Therefore, in the sentence *apiṣtuyād vr̥ṣalam* 'One may praise even an outcaste', wherein no disgust is conveyed, *api* causes cerebralization of the initial dental of the following root (P.8.3.65). The phonology of the construction and the semantic function of *api* are thus directly connected. It is the emotive meaning that distinguishes between the two usages of *api* and the corresponding formal structure of the two expressions.

Impatience or urgency is conveyed by the *kṛt* suffix *ṆamUL* according to P.3.4.52.[14] The illustration given in the *Kāśikā* on the above rule is *śayyotthāyaṃ dhāvati* '[He] runs hurriedly from his bed'. The emotional overtone implied here is that he is so impatient that he does not care even to dress after getting out of bed. When, however, no hurry or impatience is to be conveyed, the expression would be *śayyāyā utthāya dhavāti* '[He] runs after having got up from the bed'.

The feeling of appreciation is transmitted through some secondary suffixes. The suffix *rūpa*[15] in the derivative *vaiyākaraṇarūpaḥ* 'a praiseworthy grammarian', for instance, conveys the speaker's appreciation of a grammarian. In the absence of appreciation the speaker uses merely the form *vaiyākaraṇaḥ* 'grammarian'.

The primary suffixes also convey various emotions. For instance, blessing or benediction is conveyed by the primary suffix *vuN* according to P.3.1.150.[16] The word *jīvakaḥ* 'one who lives' suggests the blessing in the mind of the speaker, "Let him live long." Similarly, the *kṛt* suffix *Ḍa*[17] in the form *śatruhaḥ* 'killer of enemies' conveys the blessing that he should always be victorious in his fights with enemies.

A is eating and B does not like it. B finds fault with A's manner of eating. A does not like B's undue criticism. He retorts, *yathākāram aham bhokṣye tathākāram aham, kiṃ tavānena* 'I will eat as I will. What have you got to do with it?'. The intention of the speaker to retaliate is conveyed by the primary suffix *ṆamUL* added after the root *kṛ* in the form *yathākāram.*[18] The ordinary statement of fact would be *yathā kṛtvāhaṃ bhokṣye tathā tvaṃ drakṣyasi* 'You will see how I eat'.

Many more illustrations can be added. All show how minutely Pāṇini has observed the nuances and their correspondence with the formal structure of linguistic expressions. He has linked feelings such as anger, jealousy, love, hatred, and insult with diverse linguistic elements. His treatment of a large number of word formations that are linked with the *dhvani* indicates that the emotive and attitudinal meanings can be formalized at least to a certain extent. Thus *vyañjanā*, which often expresses the speaker's intention or presupposition towards an object or a situation, plays a crucial role in the derivational system of Pāṇini. It is incorporated in the formal analysis of the language.

In this structural approach the suggested meaning of a linguistic expression is fixed and does not vary from listener to listener. The *vyañjanā* theory developed by the poeticians fails to explain this correlation between the linguistic forms and the emotive meanings, which is clearly pointed out by Pāṇini's grammar.

The questions that emerge from the foregoing observations are: Can the *dhvani* language of the poets, which is deliberately rendered ambiguous to create a charming effect, be put to a uniform objective analysis, at least to a certain extent, as Pāṇini did? Is it possible to bring about uniformity in the comprehension of *dhvani* by all readers by establishing a correlation between emotive meanings and the formal structure of the language? Can such formalization render poetics more theoretical than intuitive? And is it really expected to be so?

One has to admit that the structural approach to *vyañjanā* has its limitations. The meaning of poetry is not a fixed thing and is open to interpretation. The true *sahṛdayas*, people of taste, always consider the best poetry to be like a veiled beauty, concealing its grace and charm and allowing the aesthetes to discover it in their own way. Intuitive communication cannot be fastened to the rules of grammar. Nevertheless, a preliminary claim can be made on the basis of the observations made above that linguistic analysis carried out in the Pāṇinian way may provide some insights for the exploration of *dhvani* and bring about uniformity, at least on the initial level, in applied criticism related to Sanskrit poetry.

Notes

1. The *Dhvanyāloka* of Ānandavardhana, ed. Nagendra (Benares 1971), 53.
2. The *Dhvanyāloka* with *Locana*, ed. P. N. Virkar and M. V. Patwardhan (Bombay, 1983), pt. 1, 233-34.
3. Ibid., 1:4: *pratīyamānaṃ punar anyadeva vastv asti vāṇīṣu mahākavīnām / yat tat prasiddhāvayavātiriktaṃ vibhāti lāvaṇyam ivāṅganāsu //*
4. The *Vaiyākaraṇasiddhāntamañjūṣā* of Nāgeśa Bhaṭṭa, ed. K. D. Shastri (Kurukshetra, 1985), 30-31.
5. Basically, *dhvani* is divided into *vastudhvani*,

alaṃkāradhvani, and *rasadhvani* by the ancient rhetoricians. This division is based on the nature of the content that is suggested. Another threefold division of *dhvani* into *śabdaśaktimūla*, *arthaśaktimūla*, and *ubhayaśaktimūla* is based on the nature of the poetic element, either word or meaning, which is the conveyor of *dhvani*. Many other kinds of *dhvani* have also been described. However, it is not the aim of the present paper to give a detailed exposition of the doctrine of *dhvani*.

6. The *Kāvyaprakāśa*, ed. Karmarkar (B.O.R.I., Poona, 1950), 72:
vaktṛboddhavyakākūnāṃ vākyavācyānyasaṃnidheḥ /
prastāvadeśakālāder vaiśiṣṭyāt pratibhājuṣām /
yo 'rthasyānyārthadhīhetur vyāpāro vyaktir eva sā //
7. The *Dhvanyāloka* with *Locana*, 3:16:
suptiṅvacanasambandhais tathā kārakaśaktibhiḥ /
kṛttaddhitasamāsaiś ca dyotyo 'lakṣyakramaḥ kvacit /
8. The *Kālidāsagranthāvali*, critically ed. by R. P. Dvivedi (Benares, 1976), 474.
9. The *Sāhityadarpaṇa*, ed. Panduranga Javaji (Bombay, 1931), 231.
10. The *Locana* on the *Dhvanyāloka*, ed. R. S. Tripathi (Delhi, 1963), pt. 2, 841: *tālair iti bahuvacanam anekavidhaṃ vaidagdhyaṃ dhvanat vipralambhoddīpakatām eti* /
11. The *Nyāyamañjarī*, ed. K. S. Varadāchārya (Mysore, 1969), 129:
etena śabdasāmarthyamahimnā so 'pi vāritaḥ /
yam anyaḥ paṇḍitammanyaḥ prapede kañcana dhvanim //

12. P.3.3.161, 163, 166, etc.
13. P.1.4.96, *apiḥ padārthasambhāvanānvavasargagarhā-samuccayeṣu* '*api* is called *karmapravacanīya* when it conveys the meaning of a word, possibility, permission, censure, or collection'.
14. P.3.4.52, *apādane parīpsāyām* '[the suffix *ṆamUL* is added after a root accompanied by] a word in the ablative when hurry is to be conveyed'.
15. P.5.3.66, *praśaṃsāyāṃ rūpap* '[The suffix] *rūpaP* is added [after a stem] when appreciation is to be conveyed'.
16. P.3.1.150, *āśiṣi ca* 'And to convey benediction [the primary suffix *vuN* is added after a root]'.
17. P.3.2.49, *āśiṣi hanaḥ* '[The suffix *Ḍa* is added after the root *han* preceded by an object as an *upapada*] to convey benediction'.
18. P.3.4.28, *yathātathayor asūyāprativacane* '[The suffix *ṆamUL* is added after *kṛ* preceded by] *yathā* or *tathā* when a retort [to a person who is] jealous [is intended]'.

ON PAŚYA MṚGO DHĀVATI

Gopikamohan Bhattacharya

In language-generated awareness (*śābdabodha*), syntactic expectancy plays a decisive role. Syntactic expectancy (*ākāṅkṣā*), competency (*yogyatā*), congruency (*āsatti*) and the speaker's intention (*tātparya*) are the determining factors in verbal awareness. Nāgeśa defines *ākāṅkṣā* as "The speaker's intention to know the meaning of a word, which is appropriate to be syntactically related with the meaning of another word of which the meaning is already known."[1] Suppose that, if I know the meaning of a word, say *cow*, I desire to know: what shall I do with the cow? I need to know the meaning of another word, *bring*. I search for a meaning for *bring* that is syntactically related to the meaning of *cow*. As long as this search continues I do not have *śābdabodha*. But, on hearing the second word and understanding its meaning, my desire is fulfilled and I become aware of the syntactic connection between the two word-meanings. Nyāya says: "Awareness of this connectedness [*saṃsarga*] is language-awareness [*śābdabodha*]."

Here it may be pointed out that this property of generating (*uthāpakatā*) a desire to know the meaning of the other word may be reciprocal or one-way. Consider the sentence *pacati taṇḍulaṃ Devadattaḥ* 'Devadatta cooks rice'. When I say the word *cooks*, a sympathetic hearer will ask: what is being cooked? Likewise, if I say *taṇḍulam* ('rice' + accusative case-suffix), the hearer will ask: what is being done with this rice? Here the awareness of one prompts the hearer to ask for the other and vice versa. But when I hear somebody saying "Look," I wish to know "Look at what." When I hear the sentence "The deer runs," my desire to know is fulfilled. If I hear the expression *mṛgo dhāvati* 'The deer runs', I do not ask "What should I do about it?" because the awareness of the sentence-meaning is complete. In this case it is not a reciprocal but a one-way determination.

I may point out here that, if I say "Look" and simply point out with my finger that the deer is running, this will not generate verbal awareness because the second half is not verbally expressed. These elliptical sentences, says the Grammarian, do not generate verbal awareness unless the other part is uttered verbally.

Now let us consider the sentence *paśya mṛgo dhāvati* 'Look, the deer runs' and the nature of the awareness that follows upon hearing it. The Nyāya and the Grammarian have suggested two different models of semantic analysis of a sentence. In the Nyāya view, the connected sentence-meaning structure is dominated by the meaning of the nominative but, according to the Grammarian, the verbal phrase is the principal element, "the center of interest," and all other word-meanings are subsidiary to it. These meaning-elements, being interrelated, finally qualify the principal meaning-element. An example will make the point clear. In the awareness generated upon hearing the expression *caitro 'nnam pacati* 'Caitra cooks rice', the Nyāya says that the meaning of the word *Caitra* is the center of interest and the chief qualificand (*mukhya viśeṣya*). One may ask: how does the meaning of *Caitra* get predominance over other meaning-instances? Perhaps the Nyāya has in mind the Vaiśeṣika notion of substance (*dravya*), which is the central element to which all other qualifiers, e.g., quality (*guṇa*), action (*kriyā*), etc., relate. Thus, the Nyāya says, the word *pacati* ('cooks') has two parts: the root *pac* and the verbal suffix *tip*. The root *pac* denotes the action of cooking and the meaning of the *tip* suffix is 'effort'. In our verbal knowledge of this sentence, the meaning of *effort* is connected with the meaning of *Caitra* as a *prakāra* 'qualifier',[2] and the meaning of the root *pac* ('to cook') is connected with *effort* through the relation of conduciveness (*anukūlatā*) because effort generates the activity of cooking. Navya-Nyāya says that the meanings of the word *Caitra*, the root *pac*, and the suffix *tip* figure (lit. *bhāsate* 'floats') in our verbal awareness in the following manner: the meaning of *Caitra* as the chief qualificand (*mukhya viśeṣya*) is qualified by the meaning of the *tip* suffix, i.e., 'effort', and the effort is qualified by the meaning of the act of cooking. So the verbal awareness of the sentence "Caitra cooks rice" would be semantically interpreted as "*Caitra* is the location of effort conducive to action, which generates the act of cooking, which has *rice* as the object" (*anna-karmaka-pākānukūla-vyāpārānukūla-kr̥ty-āśrayaś caitraḥ*). To cut a long story short, for Nyāya the meaning of the chief qualificand enjoys primacy over other meanings. It is the word inflected with a nominative case ending (*prathamānta*).

More observations on this issue may be in order. If an object, say X, figures in my verbal awareness, it is always presented as being qualified by a property. X is the qualificand (*viśeṣya*), which possesses the relational abstract *viśeṣyatā* 'qualificandness'. Likewise, that which figures in our verbal awareness as the *prakāra* 'property' also has *prakāratā* 'propertyhood'. An example will make the point clear. In our verbalized awareness of the sentence *parvato vahnimān* 'The mountain is possessed of fire', both the mountain and the fire are qualificands (*viśeṣya*). But the mountain is said to be the chief qualificand, whereas the fire is not. The principle may be formulated as follows: "Something is the chief qualificand if and only if it figures in our verbal awareness only as a qualificand (i.e., if it has only qualificandness) and not also as a qualifier." Gadādhara defines it thus: "The primacy of the qualificand consists in its not being delimited by qualifierness or being different from qualifierness" (*mukhyatvaṃ ca viśeṣyatāyāṃ prakāratānavacchinnatvaṃ prakāratābhinnatvaṃ vā*).[3] Now, in the above example the meaning of the mountain is limited by qualificandness only but the meaning of the fire is not only a qualificand but the qualifier of the mountain as well. So in fire (precisely, the meaning of the word *fire*), qualifierness and qualificandness co-locate. The meaning of *fire* stands in a double capacity, as qualificand (*viśeṣya*) and as qualifier (*prakāra*). The qualificandness (*viśeṣyatā*) is determined by "fireness" and the qualifierness is determined by the mountain (*parvata-nirūpita-prakāratā*). So *fire* cannot be the chief qualificand. *Mountain* is the chief qualificand (*mukhya viśeṣya*).

One more point before I proceed further. In the sentence-generated awareness there would be only one chief qualificand. This means that in the meaning of a sentence there can be only one "center of interest." The chief characteristic of a sentence is that it should have the identity of meaning, i.e., a sentence denotes a connected (lit. *viśiṣṭa* 'qualified') meaning. All the words in a sentence conjointly denote a single meaning, which is the meaning of the sentence. This is called *ekavākyatā*. Jaimini describes it as follows: "[A sequence of words is considered to be] a single sentence because of identity of its meaning, [such that] on being separated [its words] stand in expectancy [i.e., seem incomplete]" (*arthaikatvād ekaṃ vākyam, sākāṃkṣaṃ ced vibhāge syāt*).[4] Raghunātha says: "The usage of one-sentence-ness is only for denoting the cognition of a qualified meaning" (*ekavākyatā-vyavahāras tu viśiṣṭaikārtha-pratipatti-paratā-mātreṇa*).[5] Gadādhara agrees with Raghunātha.[6]

Now I shall discuss how the nature of language-generated awareness, as emphasized in Nyāya, leads to several unwanted situations. Consider the sentence *paśya mr̥go dhāvati* 'Look, the deer runs'. According to Nyāya, the awareness generated from the word *look* would be "You are the location of the act of seeing." From the words *the deer runs* the awareness would be "The deer is possessed of effort conducive to the act of running" (*dhāvanānukūla-kr̥timān mr̥gaḥ*). If so, we have here two chief qualificands, *tvam* 'you' and *mr̥gaḥ* 'deer'. This runs counter to the principle of *ekavākyatā* (lit. 'being a single sentence') because *ekavākyatā* implies that it should have only one meaning as the chief qualificand, whereas here we have two chief qualificands, *you* and *the deer*. Two chief qualificands imply two sentences, whereas the sentence "Look, the deer runs" is considered to be a single sentence having a qualified meaning (*viśiṣṭārtha*).[7]

In the Nyāya view, the sentence under consideration has a unified meaning. A Naiyāyika would not agree that there are two completely independent meanings, as the Grammarian interprets the Nyāya theory. In Nyāya, the semantic analysis of the sentence would be as follows: "You are the location of effort conducive to the act of seeing of which *deer* is the object, which is the location of effort conducive to the act of running" (*dhāvanānukūla-kṛty-āśraya-mṛga-karmaka-darśanānukūla-kṛty-āśrayas tvam*). It is clear that, in this analysis, *tvam* 'you' is the only chief qualificand. In this way the charge of *vākya-bheda* 'a split sentence' due to the absence of *ekavākyatā* is answered.

The Grammarian's usual counterargument is this. It may be true that the principle of *ekavākyatā* will not be violated, but the meaning of *mṛga* 'deer', being the object of the act of seeing, would then have an accusative case-suffix. That is to say, instead of saying *paśya mṛgo dhāvati*, the Naiyāyika would be forced to use an absurd expression such as *paśya mṛgaṃ dhāvati*. To resolve the impasse, Nyāya could invite a new word *tam* ('it') and divide the whole sentence-generated awareness into two awareness-instances: (i) the deer is possessed of effort, which causes the act of running (*dhāvana-janaka-kṛtimān mṛgaḥ*); and (ii) you are the location of the act of seeing, which has *that (tat)*, i.e., *deer*, as the object (*tat-karmaka-darśanāśrayas tvam*). But in that case the principle of unity of a sentence (*ekavākyatā*) is violated.

The Naiyāyika may still argue that: when I say "Look, the deer runs," what I wish to be seen is not simply "the deer" but that "the deer runs." Actually, the verbalized expression of the object of seeing is "the deer runs" (i.e., in Nyāya analysis, "the deer possessed of effort generating the act of running"). It is a qualified meaning, which as a whole is the object of seeing. A part of that meaning-complex cannot be taken out and said to be the object (*karma*). So we cannot isolate the meaning-element "deer" and say that it is the object of seeing. Hence the possibility of the word *mṛga* taking an accusative case-suffix can be ruled out.

The Grammarian counters this as follows: there is no question that the meanings of both *dhāvati* and *mṛgaḥ* constitute the object-complex of the act of seeing (i.e., both the "act of running" and the "deer" are objects of the act of seeing). But *dhāvati* cannot obviously take an accusative case-ending because it is a verbal form. Obviously, then, the accusative case-suffix should go to the word *mṛga*.

The Grammarian himself, however, would not face such a situation. He says that in sentence-generated awareness (*śābdabodha*), the chief qualificand is action (*vyapāra*). As "Look, the deer runs" is an imperative sentence, the act of seeing (*darśana-kriyā*) is the chief qualificand, "the center of interest," and its object is "the act of running of the deer" (*mṛga-kartṛkaṃ dhāvanam*). Thus, the awareness may be analyzed as: the act of seeing, of which "you" is the agent and "the act of running by the deer" is the object. The "act of running," although it is a qualificand, is expressed through a verbal form, e.g., *dhāvati.* Hence, it cannot take an accusative case-suffix.

One may ask: how, then, without an accusative case-suffix, could "the act of running" be identified as the object (*karma*)? Nāgeśa replies that the "act of running" will figure in our verbal awareness as the *object* through syntactic expectancy (*ākāṃkṣā*) or, to be precise, through relational seam (*saṃsargamaryādā*).[8]

Moreover, the way in which Nyāya analyzes the verbal awareness from a sentence leads also to problems other than *vākyabheda.* Let us explain the point further. The Grammarian works here with the following principle: if something, say X, is related with something else, say Y, as a qualifier, then X cannot be related with another something, say Z, as a qualifier (*ekatra viśeṣaṇatvenānvitasyāparatra viśeṣaṇatvāyogāt*).[9] Now, in the above sentence the act of running is related with the agent (*kartṛ*), i.e., "deer," because the Naiyāyika says "The deer is possessed of effort conducive to the act of running." Hence, the same "act of running" cannot be related to the "act of seeing" as the object (to be precise, as the qualifier). The reason behind this assumption is that when X is related with Y, the syntactic expectancy (*ākāṃkṣā*) is fulfilled. Hence, due to the absence of expectancy, X cannot be further related with Z. So the Naiyāyika cannot show *ekavākyatā* by relating the act of running with the act of seeing. He cannot get around the difficulty of the absence of *ekavākyatā.*

Notes

1. *Paramalaghumañjūṣā*, ed. K. P. Shukla (Baroda, 1961), 77: *sā ca eka-padārtha-jñāne tad-arthānvaya-yogyārthasya yaj jñānaṃ tad-viṣayecchā /*
2. For this term, see B. K. Matilal, "Awareness and Meaning in Navya-Nyāya," in *Analytical Philosophy in Comparative Perspective*, ed. Matilal and Shaw (Dordrecht: Reidel, 1985), 373.
3. Gadādhara, *Viṣayatāvāda*, ed. B. B. Das (Banaras, 1886), 17.
4. Jaimini, *Mīmāṃsāsūtra*, 2.1.46.
5. Raghunātha, *Tattvacintāmaṇidīdhiti (avayava* section), ed. V. P. Dwivedi (Benares, 1970), 1460.
6. Gadādhara, *Gādādharī (avayava* section), ed. V. P. Dwivedi (Banares, 1970), 1468: *viśiṣṭaikārtha-pratipādakatvam*; cf. *Nyāyakośa* (Poona, 1978), 188.
7. See Kauṇḍabhaṭṭa, *Vaiyākaraṇabhūṣaṇasāra*, Chowkhamba ed. (Varanasi, 1969), 47.
8. *Paramalaghumañjūṣā*, 110: *karmatvaṃ tu saṃsarga-maryādayā bhāsate.*
9. Balakr̥ṣṇa Pancholi, *Prabhā (*on *Vaiyākaraṇabhūṣaṇasāra)*, Chowkhamba ed. (Varanasi, 1969), 47.

PĀṆINI AND THE VEDA RECONSIDERED*

Johannes Bronkhorst

The relationship between Pāṇini and the Veda has been much debated.[1] The presupposition underlying a major part of this debate has been that much or even most of Vedic literature existed in its present form prior to Pāṇini. In this article an attempt will be made to establish, as far as possible, the relationship between Pāṇini and the Veda without taking the correctness of this presupposition for granted.

1.1 A fundamental question is whether Pāṇini knew the Vedic texts, i.e., the ones with which he was familiar, in the same form as we do. Were the Vedic texts that Pāṇini knew identical in all details with the editions we have now? It appears that the answer to this question must be negative.

It is not always possible to decide that a text has not reached us in its original form. In the case of metrical texts this may be possible, however, and to some extent we may be in a position to determine what the original text was like. This is the case regarding the *Ṛgveda*. In another study (Bronkhorst 1981) it has been shown that certain rules of sandhi of the *Aṣṭādhyāyī* fit an earlier stage of the text of the *Ṛgveda* than the one we now have. The conclusion was drawn that "the lack of agreement between the *Aṣṭādhyāyī* and our *R̥gveda* may henceforth have to be looked at through different eyes. Certainly, where phonetic questions are concerned, Pāṇini may describe an earlier form of the *R̥gveda*, and may not deserve to be blamed for being lacunary . . ." (pp. 91-92).

This conclusion has far-reaching implications. The *R̥gveda* has been handed down with great care, with greater care perhaps than any other Vedic text. Yet even here Pāṇini's rules of sandhi do not fully agree with the present text, although we know that at least some of them once fitted. How much less can we expect full agreement between Pāṇini's rules of sandhi and all other Vedic texts. This means that a comparison of Pāṇini's rules of sandhi and the Vedic evidence, if it is to be made at all, must be made with the greatest care. A straight confrontation of Pāṇini's rules with the Vedic facts cannot be expected to yield more than partial agreement, and says little about the state of affairs in Pāṇini's day. In the present context it is important to recall that "Pāṇini's rules on Vedic sandhi do not necessarily describe the sandhi which was actually used in the Vedic texts which Pāṇini had before him. Rather, they describe the sandhi as it ought to be according to Pāṇini. This is confirmed by the circumstance that Pāṇini sometimes gives the opinions of others besides his own, for example, in P.8.3.17-19" (Bronkhorst 1982, 275).[2]

A development in tone patterns, too, must have taken place after Pāṇini. Kiparsky (1982, 73) sums up the results of an investigation into this matter: "[T]he tone pattern described by Pāṇini represents an older stage than that described for the Vedic *saṃhitās* by the Prātiśākhyas. While the *saṃhitās* themselves are of course older than Pāṇini's grammar [?; see below], we may assume that they were accented in Pāṇini's time with the tone pattern described in the *Aṣṭādhyāyī*, and that their present tone pattern, as well as the Prātiśākhyas that codify it, are post-Pāṇinian revisions." It is true that Kiparsky derives the different tone patterns from accent properties belonging to morphemes that are stable in time. Yet it is at least conceivable, also, that these accent properties changed in the time before the tone patterns reached their final form.[3] This means that little can be concluded from such deviations from Pāṇini in the accentuation of Vedic words[4] as occur in *arya* (Thieme 1938, 91f.; Balasubrahmanyam 1964; 1969), *hāyana* (Balasubrahmanyam 1966), *jyeṣṭha* and *kaniṣṭha* (Devasthali 1967, 7-8),[5] *arpita* and *juṣṭa* (Balasubrahmanyam 1974),[6] *śriyase* (Balasubrahmanyam 1969; 1972), *voḍhave* (Balasubrahmanyam 1983), and *vṛṣṭi, bhūti,* and *vitti* (Keith 1936, 736).[7]

This is further supported by the fact that accents were not noted down until very late (Thieme 1935, 120f., 129f.). A passage in the *Śatapatha Brāhmaṇa* (1.6.3.10) gives further proof for this. There Tvaṣṭṛ pronounces a mantra wrongly, and as a result Vṛtra is killed by Indra instead of the reverse. The mantra concerned is *indraśatrur vardhasva.* The later tradition--Patañjali's *Mahābhāṣya* (1:2, l. 12), *Pāṇinīya Śikṣā* (verse 52), Bhaṭṭabhāskara and Sāyaṇa (on TS 2.5.2), etc.--agrees that the mistake concerned the accent: an intended *Tatpuruṣa* compound 'killer of Indra' becomes a *Bahuvrīhi* 'whose killer is Indra'. The formulation of TS 2.5.2.1-2--*yad abravīt svāhendraśatrur vardhasveti tasmād asyendraḥ śatrur abhavat*--fully agrees with this. MS 2.4.3 is even clearer: *svāhendraśatrur vardhasva itīndrasyāhainaṃ śatrum acikīrṣad indram asya śatrum akarot.* Yet the *Śatapatha Brāhmaṇa* formulates the story in a way that can only be explained on the assumption that there was no way to make the difference in accentuation visible. Rather than writing (or reciting!) the *Tatpuruṣa* compound with the appropriate accent, it analyzes the compound into *indrasya śatruḥ.* The passage then reads: *atha yad abravīd indra-śatrur vardhasveti tasmād u hainam indra eva jaghāna / atha yaddha śaśvad avakṣyad indrasya śatrur vardhasveti śaśvad u ha sa indram evāhaniṣyat /.*

These considerations show that any comparison between the linguistic data in Pāṇini and those in the Veda must be extremely careful in the fields of sandhi and accentuation. They also suggest that in other respects the Vedic texts known to Pāṇini *may* have undergone modification since Pāṇini's time.

As an example of a feature that *may* have changed since Pāṇini, consider the word *rātri/rātrī* in the mantras of the *Taittirīya Saṃhitā.* According to P.4.1.31 (*rātreś cājasau*), *rātrī* occurs in ritual literature (*chandasi*, see below) before all endings except the nominative plural (cf. Bhat 1968; Wackernagel 1896-1930, 3:185f.).[8] Five times the mantras of the *Taittirīya Saṃhitā* contain the word in a form that allows us to determine whether *rātri* or *rātrī* is used. Twice (TS 4.3.11.3 and 5.7.2.1) it is *rātrī*, thrice *rātri.* However, it is not impossible that originally all five occurrences had a form of *rātrī.* TS 4.1.10.1 (*rātriṃ rātrim aprayāvaṃ bharantaḥ*) recurs as *rātrīṃ rātrīm* (at MS 2.7.7

and 3.1.9; KS 16.7 and 19.10; and ŚB 6.6.4.1). TS 4.4.1.1 (*rātriṃ jinvośigasi*) occurs as *rātrīṃ jinvo* at KS 17.7. In these two cases the shortening of *ī* to *i* was a minor change. More problematic seems to be TS 7.4.18.1 (*rātrir āsīt piśaṅgilā*), to which no parallels with long *ī* correspond (Bloomfield 1906, 823). Here a substitution of *rātrī* would lead to *rātry āsīt*, which differs rather strongly from the mantra as we know it. However, no such objection can be raised against an earlier **rātri āsīt*; this in its turn might be looked upon as the result of sandhi applied to *rātrī āsīt*, by P.6.1.127 (*iko' savarṇe śākalyasya hrasvaś ca*), a rule of sandhi that also held in the *R̥gveda*, at least according to Śākalya (see Bronkhorst 1982a, 181).

1.2 The second introductory question we have to ask is whether or not Pāṇini's Vedic rules were meant to be universally valid in the Vedic texts. Our observations on sandhi have made it clear that here, at least, there is nothing to contradict the supposition that Pāṇini's rules were meant to be adhered to throughout. (This does not necessarily mean, however, that the texts known to Pāṇini always had Pāṇini's kind of sandhi.) It is at least conceivable that all the Vedic rules of the *Aṣṭādhyāyī* were meant to be strictly followed unless the opposite is explicitly stated.

This takes us to the main point of this subsection. If Pāṇini's Vedic rules were not meant to be followed strictly, this should have been indicated in the *Aṣṭādhyāyī*. Kiparsky (1980) has shown that Pāṇini distinguished three kinds of optionality: *vā* 'preferably', *vibhāṣā* 'preferably not', and *anyatarasyām* 'either way'. This means that Pāṇini used various means to indicate optionality. As a matter of fact, option is indicated in a number of Vedic rules. P.1.2.36, 6.2.164, and 7.4.44 read *vibhāṣā chandasi*, P.1.4.9 (*ṣaṣṭhī-yuktaś chandasi vā*), P.8.3.49 (*chandasi vā'prāmreḍitayoḥ*), P.5.3.13 (*vā ha ca chandasi*), P.3.4.88 and 6.1.106 (*vā chandasi*), P.6.4.5 and 6.4.86 (*chandasy ubhayathā*), P.6.4.162 (*vibhāṣarjoś chandasi*), P.8.2.70 (*amnarūdharavar ity ubhayathā chandasi*), P.8.3.104 (*yajuṣy ekeṣām*), P.8.3.119 (*nivyabhibhyo'ḍ vyavāye vā chandasi*), P.8.3.8 (*ubhayatharkṣu*), and P.6.4.9 (*vā ṣapūrvasya nigame*). The words *bahulaṃ chandasi* 'variously in ritual literature' occur no less than seventeen times together,[9] not counting the rules wherein they may have to be continued. In P.1.2.61 (*chandasi punarvasvor ekavacanam*) and 62 (*viśākhayoś ca [chandasi]*), the word *anyatarasyām* is in force from P.1.2.58, and is not cancelled until *nityam* in 1.2.63. In P.6.1.52 (*khideś chandasi*) there is continuation of *vibhāṣā* from *sūtra* 51, cancelled by *nityam* in 6.1.57. P.3.1.85 (*vyatyayo bahulam*) continues *chandasi* from 3.1.84 (*chandasi śāyaj api*), which itself indicates optionality by means of the word *api*. Similar devices are used in P.1.4.81 (*chandasi pare'pi*), and 82 (*vyavahitāś ca*); P.3.3.130 (*anyebhyo'pi dr̥śyate* [*chandasi* 129]); P.5.3.14 (*itarābhyo'pi dr̥śyante* [*chandasi* 13]); P.6.3.137 (*anyeṣām api dr̥śyate* [*r̥ci* 133][?]); P.6.4.73 and 7.1.76 (*chandasy api dr̥śyate*); P.7.1.38 (*ktvāpi chandasi*); P.5.2.50 (*thaṭ ca chandasi*); P.5.3.20 (*tayor dārhilau ca chandasi*); P.5.3.33 (*paśca paścā ca chandasi*); P.5.4.12 (*amu ca chandasi*); and P.5.4.41 (*vr̥kajyeṣṭhābhyāṃ tiltātilau ca chandasi*). P.3.2.106 (*liṭaḥ kānaj vā*) is confined to ritual literature because only there *liṭ* occurs (P.3.2.105 [*chandasi liṭ*]). P.8.1.64 (*vaivāveti ca chandasi*) continues *vibhāṣā* (63), cancelled by *nityam* in 8.1.66. P.6.1.209 (*juṣṭārpite ca chandasi*) continues *vibhāṣā* from 208, discontinued by 6.1.210 (*nityaṃ mantre*). In P.6.3.108 (*pathi ca chandasi*) the word *ca* continues *vibhāṣā* from 6.3.106 (cf. Kiparsky 1980, 62). P.8.3.105 (*stutastomayoś chandasi*) appears to continue *ekeṣām* from 8.3.104. P.4.4.113 (*srotaso vibhāṣā ḍyaḍḍyau*) continues *chandasi* from 4.4.110.

Nityam in P.4.1.29 (*nityaṃ saṃjñāchandasoḥ*), in 4.1.46 and 7.4.8 (*nityaṃ chandasi*), and in 6.1.210 (*nityaṃ mantre*), does not indicate that here, exceptionally, some Vedic rules are universally valid. Rather, it is meant to block the option that is valid in the preceding rules, as so often occurs in the *Aṣṭādhyāyī*. We have no alternative but to assume that, just as in his other rules, Pāṇini's Vedic rules not indicated as being optional were meant to be generally valid.[10]

From this we must conclude that deviations from Pāṇini in the Vedic texts known to Pāṇini either did not exist in his time or were not considered correct by him.

1.3 We now come to the question of what range of literature Pāṇini considered "Vedic" in one way or another. This is best approached by studying Pāṇini's use of the word *chandas* by which he most often refers to Vedic literature. It is clear that Pāṇini employs this word in a special way. The most common meaning of *chandas* is 'meter', and then 'metrical text'. But this is not the only sense in which Pāṇini uses it. Thieme (1935, *passim*, esp. 67-69) showed that rules given under *chandasi* 'in *chandas*' are also valid for prose passages (*brāhmaṇa* and *yajus*). He therefore rendered *chandasi* as 'in Sacred Literature'. Thieme criticizes

Liebich's (1891, 26) translation 'pre-classical language', saying: "I do not think it an appropriate translation, since it appears to endow Pāṇini with a historical perspective he hardly could have possessed" (p. 67).

This makes sense, but a major difficulty remains. Many of the forms taught under the heading *chandasi* occur in *Sūtra* texts. Instances are numerous and only a few will be given here. The name *Punarvasu*, used optionally in the singular in *chandas* according to P.1.2.61 (*chandasi punarvasvor ekavacanam* [*anyatarasyām* 58]), is so found at *Viṣṇusmṛti* (78.12) and VāŚS (1.5.1.5), besides several places in the *Black Yajurveda.* The singular of *viśākhā*, only allowed *chandasi* by P.1.2.62 (*viśākhayoś ca*), occurs similarly at VāŚS 2.2.2.14. The grammatical object of the root *hu* can have an instrumental ending in *chandas*, according to P.2.3.3 (*tṛtīyā ca hoś chandasi*). One instance is MŚS 1.6.1.23 (*payasā juhoti dadhnā yavāgvājyena vā* [cf. Thieme 1935, 10]). Some forms are *only* attested in *Sūtras. Khānya-* (P.3.1.123) only occurs in LŚS 8.2.4 and 5; (*pra-)stāvya-* (id.) in LŚS 6.1.20; *unnīya* (id.) in ŚāGS 4.14.4; and *yaśobhagīna* (P.4.4.132) in HiŚS 2.5.43, 6.4.3.

It seems safe to conclude that Pāṇini's term *chandas* covered more than just 'Sacred Literature'. We may have to assume that certain works, primarily the ritual *Sūtra*s, and among those first of all the *Śrauta Sūtra*s, belonged to a fringe area wherein Vedic usage was sometimes considered appropriate. The effect of this assumption for our investigation is that, where a *chandas* word prescribed by Pāṇini is attested in one Vedic text and in one or more *Sūtra*s, we are not entitled to conclude that Pāṇini certainly knew that Vedic text.

1.4 The final introductory question we have to consider is the following. Are Pāṇini's Vedic rules descriptive or prescriptive? To be sure, to some extent they describe the language that Pāṇini found in Vedic texts, and are therefore descriptive. But are they exclusively so? It may well be that Vedic texts were still being composed in Pāṇini's day, and that he gives in his grammar guidelines regarding correct Vedic usage. This possibility has been discussed elsewhere (Bronkhorst 1982, 275f.) and is further strengthened by the evidence to be provided in the following sections of this article. Here attention may be drawn to another reason to conclude that at least some of Pāṇini's rules may have been meant to be prescriptive, besides, or rather than, being descriptive. They may have been composed with something like *ūha* in mind.

Ūha[11] is the term used to describe the adjustments Vedic mantras undergo to make them fit for other ritual contexts. An original mantra such as *agnaye tvā juṣṭaṃ nirvapāmi*, directed to Agni, can become modified into *sūryāya tvā juṣṭaṃ nirvapāmi*, directed to Sūrya.[12] *Devīr āpaḥ śuddhā yūyam* (MS 1.1.11, 1.2.16, 3.10.1; KS 3.6), directed to the waters, becomes *deva ājya śuddhaṃ tvam* when directed to clarified butter (*ājya*). Sometimes only the number needs adjustment, as when *āyur āśāste* (MS 4.13.9; TS 2.6.9.7; TB 3.5.10.4) becomes *āyur āśāsāte* or *āyur āśāsate*. Only the gender is modified when *jūr asi dhṛtā manasā juṣṭā viṣṇave tasyās te satyasavasaḥ* (MS 1.2.4, 3.7.5; KS 2.5, 24.3; TS 1.2.4.1, 6.1.7.2; VS 4.17; ŚB 3.2.4.11; ŚBK 4.2.4.9) becomes *jūr asi dhr̥to manasā juṣṭo viṣṇave tasya te satyasavasaḥ* because a bull is under discussion.

Another interesting question is whether modified mantras are in fact mantras themselves. The later Mīmāṃsā tradition appears to be unanimous in its opinion that they are not. PMS 2.1.34 and Śabara's *Bhāṣya* thereon state explicitly that the result of *ūha* is not a mantra, and all later authorities in this field seem to have followed their example. This opinion is found, perhaps for the first time, in ĀpŚS 24.1.35, which reads *anāmnātās tv amantrā yathā pravaroha-nāmadheyagrahaṇānīti* "Die nicht (im Mantra- oder Brāhmaṇa-teile) überlieferten Teile sind indessen nicht als Mantra zu betrachten, z.B. der Pravara, die 'Verschiebung' (*ūha*), die Nennung eines Namens" (tr. Caland 1928a, 387).

It is not surprising that modified mantras were not considered mantras in their own right from an early date onward. After all, the opposite opinion would leave almost unlimited scope for creating new mantras. At a time when efforts had been made to gather all mantras into Vedic collections this must have been undesirable.

Yet there are clear traces of evidence that modified mantras were not always considered nonmantras. As late an author as Bhartr̥hari (fifth century A.D.),[13] who includes a long discussion on *ūha* in his commentary on the *Mahābhāṣya* (Ms 2b9 f.; AL 5.18 f.; Sw 6.17 f.; CE Āhn. 1, 5.1 f.) mentions "others" who think that modified mantras are themselves mantras.[14] And several *Śrauta Sūtras* make no mention of the nonmantric nature of modified mantras in contexts in which that would have been appropriate, for example, BhāŚS (6.15), MŚS (5.2.9), and ŚŚS (6.1). Moreover, HiŚS (1.1.13-

14) specifies that which is not a mantra without mentioning *ūha*! Apparently, at one time, modified mantras were mantras.

This view is supported by the fact that modified mantras have actually been included in the Vedic collections as mantras. A particularly clear example is the long *adhrigu* passage that occurs, or is discussed, in MS 4.13.4, KS 16.21, TB 3.6.6, AB 2.6-7 (6.6-7), KB 10.4, ĀśvŚS 3.3, and ŚŚS 5.17, with this difference: TB, AB, KB, and ŚŚS have *medhapatibhyām* where MS and KS have *medhapataye*. Interestingly, the difference is explained in AB 2.6.6 (6.6.6) in the following words:

> *sa yady ekadevatyaḥ paśuḥ syān medhapataya iti brūyāt yadi dvidevatyo medhapatibhyām iti yadi bahudevatyo medhapatibhya ity etad eva sthitam*
> If the victim be for one deity, 'for the lord of the sacrifice' [*medhapataye*] he should say; if for two deities, 'for the two lords of the sacrifice' [*medhapatibhyām*]; if for many deities, 'for the lords of the sacrifice' [*medhapatibhyaḥ*]. That is the rule. (Tr. Keith 1920, 138)

This is as clear a case of *ūha* as is possible.[15]

TS 2.3.10.1-2 repeats the same sacrificial formula four times, with differences in number, in a single passage in order to adjust it to different numbers of gods:

> *aśvinoḥ prāṇo'si tasya te dattāṃ yayoḥ prāṇo'si svāhā*
> *indrasya prāṇo'si tasya te dadātu yasya prāṇo'si svāhā*

mitrāvaruṇayoḥ prāṇo'si tasya te dattāṃ yayoḥ prāṇo'si svāhā viśveṣāṃ devānāṃ prāṇo'si tasya te dadatu yeṣāṃ prāṇo'si svāhā

The question we must now consider is to what extent the Vedic rules of the *Aṣṭādhyāyī* can be looked upon as having been composed with this kind of *ūha* in mind. Obviously, it cannot be maintained that this was the only purpose of these Vedic rules, for some were undoubtedly intended to describe isolated Vedic facts. But this does not exclude the possibility that *ūha* was one of the purposes for which some of the Vedic rules of the *Aṣṭādhyāyī* were formulated.

There is some reason to accept this last view. Some *Śrauta Sūtras* lay down rules pertaining to the modification of certain verbal forms. MŚS 5.2.9.6, for example, lists the following acceptable modified forms: *adat, adatām, adan, ghasat, ghastām, ghasan, aghasat, aghastām, aghasan, karat, karatām, karan, agrabhīt, agrabhīṣṭām, agrabhīṣuḥ*, and *akṣan*. ĀśvŚS 3.4.15, similarly, lists *ādat, ghasat, karat, juṣatām, aghat, agrabhīt* and *avīvṛdhata*. ŚŚS 6.1.5, finally, lists *ādat, ādan, ghastu, ghasantu, aghasat, aghasan*, or *aghat, akṣan, agrabhīt, agrabhīṣuḥ, avīvṛdhata, avīvṛdhanta*, and others. This shows that there was concern in ritual circles regarding the correct use of certain verbal forms in modified mantras. Among the recurring forms are the aorists of the roots *ghas, ad,*[16] and *kṛ*.

The shared concern of ĀśvŚS 3.4.15, ŚŚS 6.1.5, and MŚS 5.2.9.6 is explained by the fact that most of the modifications are meant for virtually identical texts, the so-called *Praiṣa sūktas*, in particular RV Khila 5.7.2 (f and l), which correspond to MS 4.13.7 (p. 208, 1.3-7) and 4.13.9 (p. 211, 1.5-12).

It is very probable that Pāṇini knew the *Praiṣa sūktas* in which these modifications were to take place, for Scheftelowitz (1919, 47f.) has adduced reasons to believe that the *Praiṣas* are among the oldest Vedic texts in prose. This allows us to surmise that a Pāṇinian *sūtra* may have been composed partly to solve this same problem. This *sūtra* would then be P.2.4.80 (*mantre ghasahvaraṇaśavr̥dahādvr̥ckr̥gamijanibhyo leḥ*), which deals with the aorists of a number of roots, among them *ghas* and *kr̥, in a mantra.* It favors here such forms as *(a)ghat, (a)ghastām, akṣan* and *akaḥ,* and *akran* (not in all cases the same forms as the above *Śrauta Sūtras*).

If it can be accepted that P.2.4.80 was composed to serve the purpose of *ūha* (besides other purposes), the same may be true of other rules of the *Aṣṭādhyāyī.* This, in turn, would mean that these rules not only *describe* Vedic data but also *prescribe* the means for modifying Vedic mantras when necessary. This implies that we cannot always be sure that Pāṇini's Vedic rules describe forms that occurred in Vedic texts known to Pāṇini. Unattested forms accounted for by rules in the *Aṣṭādhyāyī* do not, then, in all cases have to have been part of texts that are now lost.

2. We can now turn to the main part of the present investigation: an attempt to determine which Vedic texts Pāṇini knew and which he did not. The above considerations make it clear that in this context Pāṇini's rules on sandhi and accent will be of little help. Moreover, none of the rules that concern details of the phonetic shape of words, i.e., the orthoepic diaskeuasis of texts, can be relied upon to determine which texts Pāṇini knew, for the simple reason that these features may have changed, and in some cases certainly changed, after him. Our enquiry must in the main rely on word-forms prescribed in the *Aṣṭādhyāyī*.

Here another consideration arises. We have decided to take Pāṇini seriously, but this does not mean that we demand his grammar to be complete. Nor does it exclude the possibility that he made occasional mistakes. It does, however, imply that, where Pāṇini clearly and explicitly excludes certain features from the Vedic language, we must regard with suspicion the Vedic texts containing those features.

We proceed in a twofold manner. On one hand, we collect forms prescribed by Pāṇini for Vedic and attested in but one Vedic text and nowhere else. If a sufficient number of such forms are found for a particular Vedic text and nothing else pleads against it, we may then assume that this Vedic text was known to Pāṇini. On the other hand, we shall look for Vedic texts that contain features excluded by Pāṇini. If the number of such features is sufficiently large, we may consider the possibility that Pāṇini did not know these texts. This double approach will provide us with the material to be evaluated in subsequent sections.

2.1 Many words prescribed by Pāṇini are found only in the *R̥gveda*. Some examples are *vr̥kati* (P.5.4.41) at RV 4.41.4; *cicyuṣe* (P.6.1.36) at RV 4.30.22; *yajadhvainam* (P.7.1.43) at RV 8.2.37; *jagr̥bhma* (P.7.2.64) at RV 1.139.10 and 10.47.1;[17] *vr̥ṣaṇyati* (P.7.4.36) at RV 9.5.6; *tetikte* (P.7.4.65) at RV 4.23.7; and *svatavāṃḥ pāyuḥ* (P.8.3.11) at RV 4.2.6.

2.2 Three words prescribed by Pāṇini for Vedic are only found in the *Taittirīya Saṃhitā: khanya-* (P.3.1.123) at TS 7.4.13.1; the denominative *kavya-* (P.7.4.39) at TS 7.1.20.1; and *ānr̥huḥ* (P.6.1.36) at TS 3.2.8.3. Note that all three words occur in mantras. Thieme (1935, 64) was of the opinion that a fourth word, *brahmavādya (*P.3.1.123), is found only in the *Taittirīya Saṃhitā.* This word occurs in a *brāhmaṇa* portion (at TS 2.5.8.3) but not only there; it is also found at JUB 3.2.3.2; ĀpŚS 21.10.12; and VādhŚS (Caland 1928, 176). Thus, no direct evidence remains that Pāṇini knew the *brāhmaṇa* portion of the *Taittirīya Saṃhitā.*

2.3 Not all the evidence produced by Leopold von Schroeder (1879, 194f.; 1881-86, 1:xi f., 2:viii f.) to show that Pāṇini knew the *Maitrāyaṇī Saṃhitā* can stand scrutiny. Some cases are derived not from Pāṇini but from his commentators. Others correspond to rules of Pāṇini that are not confined to Vedic usage; these cases do not prove that Pāṇini knew the *Maitrāyaṇī Saṃhitā,* or a part thereof, for the simple reason that the words concerned were apparently also in use in other than ritual contexts. Finally, there are cases wherein Schroeder was mistaken in thinking that certain Vedic words prescribed by Pāṇini occurred only in the *Maitrāyaṇī Saṃhitā* and not in other texts.

However, the following cases can be used to establish Pāṇini's acquaintance with at least certain parts of the *Maitrāyaṇī Saṃhitā.* P.3.1.42 teaches the Vedic (*chandasi,* but *amantre*) verbal forms *abhyutsādayām akaḥ, prajanayām akaḥ,* and *pāvayāṃ kriyāt.* They occur at MS 1.6.5, 1.6.10 and 1.8.5, and 2.1.3, respectively, and nowhere else. The Vedic (*nigame*) forms *sāḍhyai* and *sāḍhvā* (P.6.3.113) are nowhere found except in MS 1.6.3 and 3.8.5, respectively. *Agrīya-* (P.4.4.117) is only attested at MS 2.7.13, 2.9.5, and in the colophon to 3.1.10. Noncompounded *bhaviṣṇu* (P.3.2.138) is found only at MS 1.8.1. *Praṇīya-* (P.3.1.123) is found at MS 3.9.1 and nowhere else; *ucchiṣya-* occurs only at MS 3.9.2. *Purīṣyavāhana* (P.3.2.65) is found only at MS 2.7.4.

2.4 Vedic forms attested only in the *Kāṭhaka Saṃhitā* are the following (cf. Schroeder 1880; 1895): *ramayām akaḥ* (P.3.1.42) at KS 7.7; *upacāyyapr̥ḍa* (P.3.1.123) at KS 11.1; and *kṣariti* (P.7.2.34) at KS 12.11. One word occurs only in the *Kāṭhaka Saṃhitā* and in the *Kapiṣṭhala Saṃhitā*. Since the latter "is practically a variant of the *Kāṭhaka*" (Gonda 1975, 327), it is here included: *jagatya-* (P.4.4.122) at KS 1.8 ≈ KapS 1.8, and at KS 31.7. *Adhvarya* in P.3.1.123 may indicate acquaintance with KS 35.7 = KapS 48.9 (Thieme 1935, 23-24; Gotō 1987, 191, n. 355).

2.5 A Vedic form found exclusively in the *Atharvaveda* is *ailayīt* formed by P.3.1.51 (cf. Thieme 1935, 64); it occurs at AVŚ 6.16.3.[18] *Śivatāti* (P.4.4.143) is only found at AVP 5.36.1-9. The word *māmakī*, formed by P.4.1.30, occurs only AVP 6.6.8.[19]

2.6 Two Vedic forms occur in the *Lāṭyāyana Śrauta Sūtra* of the *Sāmaveda* and nowhere else (except, of course, in the later *Drāhyāyaṇa Śrauta Sūtra*, which is often no more than a recast of the former): *khānya-* (P.3.1.123) at LŚS 8.2.4 and 5 (DrŚS 22.2.5 and 6); and *(pra-)stāvya-* (id.) at LŚS 6.1.20 (DrŚS 16.1.22 and 18). *Hvarita* (P.7.2.33) occurs only in a mantra in MŚS 2.5.4.24d and 4.4.39. *Saniṃ sasanivāṃsam* (P.7.2.69) occurs in mantras in MŚS 1.3.4.2 and VāŚS

1.3.5.16 (cf. Hoffmann 1974). *Dādharti* is only attested in JB 2.37.[20] *Yaśobhagīna* (P.4.4.132) is only attested HiŚS 2.5.43 and 6.4.3.

3.1 We now turn to forms excluded by Pāṇini.

P.3.1.35 (*kāspratyayād ām amantre liṭi*) forbids a periphrastic perfect to occur in a mantra, yet AVŚ 18.2.27 has *gamayāṃ cakāra* (cf. Whitney 1893, 249). AVP 18.65.10 has *gamayāṃ cakartha.*

P.5.1.91 (*vatsarāntāc chaś chandasi*) prescribes *-īya* after words ending in *-vatsara*, resulting in forms like *saṃvatsarīya.* The next rule, 5.1.92 (*saṃparipūrvāt kha ca*), adds *-īna* in the same position, provided that *-vatsara-* is preceded by *sam-* or *pari-*. This means that Pāṇini did not know, or approve of, forms wherein *-vatsarīṇa-* is not preceded by *sam-* or *pari-*. Yet such forms occur: *idāvatsarīṇa* at TB 1.4.10.2 and *anuvatsarīṇa* at TB 1.4.10.3.

P.5.4.158 (*r̥taś chandasi*) forbids the addition of *kaP* after a *Bahuvrīhi* compound ending in *-r̥*. An exception is *brāhmaṇabhartr̥ka* (AA 5.3.2).

P.6.3.84 (*samānasya chandasy amūrdhaprabhr̥tyudarkeṣu*) forbids substitution of *sa-* for *samāna* before *mūrdhan, prabhr̥ti,* and *udarka.* Yet this substitution has taken place in *saprabhr̥ti* (PB 15.1.6 and KB 20.4, 21.4, etc.); *sodarka* (PB 13.7.9, 13.8.1, 13.8.4, and 13.8.5; and KB 20.4, 21.4, etc.).

P.7.1.26 (*netarāc chandasi*) prohibits the use of neuter *itarad* in ritual literature. Yet it occurs at AB 6.15; KB 12.8; ŚB 4.5.8.14 and 13.8.2.9; TB 3.10.11.4; JB 1.213, 2.75, and 2.249; and at ṢaḍB 4.3.7, 4.4.10, and 4.5.8.

P.7.2.88 (*prathamāyāś ca dvivacane bhāṣāyām*) prescribes the nominatives *āvām* and *yuvām* with long penultimate *ā* for secular language, thus excluding these nominatives from the Vedic language. Yet they occcur in *āvām* (AB 4.8; ŚāṅA 5.7; ŚB 4.1.5.16 and 14.1.1.23; BAU[K] 3.2.13; ChU 8.8.1) and *yuvām* (PB 21.1.1).

3.2 We obtain further results by applying more strictly our rule that Pāṇini's grammar is to be taken seriously. Grammatical *sūtras* that are not indicated as being optional must be accepted as intended to be of general validity. In incidental cases this may give rise to doubts,[21] but no such doubt seems to attach to the following cases.

P.2.3.61 (*preṣyabruvor haviṣo devatāsaṃpradāne*) is a rule valid for *Brāhmaṇa* literature (*anuvṛtti* of *brāhmaṇe* from rule 60; see Joshi and Roodbergen 1981, 101, n. 331), prescribing a genitive for the object of *preṣya* and *brū*, if it is an oblation in an offering to a deity. It thus excludes the use of the accusative in such cases. Yet the accusative is often used in the *Śatapatha Brāhmaṇa*, most clearly in *agnīṣomābhyāṃ chāgasya vapāṃ medaḥ preṣya* (ŚB 3.8.2.27; ŚBK 4.8.2.21), *agnīṣomābhyāṃ chāgasya haviḥ preṣya* (ŚB 3.8.3.29; ŚBK 4.8.3.18), *indrāya somān prasthitān preṣya* (ŚB 4.2.1.23; ŚBK 5.2.1.20), and *chāgānāṃ haviḥ prasthitaṃ preṣya* (ŚB 5.1.3.14).[22]

P.3.1.59 (*kṛmṛdṛruhibhyaś chandasi*) is a nonoptional rule (cf. Kiparsky 1980, 62) prescribing *aṅ* as an aorist marker after the roots *kṛ*, *mṛ*, *dṛ*, and *ruh* in ritual literature. It excludes in this way the forms *akārṣīt, akārṣīḥ, akārṣam,* and *arukṣat* from Vedic literature. Yet these forms occur, as follows: *(a)kārṣīt* (GB 1.3.4; ChU 6.16.1); *akārṣīḥ*

(ŚB 10.5.5.3; GB 1.3.11); *akārṣam* (AVP 20.1.6; TB 3.7.5.5; TA 10.24.1, 10.25.1; GB 1.3.12); and *arukṣat* (AVŚ 12.3.42; AVP 17.40.2).

P.4.4.105 (*sabhāyāḥ yaḥ*) prescribes the suffix *ya* after *sabhā* in the sense *tatra sādhuḥ* (4.4.98). The next rule, P.4.4.106 (*ḍhaś chandasi*), makes an exception for ritual literature. The form *sabhya* derived by P.4.4.105 should apparently not occur in Vedic literature. It does, though, at the following places: AVŚ 8.10.9, 19.55.5; AVP 16.133.5; MS 1.6.11; TB 1.2.1.26, 3.7.4.6; and ŚB 12.9.2.3.

P.5.4.103 (*anasantān napuṃsakāc chandasi*) prescribes for ritual literature the addition of *ṭac* to neuter *Tatpuruṣa* compounds the last member of which end in *-an* or *-as*. Patañjali in his *Mahābhāṣya* (2:441) makes this rule optional, in order to account for words like *brahmasāman* and *devacchandas*, but this merely emphasizes the fact that Pāṇini's rule is not optional. Yet there are numerous exceptions, some of which occur in the following texts:[23]

AVŚ 5.10.1-7 (*aśmavarman*), 19.7.2 (*mr̥gaśiraś*), 19.30.3 (*devavarman*).

AVP 5.29.1 (*sūryavarcas*), 6.12.9-11 and 6.13.1-3 (*aśmavarman*), 13.11.21 (*devavarman*), 19.48.14 (*hiraṇyanāman*).

MS 3.6.7 (*dīkṣitavāsas*), 3.11.9 (*vyāghraloman*).

VSM 19.92 (*vyāghraloman* = MS 3.11.9).

VSK 21.6.13 (*vyāghraloman* = MS 3.11.9 and VSM 19.92).

AB 1.26 (*devavarman*), 4.19 (*brahmasāman, agniṣṭomasāman*), 7.19 (*iṣudhanvan*), 8.5 and 8.6 (*vyāghracarman*).

KB 2.1, 5.7, and 27.1 (*devakarman*), 5.5 (*pūrvedyuḥkarman* and *puṣṭikarman*), 5.7 (*pitr̥karman*), 8.7 (*paśukarman*), 27.1 (*agniṣṭomasāman*), 30.11 (*rātricchandas*).

GB 1.3.16 (*sarvacchandas*), 1.5.25 (*svakarman*), 2.1.23 (*puṣṭikarman, pūrvedyuḥkarman*), 2.6.6 (*yajñaparvan*).

TB 1.7.8.1 (*śārdūlacarman*).

ŚB 4.6.6.5 and 13.3.3.5 (*brahmasāman*), 5.3.5.3, 5.4.1.9, and 11 (*śārdūlacarman*), 6.6.1.4, 7.3.1.4, etc. (*adhvarakarman, agnikarman*), 13.3.3.4 (*maitrāvaruṇasāman*), 13.3.3.6 (*acchāvākasāman*), 13.5.1.1 and 13.5.3.10 (*agniṣṭomasāman*), 14.3.1.35 (*patnīkarman*).

ŚBK 1.1.2.5-6 (*mr̥gaśiras*), 7.2.4.3 and 7.3.1.9-10 (*śārdūlacarman*).

JB 1.149, etc. (*rathantarasāman*), 1.155, etc. (*acchāvākasāman*), 1.172, etc. (*agniṣṭomasāman*), 2.240 (*uttaravayas*), 2.276 (*ācāryakarman*), etc.

PB 4.2.19, etc. (*agniṣṭomasāman*), 4.3.1, etc. (*brahmasāman*), 8.10.1, etc. (*acchāvākasāman*), 9.2.7 and 15 (*kṣatrasāman*), 9.2.20, etc. (*rātriṣāman*), 11.3.8 and 9 (*somasāman*), 13.9.22 and 23 (*varuṇasāman*).

ṢaḍB 4.2.12-14 (*brahmasāman*).

ĀrṣB 1.378 (*varuṇasāman*), 2.3.11 (*arkaśiras*), etc.

JĀB 5.3, etc. (*somasāman*), *Arkaparvan* 3.9 (*arkaśiras*), etc.

SāB 1.5.15 (*svakarman*), 2.1.6 (*setuṣāman*), 2.3.3 (*sarpasāman*), 2.3.6 (*arkaśiras*).

ŚāṭyB, p. 72 (*brahmasāman, acchāvākasāman*).

VaṃśaB 1 (*giriśarman*).

ŚāṅA 1.5 (*devacchandas*), 3.5 (*brahmayaśas, brahmatejas*).

TA 1.15.1, etc. (*svatejas*).

P.5.4.142 (*chandasi ca*) prescribes substitution of *datR̥* for *danta* final in a *Bahuvrīhi* compound in ritual literature. It excludes from the Vedic language *Bahuvrīhi* compounds ending in *danta*. Yet there are some: *kṛṣṇadanta* at AA 3.2.4 and ŚāṅA 11.4; *viṣadanta* at AVP 5.9.8; *iṣīkādanta* at AVP 1.44.2; *ubhayatodanta* at AA 2.3.1, ŚB 1.6.3.30, ŚBK 2.6.1.21, JB 1.128, 2.84, and 2.114, and SāB 1.8.2; and *anyatodanta* at ŚBK 2.6.1.21 and JB 1.128, 2.84, and 2.114.

P.7.1.56 (*śrīgrāmaṇyoś chandasi*) determines the form of the genitive plural of *śrī* and *grāmaṇī* as *śrīṇām* and *grāmaṇīnām*, respectively. But genitive *sūtagrāmaṇyām* occurs at ŚB 13.4.2.5 and 13.5.2.7.

P.6.4.141 reads *mantreṣv āṅy āder ātmanaḥ (lopaḥ* 134) "In mantras there is elision of the initial [sound *ā*] of *ātman* when [the instrumental singular ending] *āṅ* follows." It is not easy to determine the precise meaning of this *sūtra*. It may not imply that *ātman* never loses its initial *ā* before other case endings, since for all we know Pāṇini may have looked upon *tman* as a separate vocable, but this *sūtra* clearly excludes the occurrence of *ātmanā* in mantras. This form is found, however, in mantras at the following places: AVŚ 3.29.8; AVŚ 5.29.6-9 ≈ AVP 13.9.7-8; AVŚ 8.2.8 ≈ AVP 16.3.9; AVŚ 9.5.31-36 ≈ AVP 16.99.8; AVŚ 18.2.7; AVŚ 19.33.5 ≈ 12.5.5; AVP 3.28.1, 16.100.5-11, and 16.119.1-3; VSM 32.11 ≈ VSK 35.3.8; and MS 2.8.14.

To the above cases the following may be added:

P.2.4.48 (*hemantaśiśirāv ahorātre ca chandasi*) implies, as Thieme (1935, 13) rightly pointed out, that Pāṇini "must have known *śiśira-* as a *neuter*." However, *śiśira* is masculine at SVK 3.4.2; SVJ 2.3.3; AVŚ 6.55.2 and 12.1.36; AVP 17.4.6 and 19.9.3; ŚB 2.1.3.1, 2.6.1.2, 8.7.1.7 and 8, 13.6.1.10 and 11; ŚBK 1.1.3.1 and 1.2.3.6; JB 1.313, 2.51, 2.211, 2.356; and TA 1.6.1.

P.3.1.118 (*pratyapibhyāṃ graheḥ* [without *chandasi*; see Kielhorn 1885, 192 (195); Thieme 1935, 16]) prescribes *pratigr̥hya-* and *apigr̥hya-*. Kātyāyana's *vārttika* on this *sūtra* confines it to Vedic literature (*chandas*) and Patañjali mentions the alternatives *pratigrāhya-* and *apigrāhya-*. The last two forms were apparently not known to Pāṇini, yet *apratigrāhya-* occurs at SāB 1.7.2.

4. What patterns arise from these data? Which Vedic texts did Pāṇini know, and which did he not know? We shall try to arrive at an opinion on the basis of the forms emphatically accepted or rejected by Pāṇini himself.[24]

4.1 Pāṇini records a number of forms that occur in the *R̥gveda* and nowhere else. Among the forms he clearly rejects, not one occurs in the *R̥gveda*. To this must be added the fact that P.1.1.16-18 refer to Śākalya's *Padapāṭha*. The *Padapāṭha* was added to the collection of hymns (excepting six verses; see Kashikar 1951, 44) and presupposes the latter. We may safely assume that Pāṇini knew the collected *R̥gveda*, not just the individual hymns.

Note that this is in no way obvious. Pāṇini knew Vedic stanzas (*r̥c*) and sacrificial formulas in prose (*yajus*)--both of these went by the term *mantra*--besides *brāhmaṇa* and *kalpa*. He nowhere says that he knew the mantras in collections. In this connection it is interesting to observe that the term that came to designate such collections (*saṃhitā*) did not yet have this meaning in Pāṇini's grammar and in the Vedic scriptures. There it is synonymous throughout with *sandhi*. The *saṃhitā-pāṭha*, as opposed to the *pada-pāṭha*, is the version of the text with sandhi.

4.2 The question as to whether the Vedic collections,

the *Saṃhitās*, existed in Pāṇini's time as collections becomes pertinent with regard to the *Taittirīya Saṃhitā*. We saw that three forms prescribed by Pāṇini occur in the *Taittirīya Saṃhitā* and nowhere else (**2.2**, above). All these words occur in mantras. This means that possibly Pāṇini *may* not have known the *brāhmaṇa* portions of the *Taittirīya Saṃhitā*. This possibility is supported by the fact that these *brāhmaṇa* parts frequently contain a conspicuous non-Pāṇinian feature, viz., the ending *-ai* instead of *-ās* (see Caland 1927, 50; Keith 1914, 1:cxlv f.). Note also that the *brāhmaṇa* portion of the *Taittirīya Saṃhitā* refers twice (6.1.9.2, 6.4.5.1) to Aruṇa Aupaveśi, whose grandson Śvetaketu Āruṇeya is characterized as modern in the *Āpastamba Dharma Sūtra* (1.5.5).

All this suggests that the *Taittirīya Saṃhitā* was collected in its more or less final form at a late date, perhaps later than Pāṇini. This agrees with some facts regarding the *Taittirīya Brāhmaṇa* and *Taittirīya Āraṇyaka*, to which we now turn.

Both the *Taittirīya Brāhmaṇa* and the *Taittirīya Āraṇyaka* contain forms that are explicitly rejected by Pāṇini. The *Taittirīya Brāhmaṇa* has *idāvatsarīṇa, anuvatsarīṇa, itarad* (**3.1**, above), *akārṣam, sabhya,* and *śārdūlacarman* (**3.2**). The *Taittirīya Āraṇyaka* has *akārṣam, svatejas,* and *śiśira* (m.) (**3.2**). It seems safe to conclude that these works were not known to, or accepted by, Pāṇini. The *Baudhāyana* and *Āpastamba Śrauta Sūtras* "accord in recognizing the whole content both of the *Brāhmaṇa* and of the *Āraṇyaka*" (Keith 1914, 1:lxxviii). Yet "it would be impossible, so far as can be seen, to prove that to [these *Sūtras*] even the

Saṅhitā was yet a definite unit" (ibid., lxxix-lxxx). The *sūtras* only distinguish between mantra and *brāhmaṇa*, which occur in each of the three, *Taittirīya Saṃhitā*, *Taittirīya Brāhmaṇa*, and *Taittirīya Āraṇyaka*.[25]

The interrelationship of mantras and *brāhmaṇa* portions of the three *Taittirīya* texts suggests that they, or parts of them, once existed as an undivided whole. We see, for example, that the *brāhmaṇa* portions of TS 2.5.7 and 8 comment on the mantras of TB 3.5.1 and 2; TS 2.5.9 on TB 3.5.3.1-4.1; TS 2.6.1 and 2 on TB 3.5.5-7; TS 2.6.7 on TB 3.5.8; TS 2.6.9 on TB 3.5.10; and TS 2.6.10 on TB 3.5.11 (Keith 1914, 1:lxxxiv). TS 3.5.11 supplements TB 3.6.1, giving the mantras for the *hotṛ* for the animal sacrifice (Keith 1914, 1:286, n. 4). Keith (1914, 1:lxxix) comes to a similar conclusion on the basis of the *Śrauta Sūtras*: "So far as we can judge there is no trace of any distinction being felt by the Sūtrakāras between the nature of the texts before them."

It is not impossible that the creation of a *Padapāṭha* differentiated the *Taittirīya Saṃhitā* from *Taittirīya Brāhmaṇa* and *Taittirīya Āraṇyaka*, just as the *Ṛgveda* may conceivably have been collected by the author of its *Padapāṭha* (Bronkhorst 1982a, 187).

The fact that Pāṇini derives the term *Taittirīya*, in the sense 'uttered by Tittiri', in P.4.3.102 does not, of course, prove that the *Taittirīya* texts, as now known, were known to him. Pāṇini probably knew the mantras, or a number of them, that are now part of the *Taittirīya Saṃhitā*, and he may indeed have considered them *taittirīya* 'uttered by Tittiri'.

Note, finally, that the *Taittirīya Saṃhitā* appears to borrow from the *Aitareya Brāhmaṇa* 1-5, as argued by Keith (1914, 1:xcvii f.); see also Aufrecht (1879, vi, 431f.) and Keith (1920, 46). The *Aitareya Brāhmaṇa* itself, including its first five chapters, deviates in a number of points from Pāṇini (**4.5**, below).

4.3 Some of the other *Saṃhitās* of the *Yajurveda* sin occasionally against Pāṇini.

The *Vājasaneyi Saṃhitā* has *ātmanā*, masculine *śiśira*, and one *Tatpuruṣa* compound in *-an (vyāghraloman)*. It shares this, however, with the *Maitrāyaṇī Saṃhitā*.

The *Maitrāyaṇī Saṃhitā* has *sabhya*, some *Tatpuruṣa* compounds in *-as* and *-an*, *ātmanā*; note further *dādhrati* (see note 19, above). These deviations from Pāṇini in the *Maitrāyaṇī Saṃhitā* are most surprising because Pāṇini appeared to know both the mantra and *brāhmaṇa* portions of this text (see **2.3**, above). This warns us once again that we cannot assume that the texts we know now existed in the same form in Pāṇini's day.

4.4 Did Pāṇini know the *Atharvaveda*? Two forms prescribed by him are found only there, one in the *Śaunakīya* version and one in the *Paippalāda* version. However, opposed to these two forms are numerous others forbidden by Pāṇini. They include *gamayāṃ cakāra, gamayāṃ cakartha* (**3.1**), *akārṣam, arukṣat, sabhya*, several neuter *Tatpuruṣa* compounds ending in *-an* and *-as*, *viṣadanta* and *iṣīkādanta, haricandra, ātmanā*, and *śiśira* (masc.) (**3.2**).

One might raise the question of whether the word-forms in the *Atharvaveda* may not have been Vedic in Pāṇini's opinion, that is, whether, perhaps, they were covered by non-Vedic rules of the *Aṣṭādhyāyī*. This is suggested by Balasubrahmanyam's remark (1984, 23):

> Among the seven *khyun-* derivatives taught by P[āṇini] in A[*ṣṭādhyāyī*] 3.2.56, *subhagaṃkaraṇī* and *priyaṃ-karaṇam* are only attested in the *Saṃhitā* texts of the [*Atharvaveda*]--the former occurring at [AVŚ] 6.139.1 and AVP 7.12.5, and the latter at the *Paippalāda Saṃhitā* (3.28.5; 6). Neither in the other Vedic *Saṃhitās* nor in the *Brāhmaṇa-Āraṇyaka* texts, do we come across these derivatives.

Balasubrahmanyam's observation is misleading in that *subhagaṃkaraṇī* is not taught in P.3.2.56 nor anywhere else in the *Aṣṭādhyāyī*. This is so because a *vārttika* of the *Saunāgas* (Mbh, 2:105, 1.8; on P.3.2.56) is required to provide *subhagaṃkaraṇa* with its feminine ending, *ī*, as shown by Balasubrahmanyam himself. Thus, P.3.2.56 did not derive *subhagaṃkaraṇī* in the *Atharvaveda*. The fact that the *Atharvaveda* contains two more words of the same kind (*ayakṣmaṃkaraṇī* at AVŚ 19.2.5 and AVP 8.8.11; *sarūpaṃkaraṇī* at AVŚ 1.24.4 and AVP 1.26.5; see Balasubrahmanyam 1984, 25f.) and that these words are not even partially[26] derived in Pāṇini's grammar, makes it less than likely that the *priyaṃkaraṇam* of AVP 3.28.6 was meant to be explained in P.3.2.56.

An interesting confirmation that the *Atharvaveda* did not exist as a collection until long after the other three Vedas were collected is found in the *Chāndogya Upaniṣad*. Sections 3.1-5 make a number of comparisons, or rather identifications, of which the following are of interest to us.

Section 3.1 states that the bees are the *ṛcs*, the flower is the *Ṛgveda*; in 3.2 the bees are the *yajus* (pl.), the flower is the *Yajurveda*; and in 3.3 the bees are the *sāmans*, the flower is the *Sāmaveda*. The interesting observation comes in section 3.4, where the bees are the *atharvāṅgirasaḥ* and the flower is *itihāsapurāṇam*. In 3.5, finally, the bees are the hidden teachings (*guhyā ādeśāḥ*), which may be the *Upaniṣads*, and the flower is *Brahman* (n.). Since the *atharvāṅgirasaḥ* constitute the *Atharvaveda* as we know it, the logic of the situation would have required that the flower in 3.4 be identified with the *Atharvaveda*. The fact that it is not hardly allows an explanation other than that the author of this passage did not know of such a definite collection of *atharvans* and *aṅgirases*. *Itihāsa* and *purāṇa* certainly do not designate the *Atharvaveda*, neither separately nor jointly (see Horsch 1966, 13f.).

Bloomfield (1899, 2f.), too, came to the conclusion "that many hymns and prose pieces in the AV. date from a very late period of Vedic productivity." Indeed, "there is nothing in the way of assuming that the composition of such texts as the AB. and ŚB. preceded the redactions of the Atharvan Saṃhitās."

Patañjali's *Mahābhāṣya* cites in its opening passage the first lines of the four Vedas; these apparently existed as collections in those days (second century B.C.). The first line is *śaṃ no devīr abhiṣṭaye*, which begins the *Paippalāda* version of the *Atharvaveda*. Patañjali even informs us of the size of the *Atharvaveda* known to him, saying (Mbh, 2:378, 1.11; on P.5.2.37): *viṃśino'ṅgirasaḥ*. This fits the twenty books of the *Paippalāda Saṃhitā*.[27] We may conclude from this that the *Paippalāda Saṃhitā* existed in its present form, at any rate, in the second century B.C.

4.5 The *Aitareya Brāhmaṇa* transgresses Pāṇini's rules in containing *itarad*, nominative *āvām* (**3.1**), and several neuter *Tatpuruṣa* compounds in *-an* (**3.2**). It is also interesting that AB 7.17 has the periphrastic perfect *āmantrayām āsa*, as opposed to P.3.1.40, which allows only *kr̥* in such formations (Keith 1936, 747). We also find optatives in *-(ay)īta* instead of *-(ay)eta* (Renou 1940, 11), and the ending *-ai* for both genitive and ablative *-ās* (Caland 1927, 50), not prescribed by Pāṇini.

By way of exception some older arguments adduced by Keith (1920, 42f.) to determine the date of the *Aitareya Brāhmaṇa* will be reviewed here (see also Bronkhorst 1982, 276). The language of this *Brāhmaṇa* is said to be "decidedly older than the Bhāṣā of Pāṇini," on the basis of Liebich's Pāṇini (1891). The circularity of Liebich's arguments has been shown elsewhere (Bronkhorst 1982, 275f.). The fact that Yāska knew the *Aitareya Brāhmaṇa* is irrelevant, since it is very likely that he is later than Pāṇini (Bronkhorst 1984, 8f.). The *Aitareya Brāhmaṇa* contains indications that it knew the *R̥gveda* before the completion of the orthoepic diaskeuasis but this implies nothing in view of the fact that the orthoepic diaskeuasis of the *R̥gveda* was not completed until long after Pāṇini (Bronkhorst 1981). The absence of reference to metempsychosis must be viewed against the background of the unwillingness of orthodox Brahmanism to let these ideas find entrance into their sacred texts even at a time when they had become generally known and widely accepted (Bronkhorst 1989, 125).

4.6 The other *Brāhmaṇas* that are considered early are the *Kauṣītaki Brāhmaṇa, Pañcaviṃśa Brāhmaṇa, Jaiminīya Brāhmaṇa,* and *Śatapatha Brāhmaṇa* (Renou 1957, 14). We can be brief about them.

The *Kauṣītaki Brāhmaṇa* has a number of forbidden words: *saprabhṛti, sodarka,* and *itarad,* besides many neuter *Tatpuruṣa* compounds in *-an* and at least one in *-as.* Like the *Aitareya Brāhmaṇa*, it has optatives in *-(ay)īta* and *-ai* for *-ās.*

The *Pañcaviṃśa Brāhmaṇa*, too, has *saprabhṛti* and *sodarka,* as well as nominative *yuvām,* and many neuter *Tatpuruṣa* compounds in *-an.*

The *Jaiminīya Brāhmaṇa* goes against Pāṇini's grammar in having *itarad,* many neuter *Tatpuruṣa* compounds in *-an* and *-as, ubhayatodanta* and *anyatodanta,* and masculine *śiśira.*

The *Śatapatha Brāhmaṇa* deviates from Pāṇini's grammar in the words *itarad,* nominative *āvām, akārṣīḥ, sabhya,* an accusative rather than a genitive for the object of *preṣya,* many neuter *Tatpuruṣa* compounds in *-an, ubhayatodanta,* genitive plural *-grāmaṇyām,* and masculine *śiśira.*

The *Kāṇva* version of the *Śatapatha Brāhmaṇa*, finally, deviates in fewer respects, containing a few neuter *Tatpuruṣa* compounds in *-an* and *-as, ubhayatodanta* and *anyatodanta,* an accusative rather than a genitive for the object of *preṣya,* and masculine *śiśira.*

5. The above considerations must be treated with caution. For one thing, it is not known in any detail what changes were made in the texts during the process we refer to as their "orthoepic diaskeuasis." This implies that we cannot be altogether sure what features of those texts can be used to determine their relationship with Pāṇini's *Aṣṭādhyāyī*. We also do not know how many serious deviations from Pāṇini's explicit statements must be considered evidence that Pāṇini was ignorant of a particular text. Further, we should remember that we made an assumption, which may not be acceptable to everyone, that Pāṇini's grammar can be taken seriously.

Neither should we be rash in concluding that Vedic texts that transgress the rules of Pāṇini repeatedly were for that reason completely unknown to Pāṇini. The problem is that, probably, no Vedic text has a single author. All are collections of parts of more or less heterogeneous origin. This applies to the *Saṃhitās* as well as to the *Brāhmaṇas* and *Āraṇyakas*. The most we can conclude from the deviations between the majority of Vedic texts and Pāṇini's grammar is that Pāṇini did not know much of Vedic literature in its present form, that is, in the collections known to us. Much of Vedic literature was still in a state of flux in Pāṇini's day, and had not yet reached the unalterable shape in which we know it.

These considerations are of value with regard to the texts that would seem to have been unknown to Pāṇini on the basis of the evidence reviewed in this article. They are, however, of equal value where the texts that appear to have been known to Pāṇini are concerned. The *Ṛgveda* may be an exception; it was known to Pāṇini along with its *Padapāṭha*, which leaves little room for major changes other than sandhi. But we must be cautious with respect to such texts as the *Maitrāyaṇī Saṃhitā* and *Kāṭhaka Saṃhitā*. It is true that they contain words prescribed by Pāṇini, which occur nowhere else, but this proves no more than that Pāṇini was acquainted with certain portions of them, if it proves anything at all.

The regional origin and early spread of most of the Vedic texts may account for Pāṇini's lack of acquaintance with some of them. Pāṇini is held to have lived in northwest India. Texts from other parts of the country may only have become known to him if they were generally accepted as Vedic in their region and beyond it.

Notes

* This study was carried out as part of a project of professors M. Witzel and T. E. Vetter, which was financed by the Netherlands Organization for the Advancement of Pure Research (Z.W.O.). In particular, Professor Witzel took a lively interest in the project. One of his own fields of specialization is the geographical distribution of Vedic schools in different periods. It is hoped that from that side additional evidence will come forth to shed light on the problems discussed here. Meanwhile, Witzel's "Tracing the Vedic Dialects" (1989) has appeared, which, unfortunately, could not be taken into consideration for the present article.

1. For a survey, see Cardona (1976, 226-28). Some important articles have been reproduced and discussed in Staal (1972, 135-204).
2. This means that one cannot conclude from certain peculiarities of sandhi in the *Maitrāyaṇī Saṃhitā* which are

not described by Pāṇini, that they "escaped his observation," as Palsule (1982, 188) claims.

3. Balasubrahmanyam (1981, 400) notes that in the sample studied by him, "three per cent of the exclusive Vedic vocabulary differs from P[āṇini]'s accentual system, and four per cent of the common vocabulary manifests the apparent difference between P[āṇini] and the Veda with reference to the systems of *Kr̥t* accentuation."
4. Even Kātyāyana and Patañjali sometimes ascribe an accent to a Vedic word that deviates from the accent found in the surviving texts (see Balasubrahmanyam 1974, 3, on *sthāsnu*).
5. The fact that the *Phiṭsūtra*s of Śāntanava ascribe to *arya, jyeṣṭha,* and *kaniṣṭha* the accents found in the extant Vedic literature is reason to think that Śāntanava is later rather than earlier than Pāṇini; cf. Kielhorn (1866, 1f.) and Devasthali (1967, 39f.). Kapila Deva Shastri (Saṃ 2018, 28f.) argues for an earlier date of the *Phiṭsūtra*s on insufficient grounds (Cardona 1976, 176).
6. Cf. Kiparsky (1980, 69) and Devasthali (1984, 137).
7. Thieme (1985) shows that the accents prescribed by Pāṇini in the case of words that are commonly used to address people are the initial accents of the vocative. He concludes that Pāṇini's accents are later than the (differing) Vedic ones. This may be correct, yet it does not by itself prove that all the texts having Vedic accentuation in these cases are older than Pāṇini. It is certainly conceivable that the Vedic texts were composed in a form of language that was kept archaic also

in its accents. Pāṇini's *bhāṣā*, too, is younger than Vedic, yet Pāṇini does not for that reason necessarily postdate scriptures that use the Vedic language.

8. Note that MS 1.5.12 (p. 81 1.2-6) uses *rātrī* in the language used by the gods and *rātri* elsewhere; this was pointed out to me by Professor Witzel.
9. P.2.3.62, 4.39, 73, 76, 3.2.88, 5.2.122, 6.1.34, 70, 133, 178, 2.199, 4.75, 7.1.8, 10, 103, 3.97, 4.78. Cf. Shivaramaiah (1969).
10. It goes without saying that the generality of such rules can be restricted in various ways such as the presence of rules that account for exceptions (*apavāda*).
11. For a brief description, see Chakrabarti (1980, 134-36) and Jha (1942, 294-99).
12. The following examples are taken from Bhartṛhari's discussion of *ūha* in his commentary on the *Mahābhāṣya* (see below).
13. We should not be misguided by this late date. Bhartṛhari made use of works on Mīmāṃsā older than Śabara's, among them probably the one by Bhavadāsa. See Bronkhorst (1989a).
14. The relevance for grammar is, of course, that in this way it can be decided whether or not Vedic rules are to be used in the modified mantras. Note that Kumārila's *Tantravārttika* on PMS 1.3.24 maintains that *ūha* is brought about without the help of grammar but rather with forms found in the Veda.
15. ŚŚS 6.1.15, similarly, prescribes substitution of *medhapataye* or *medhapatibhyaḥ* for, apparently, *medhapatibhyām*, as instances of *ūha*.

16. *ghas* replaces *ad* before aorist endings according to P.2.4.37 (*luṅsanor ghasḷ*).
17. The value of this case is somewhat in doubt since TB 2.8.2.5 cites the same mantra as RV 10.47.1 with *jagṛbhṇā*; it may have contained *jagṛbhma*.
18. My friend Dr. Harry Falk points out in a forthcoming article that Pāṇini cannot have known AVŚ 6.16.3, the reason being that Pāṇini derives *ailayīt* from *elayati*: the same mantra contains the form *ilaya* (*avelaya*), so that Pāṇini, had he known AVŚ 6.16.3 as a whole, would have derived *ailayīt* from *ilayati* rather than from *elayati*.
19. This was pointed out by Manjul Mayank in a paper read at the Seventh World Sanskrit Conference, Leiden, 1987.
20. The corresponding plural *dādhrati* occurs at TS 2.3.1.2, 5.3.9.2; MS 2.2.1; and KS 11.6. However, the juxtaposition of *dādharti, dardharti, dardharṣi*, and other finite verb forms seems to indicate that the precise form *dādharti* is meant.
21. For example, P.7.1.57 (*goḥ pādānte*) prescribes that the genitive plural of *go* at the end of a verse-foot in ritual literature is *gonām*. This is illustrated in RV 10.47.1. But the *Kāśikā* rightly observes that there are exceptions: RV 10.166.1 has *gavām* at the end of a verse-foot.
22. The *Kāṇva* parallel ŚBK 6.1.3.12 (*chāgānāṃ haviṣāṃ prasthitaṃ preṣya*) seems to be the only example in Vedic literature in which P.2.3.61 is obeyed. Note that the single *vārttika* on P.2.3.61 is intended to make the rule invalid where the oblation is *prasthita*. This would

justify all, or almost all, deviations from Pāṇini's rule, yet the fact that Pāṇini says nothing about *prasthita* in this context shows that he did not know, or accept, these counterexamples. Similarly, see Navathe (1987).

23. *bāhvojas* in RV 8.93.2 is considered a *Bahuvrīhi*, and not therefore a *Tatpuruṣa* compound, by Oldenberg (1909-12, 2:144). *somaparvabhiḥ* in RV 1.9.1 = AVŚ 20.71.7 = VSM 33.25 = VSK 32.2.8 = SVK 1.180 = SVJ 1.2.1.7.6 can be derived from *-parva*, by P.7.1.10.
24. Note that the insufficiency of Pāṇini's grammar with regard to the Vedic data has been known for a long time in the Pāṇinian tradition. Kumārila Bhaṭṭa, in his *Tantravārttika*, cites in this connection SVK 2.1006 = SVJ 4.17.11 (*madhya āpasya tiṣṭhati*), which has *āpasya* instead of *apām*.
25. Caland (1921, 3) observed that the *Āpastamba Śrauta Sūtra* refers to mantras of the *Taittirīya Saṃhitā* by way of their initial words, and to those of the *Taittirīya Brāhmaṇa* by citing them in full. Kashikar (1968, 400) has also shown that mantras from the *Taittirīya Brāhmaṇa* are often quoted by *pratīka*. The *Bhāradvāja Śrauta Sūtra* follows a similar practice (Kashikar 1968, 401).
26. That is, not even the forms *ayakṣmaṃkaraṇa* and *sarūpaṃkaraṇa*, without the feminine *ī*, are derived.
27. Note that the *Mahābhāṣya* also prefers the *Paippalāda* version of the *Atharvaveda* in some citations (see Renou 1953, 463).

Abbreviations

AA	*Aitareya Āraṇyaka*
AB	*Aitareya Brāhmaṇa*
AL	Abhyankar and Limaye's edition of Bhartṛhari's *Mahābhāṣyadīpikā*
ĀpŚS	*Āpastamba Śrauta Sūtra*
ĀrṣB	*Ārṣeya Brāhmaṇa*
ĀśvŚS	*Āśvalāyana Śrauta Sūtra*
AVP	*Atharvaveda* (Paippalāda)
AVŚ	*Atharvaveda* (Śaunakīya)
BAU(K)	*Bṛhadāraṇyaka Upaniṣad (Kāṇva)*
BhāŚS	*Bhāradvāja Śrauta Sūtra*
CE	"Critical edition" of Bhartṛhari's *Mahābhāṣyadīpikā*
ChU	*Chāndogya Upaniṣad*
DrŚS	*Drāhyāyaṇa Śrauta Sūtra*
HiŚS	*Hiraṇyakeśi Śrauta Sūtra*
JAB	*Jaiminīya-Ārṣeya-Brāhmaṇa*, edited by Bellikoth Ramachandra Sharma. Tirupati: Kendriya Sanskrit Vidyapeetha. 1967.
JUB	*Jaiminīya Upaniṣad Brāhmaṇa*
KB	*Kauṣītaki Brāhmaṇa*
KS	*Kāṭhaka Saṃhitā*
LŚS	*Lāṭyāyana Śrauta Sūtra*
Ms	Manuscript of Bhartṛhari's *Mahābhāṣyadīpikā*
MS	*Maitrāyaṇī Saṃhitā*
MŚS	*Mānava Śrauta Sūtra*
P.	Pāṇinian sūtra
PB	*Pañcaviṃśa Brāhmaṇa*
PMS	*Pūrva Mīmāṃsā Sūtra*

SāB	*Sāmavidhāna Brāhmaṇa*
ṢaḍB	*Ṣaḍviṃśa Brāhmaṇa*, edited by Bellikoth Ramachandra Sharma. Tirupati: Kendriya Sanskrit Vidyapeetha. 1967.
ŚāGS	*Śāṅkhāyana Gṛhya Sūtra*
ŚāṅA	*Śāṅkhāyana Āraṇyaka*
ŚāṭyB	*Śāṭyāyana Brāhmaṇa*
ŚB	*Śatapatha Brāhmaṇa*
ŚBK	*Śatapatha Brāhmaṇa (Kāṇva)*
ŚŚS	*Śāṅkhāyana Śrauta Sūtra*
Sw	Swaminathan's edition of Bhartṛhari's *Mahābhāṣyadīpikā*
TB	*Taittirīya Brāhmaṇa*
VaṃśaB	*Vaṃśa Brāhmaṇa*
VāŚS	*Vārāha Śrauta Sūtra*

Bibliography

Aufrecht, Theodor, 1879: *Das Aitareya Brāhmaṇa.* Bonn: Adolph Marcus.

Balasubrahmanyam, M. D., 1964: "The accentuation of *arya* in Pāṇini and the Veda." *26th International Congress of Orientalists.* New Delhi. Summaries of Papers, III, 54-55.

-------, 1966: "An accentual problem in Pāṇini and the Veda apropos of the word *hāyana-*." *Bulletin of the Deccan College Research Institute* 25, 43-58.

-------, 1969: "*Arya*-: an accentual study." *Indian Antiquary*, Third Series, 3 (R. N. Dandekar Felicitation Volume), 112-27.

-------, 1972: "Vedic *śriyase* and Pāṇini 3.4.9." *Vishveshvarananda Indological Journal* 10, 7-10.

-------, 1974: "Pāṇini 6.1.209-210." *Charudeva Shastri Felicitation Volume*. Delhi, 189-93.

-------, 1974a: "Kātyāyana and some Vedic formations." *Saṃskr̥tavimarśaḥ* 1(2), 1-4.

-------, 1981: *The System of Kr̥t Accentuation in Pāṇini and the Veda*. Tirupati: Kendriya Sanskrit Vidyapeetha (Kendriya Sanskrit Vidyapeetha Series No. 32).

-------, 1983: "An accentual note on Vedic *voḍhave*." *Surabhi*. Sreekrishna Sarma Felicitation Volume. Tirupati: Sri Venkateswara University, 229-40.

-------, 1984: "*Subhagaṃkaraṇī* in AV 6,139,1." *Amr̥tadhārā*. R. N. Dandekar Felicitation Volume. Delhi: Ajanta Publications, 21-27.

Bhartr̥hari: *Mahābhāṣya Dīpikā*. (1) Edited by K. V. Abhyankar and V. P. Limaye. Poona: Bhandarkar Oriental Research Institute. 1970 (Post-Graduate and Research Department Series No. 8). (2) Partly edited by V. Swaminathan under the title *Mahābhāṣya Ṭīkā*. Varanasi:

Banaras Hindu University. 1965 (Hindu Vishvavidyalaya Nepal Rajya Sanskrit Series Vol. 11). (3) Manuscript reproduced. Poona: Bhandarkar Oriental Research Institute. 1980. (4) "Critical edition" and translation. Poona: Bhandarkar Oriental Research Institute. To date, six volumes have been published: Āhnika 3 by G. B. Palsule (1983); Āhnika 5 by V. P. Limaye, G. B. Palsule, and V. B. Bhagavat (1984); Āhnika 6, part 1, by V. B. Bhagavat and Saroja Bhate (1986); Āhnika 1 by Johannes Bronkhorst (1987); Āhnika 2 by G. B. Palsule (1988); and Āhnika 4 by G. V. Devasthali and G. B. Palsule (1989).

Bhat, M. S., 1968: "The Vedic stem *rātri-* and Pāṇini." *Journal of the Bombay Branch of the Royal Asiatic Society* 41-42 (1966-67, N.S.), 8-11.

Bloomfield, Maurice, 1899: *The Atharva Veda.* Asian Publication Services. 1978.

-------, 1906: *A Vedic Concordance.* Delhi, Varanasi, and Patna: Motilal Banarsidass. 1964 (Harvard Oriental Series, Vol. 10).

Bronkhorst, Johannes, 1981: "The orthoepic diaskeuasis of the R̥gveda and the date of Pāṇini." *Indo-Iranian Journal* 23, 83-95.

-------, 1982: "The variationist Pāṇini and Vedic." *Indo-Iranian Journal* 24, 273-82.

-------, 1982a: "Some observations on the Padapāṭha of the Ṛgveda." *Indo-Iranian Journal* 24, 181-89.

-------, 1984: "Nirukta, Uṇādi Sūtra, and Aṣṭādhyāyī." *Indo-Iranian Journal* 27, 1-15.

-------, 1989: "L'indianisme et les préjugés occidentaux." *Études de Lettres* (Lausanne), April-June 1989, 119-36.

-------, 1989a: "Bhartṛhari and Mīmāṃsā." *Studien zur Indologie und Iranistik* 15, 101-17.

Caland, W. (tr.), 1921: *Das Śrautasūtra des Āpastamba.* Göttingen: Vandenhoeck and Ruprecht.

-------, 1927: "On a paragraph of Vaidic syntax." *Acta Orientalia* 5, 49-51.

-------, 1928: "Eine vierte Mitteilung über das Vādhūlasūtra." *Acta Orientalia* 6, 97-241.

-------, (tr.), 1928a: *Das Śrautasūtra des Āpastamba.* Sechszehntes bis vierundzwanzigstes und einunddreissigstes Buch. Amsterdam: Koninklijke Akademie van Wetenschappen.

Cardona, George, 1976: *Pāṇini: A Survey of Research.* Delhi, Varanasi, and Patna: Motilal Banarsidass. 1980.

Chakrabarti, Samiran Chandra, 1980: *The Paribhāṣās in the Śrautasūtras*. Calcutta: Sanskrit Pustak Bhandar.

Devasthali, G. V., 1967: *Phiṭsūtras of Śāntanava*. Edited with introduction, translation, and critical and exegetical notes. Poona: University of Poona. (Publications of the Centre of Advanced Study in Sanskrit, Class C, No. 1).

-------, 1984: "Pāṇini and Vedic--a critique." *Annals of the Bhandarkar Oriental Research Institute* 64 (1983), 137-48.

Gonda, Jan, 1975: *Vedic Literature (Saṃhitās and Brāhmaṇas)*. Wiesbaden: Otto Harrassowitz (A History of Indian Literature, Vol. I, Fasc. 1).

Gotō, Toshifumi, 1987: *Die "I. Präsensklasse" im Vedischen*. Wien: Verlag der Österreichischen Akademie der Wissenschaften.

Hoffman, Karl, 1974: "Pāṇini VII 2, 69 saniṃ sasanivāṃsam." *Münchener Studien zur Sprachwissenschaft* 32, 73-80.

Horsch, Paul, 1966: *Die vedische Gāthā- und Śloka-Literatur*. Bern: Francke Verlag.

Jha, Ganganatha, 1942: *Pūrva-Mīmāṃsā in its Sources*. Second edition, 1964. Varanasi: Banaras Hindu University.

Joshi, S. D., and Roodbergen, J. A. F., 1981: *Patañjali's Vyākaraṇa-Mahābhāṣya, Prātipadikārthaśeṣāhnika (P.2.3.46-2.3.71)*. Pune: University of Poona (Publications of the Centre of Advanced Study in Sanskrit, Class C, No. 14).

Kapila Deva Shastri, Saṃ 2018: *Saṃskṛta Vyākaraṇa meṃ Gaṇapāṭha kī Paramparā aura Ācārya Pāṇini*. Ajmer: Bhāratīya-Prācyavidyā-Pratiṣṭhāna.

Kashikar, C. G., 1951: "The problem of the Gaḷantas in the Ṛgvedapadapāṭha." *Proceedings of the All-India Oriental Conference* 13 (1946), 39-46.

-------, 1968: "The Taittirīya-Brāhmaṇa in relation to the Sūtrakāras." *Pratidānama*. Festschrift Franciscus Bernardus Jacobus Kuiper. The Hague and Paris: Mouton, 398-408.

Keith, Arthur Berriedale (tr.), 1914: *The Veda of the Black Yajus School entitled Taittiriya Sanhita*. 2 parts. Cambridge, Mass.: Harvard University Press (Harvard Oriental Series 18, 19).

-------, (tr.), 1920: *Rigveda Brahmanas: The Aitareya and Kauṣītaki Brāhmaṇas of the Rigveda*. Delhi, Patna, and Varanasi: Motilal Banarsidass. 1971 (Harvard Oriental Series 25).

-------, 1936: "Pāṇini and the Veda." *Indian Culture* 2, 735-48.

Kielhorn, Franz, 1866: *Çāntanava's Phiṭsūtra.* Mit verschiedenen indischen Commentaren, Einleitung, Uebersetzung und Anmerkungen herausgegeben. Genehmigter Nachdruck. Nendeln, Liechtenstein: Kraus Reprint, Ltd. 1966 (Abhandlungen der Deutschen Morgenländischen Gesellschaft, IV. Band No. 2).

-------, 1885: "Der Grammatiker Pāṇini." *Göttinger Nachr.* 1885, 185-99. Reprinted in *Kleine Schriften* I, 188-202. Wiesbaden: Franz Steiner, 1969.

Kiparsky, Paul, 1980: *Pāṇini as a Variationist.* Edited by S. D. Joshi. Pune: Centre of Advanced Study in Sanskrit, in collaboration with the MIT Press, Cambridge, Mass., and London.

-------, 1982: *Some Theoretical Problems in Pāṇini's Grammar.* Poona: Bhandarkar Oriental Research Institute.

Kumārila Bhaṭṭa: *Tantravārttika.* In: *Mīmāṃsādarśana.* Edited by Kāśīnātha Vāsudevaśāstrī Abhyaṃkara and Pt. Gaṇeśaśāstrī Jośī. Poona: Ānandāśrama. 1973-84 (Ānandāśrama Saṃskṛtagranthāvali 97).

Liebich, Bruno, 1891: *Pāṇini: Ein Beitrag zur Kenntnis der indischen Literatur und Grammatik.* Leipzig: H. Haessel.

Mayank, Manjul, 1990: "Pāṇini's acquaintance with the Atharvaveda." In: *Pāṇini and the Veda.* Edited by Madhav M. Deshpande. Leiden: E. J. Brill.

Navathe, P. D., 1987: "On the prasthitaṃ haviḥ." *Annals of the Bhandarkar Oriental Research Institute* 68 (Ramakrishna Gopal Bhandarkar 150th Birth-Anniversary Volume), 645-51.

Oldenberg, Hermann, 1909-1912: *Ṛgveda. Textkritische und exegetische Noten.* 2 vols. Berlin: Weidmannsche Buchhandlung (Abhandlungen der königlichen Gesellschaft der Wissenschaften zu Göttingen, phil.-hist. Klasse, N.F. Band XI Nro. 5 and Band XIII Nro. 3).

Palsule, G. B., 1982: "Two Vedic rules of Pāṇini: 8.3.47 and 8.3.10." *Golden Jubilee Volume.* Poona: Vaidika Saṃśodhana Maṇḍala, 185-88.

Pāṇinīya Śikṣā. Edited by Manomohan Ghosh. Calcutta: University of Calcutta. 1938.

Patañjali: *Vyākaraṇa-Mahābhāṣya.* Edited by F. Kielhorn. Third Edition by K. V. Abhyankar. 3 vols. Poona: Bhandarkar Oriental Research Institute. 1962-72.

Renou, Louis, 1940: "Sur certaines anomalies de l'optatif sanskrit." *Bulletin de la Société de Linguistique de Paris* 41, 5-17.

-------, 1953: "Le Veda chez Patañjali." *Journal Asiatique* 241, 427-64.

-------, 1957: *Altindische Grammatik: Introduction générale.* Nouvelle édition du texte (by Jacob Wackernagel) paru en 1896, au tome I. Göttingen: Vandenhoeck and Ruprecht.

Scheftelowitz, Isidor, 1906: *Die Apokryphen des Ṛgveda.* Hildesheim: Georg Olms Verlagsbuchhandlung. 1966.

-------, 1919: "Die Nividas und Praiṣas, die ältesten vedischen Prosatexte." *Zeitschrift der Deutschen Morgenländischen Gesellschaft* 73, 30-50.

Schroeder, Leopold von, 1879: "Ueber die Maitrāyaṇī Saṃhitā, ihr Alter, ihr Verhältniss zu den verwandten Çākhā's, ihre sprachliche und historische Bedeutung." *Zeitschrift der Deutschen Morgenländischen Gesellschaft* 33, 177-207.

-------, 1880: "Das Kāṭhakam und die Māitrāyaṇī Saṃhitā." *Monatsberichte der Königlich Preussischen Akademie der Wissenschaften zu Berlin* (1879), 675-704.

-------, (ed.), 1881-86: *Maitrāyaṇī Saṃhitā.* Parts I-IV. Leipzig: F. A. Brockhaus.

-------, 1895: "Das Kāṭhaka, seine Handschriften, seine Accentuation und seine Beziehung zu den indischen Lexicographen und Grammatikern." *Zeitschrift der Deutschen Morgenländischen Gesellschaft* 49, 145-71.

Shivaramaiah, B. K., 1969: "A note on 'bahulaṃ chandasi.'" *The Mysore Orientalist* 2(1), 7-11.

Staal, J. F. (ed.), 1972: *A Reader on the Sanskrit Grammarians*. Cambridge, Mass., and London, MIT Press.

Thieme, Paul, 1935: *Pāṇini and the Veda*. Studies in the early history of linguistic science in India. Allahabad: Globe Press.

-------, 1938: *Der Fremdling im R̥gveda*. Eine Studie über die Bedeutung der Worte *ari, arya, aryaman* und *ārya*. Leipzig: Deutsche Morgenländische Gesellschaft. Reprint: Kraus Reprint, Ltd., Nendeln, Liechtenstein. 1966.

-------, 1985: "Nennformen aus Anrede und Anruf im Sanskrit." *Münchener Studien zur Sprachwissenschaft* 44 (Festgabe Karl Hoffmann) I, 239-58.

Wackernagel, Jakob, 1896-1930: *Altindische Grammatik*. Göttingen: Vandenhoeck und Ruprecht.

Whitney, W. D., 1893: "The Veda in Pāṇini." *Giornale della Società Asiatica Italiana* 7, 243-54.

Witzel, M., 1989: "Tracing the Vedic dialects." In: *Dialectes dans les littératures indo-aryennes*. Edited by Colette Caillat. Paris: Institut de Civilisation Indienne (Publications de l'Institut de Civilisation Indienne, Fasc. 55), 97-265.

ON PĀṆINI, ŚĀKALYA, VEDIC DIALECTS AND VEDIC EXEGETICAL TRADITIONS[1]

George Cardona

0 Pāṇini refers in his *Aṣṭādhyāyī* to certain features of speech that are attributed to Śākalya. In particular, some of the *Aṣṭādhyāyī* rules concern aspects of Śākalya's dialect as reflected in his *padapāṭha* to the *R̥gveda*. These *sūtras* are of interest in connection with aspects of Sanskrit dialects at the times of Pāṇini and his predecessors. They establish that Śākalya, the author of the *padapāṭha* to the *R̥gveda*, antedated Pāṇini. Śākalya also gives us evidence in his *padapāṭha* for dating an important dialectal split in early Indo-Aryan. Moreover, the evidence of the *Aṣṭādhyāyī* concerning forms of the type *adukṣat* allows a perspective on how Pāṇini viewed the *saṃhitāpāṭha* and the *padapāṭha* of the *R̥gveda*.

1 Let me consider first two *sūtras* in which Pāṇini deals with features of Śākalya's *padapāṭha*.

1.1 *Aṣṭādhyāyī* 1.1.16: सम्बुद्धौ शाकल्यस्येतावनार्षे (ओत् १५, प्रगृह्यम् ११) states that, according to Śākalya, a vowel *o* whose occurrence is determined by a *sambuddhi* ending has the class name *pragr̥hya* if it is followed by *iti* that does not stem from a *r̥ṣi*. That is, *-o* of vocative singular forms is classed as a *pragr̥hya* element under these conditions. A *pragṛhya* vowel is exempt from replacements that regularly apply to vowels followed by other vowels in close junction.[2] *Aṣṭādhyāyī* 1.1.16 thus says that Śākalya has *-o* in vocative singular forms before *iti*, which does not occur in the original text attributed to a *ṛṣi*.

This accords with what is known about Śākalya's *padapāṭha* to the *Ṛgveda*. For example, corresponding to the *saṃhitāpāṭha* of *Ṛgveda* 1.2.1a, 2a: वाय॒वा याहि, उ॒क्थेभिर्जरन्ते the *padapāṭha* has वाय॒ो इति । आ । या॒हि॒ ।, वाय॒ो इति । उ॒क्थेभिः । ज॒र॒न्ते॒ ।. The *Ṛgvedaprātiśākhya* accounts for the data in question by providing that *-o* of a vocative form is called *pragṛhya*, then saying that a *pragṛhya* element remains unchanged before the *i-* of *iti* in the *padapāṭha* and before vowels in the *saṃhitā* text that stems from *ṛṣis*.[3]

1.2 Similarly, *Aṣṭādhyāyī* 1.1.17: उञ ऊँ । states that, according to Śākalya, the particle *u* is replaced by a nasalized vowel that is long and *pragṛhya*.[4] This accords both with what is known of the *padapāṭha* to the *Ṛgveda* and what is provided for in the *Ṛgvedaprātiśākhya*. For example, corresponding to the *saṃhitāpāṭha* सूर्या॑य॒ पन्था॒मन्वेतवा उ । (*Ṛgveda* 1.24.8b), the *padapāṭha* has सूर्या॑य । पन्था॑म् । अनु॑ ऽए॒त॒वै । ऊँ॒ इति ।. *Ṛgvedaprātiśākhya* 1.75 (उकारश्चेतिकरणेन युक्तो रक्तो ऽपृक्तो द्राघितः शाकलेन ।) states that, according to the teaching of Śākalya, a unisegmental element *u* that is connected with *iti*--that is, the particle *u* followed by *iti* in the *padapāṭha*--is both lengthened and nasalized.[5]

1.3 Clearly, *Aṣṭādhyāyī* 1.1.16 is best interpreted as reflecting what Śākalya does in his *padapāṭha*.[6] Moreover, although the *padas* of any *padapāṭha* are generally followed by pauses, thus placing their final segments in prepause position, Śākalya's letting *iti* directly follow *pragṛhya* -*o*, and also *ūm̐*, has a parallel in his procedure. Consider briefly some examples of words with -*ḥ* in the *Ṛgveda padapāṭha* corresponding to -*r* of the *saṃhitāpāṭha*, together with *prātiśākhya* rules that serve to relate the two. The *Ṛgvedaprātiśākhya* recognizes a rhotacizing -*ḥ*, which it calls *rephin*. In general, -*ḥ* preceded by a vowel other than *a* or *ā* is classed as *rephin*, and such a *visarjanīya* goes to -*r* before a vowel or a voiced consonant.[7] For example, the *saṃhitāpāṭha* of *Ṛgveda* 3.26.7a has अ॒ग्निरस्मि , and the corresponding *padapāṭha* text is अ॒ग्निः । अ॒स्मि॒ ।. There are also words like *prātáḥ*, however, which have -*r* before vowels and voiced consonants although they have prepause -*ḥ* following an *a*-vowel. For example, corresponding to *Ṛgveda* 7.41.1a: प्रा॒तर॒ग्निम्प्रा॒तरिन्द्रं हवामहे and 1.16.3a: इन्द्रम्प्रा॒तर्हवामह. . . , the *padapāṭha* has प्रा॒तः । अ॒ग्निम् । प्रा॒तः । इन्द्रम् । ह॒वा॒म॒हे॒ । and इन्द्रम् । प्रा॒तः । ह॒वा॒म॒हे॒ ।. Accordingly, the *Ṛgvedaprātiśākhya* provides that *prātáḥ* has a *rephin ḥ*.[8] Of course, the change to *r* does not apply for *ḥ* followed by a voiceless consonant or pause; for example, *Ṛgveda* 4.35.7a: प्रा॒तस्सु॒तमपिबो हर्यश्व॒ has *prātás*. Moreover, both *rephin* and non-*rephin ḥ* assimilate to following voiceless consonants;[9] for example, *nas*, as in *Ṛgveda* 10.128.9a: ये न॒स्स॒पत्ना॒ . . . (*padapāṭha* ये । न॒ः । स॒ऽपत्नाः । . . .), alternates with *naḥ* and *naś*, but not with **nar*. In his *padapāṭha*, Śākalya lets *prātár* and *iti* occur in close conjunction (प्रा॒तरिति । सु॒तम् । अ॒पि॒ब॒ः । . . .), thus showing that *prātáḥ* (--› *prātás*; see note 9) has a rhotacizing -*ḥ*. Naturally, if the first vowel of *iti* in the *padapāṭha* is to condition the occurrence of -*r* in an item with *rephin ḥ*, the two words have to be pronounced in close junction (*saṃhitāyām*) within the *padapāṭha*. Similarly, by letting a vocative form with *-o* be followed by *iti* in close junction, where a non-*pragṛhya* vowel *o* would go to *av*, Śākalya shows that in his dialect the vowel of such a vocative form is *pragṛhya*.[10]

2 From what has been shown up to this point, it must be accepted both that Śākalya, the author of the *padapāṭha* to the *Ṛgveda*, preceded Pāṇini and that Pāṇini refers to him explicitly. This is of import to another point, which more directly concerns some dialect variation in Vedic.

2.1 It is well known that early Vedic had variants of the types *dakṣ-* and *dhakṣ-*. It is also demonstrable that the variants belong to distinct dialects of early Vedic.[11] Given that the type *dakṣ-*, with an unaspirated base-initial consonant, shows the effects of deaspiration ("Grassmann's Law") on forms that, in early Indo-Iranian, also showed the progressive assimilation that goes under the label "Bartholomae's Law," and that the type *dhakṣ-* is immediately and plausibly accounted for as an innovation through analogic spread of variants with aspirated initials after the Indo-Aryan devoicing of clusters such as **-ghzh-*, I think it proper to consider, with earlier scholars, that the types *dakṣ-* and *dhakṣ-* are respectively archaic and modern. Now, in Śākalya's dialect, as in the language that Pāṇini describes, the modern type *dhakṣ-* is the norm. Accordingly, Śākalya consistently gives forms like *adhukṣat* instead of *adukṣat* where the *saṃhitāpāṭha* has the latter (see the paper alluded to in note 11).

2.2 Another fact concerning such variants--which, to my knowledge, has not been emphasized by earlier scholars--

is that Pāṇini does not specifically account for the type *dakṣ-*. The *Aṣṭādhyāyī* has *sūtras* accounting for the type *dhakṣ-*. Thus, *-h* of a verb is generally replaced by *-ḍh* but *-gh* substitutes for *-h* of a verb that begins with *d-*, and an aspirated stop replaces an unaspirated stop *b ḍ d g* in a syllable of a verb that ends in an aspirate at a word boundary and at a morpheme boundary before *-s-* and *-dhv-*.[12] With retroflexion and devoicing, then, forms like *adhukṣat* are derived from *aduh-sa-t*. But no special provision is made in the *Aṣṭādhyāyī* to derive forms like *adukṣat*.

2.3 This can hardly be considered simply an oversight. Forms of the type in question occur too frequently in the *R̥gveda* and other Vedic texts to allow this assumption and Pāṇini does explicitly provide for Vedic forms like *bhari-bhrat*, with aspirated *bh-* instead of unaspirated *b-* in an *abhyāsa* syllable.[13] Another possible reason is that Pāṇini may have been led to omit accounting for forms of the type *dakṣ-* because these were somehow stigmatized, parts of dialects not viewed as acceptable. This possibility can be ruled out, however, for several reasons. First, it is difficult to maintain that Pāṇini would consider stigmatized forms that were not at all uncommon in the *R̥gveda*, which is part of the accepted corpus of sacred Vedic texts. To be sure, certain pronunciations, belonging to particular recitational schools, could and were stigmatized. It is precisely within the traditions of the *R̥gveda*, moreover, that such censure is made most explicit. Two examples will suffice to bring out this point. There were some recitational traditions in which, instead of hiatus sequences *-e a-*, *-o a-*, one had *-e ĕ-*, *-o ŏ-*, with initial short vowels *ĕ- ŏ-*, which were considered the results of assimilation. In the *R̥gvedaprātiśākhya,* such pronunciation is not merely mentioned; Śaunaka explicitly remarks that the accepted tradition of recitation is different.[14] The *R̥gvedaprātiśākhya* also takes note of certain peculiarities involving the pronunciation of sequences with *yamas*, sounds produced when non-nasal stops are followed by nasals, as in *pálikniḥ* 'gray' and *ámathnāt* 'tore away'. Śaunaka gives the general rule concerning *yamas*: non-nasal stops become corresponding *yamas* when they precede nasals.[15] He goes on to note two peculiarities in the recitational tradition represented by Gārgya: a nasal vocalic segment (*nāsikyā svarabhaktiḥ*) is inserted after a *yama*, and if the *yama* is aspirated, as in *ámathnāt,* an aspirated segment follows it.[16] Moreover, Śaunaka explicitly says that one is to avoid (*varjayet*) the addition of an aspirated segment.[17]

On the other hand, Śaunaka does not suggest in any way that variants of the type *dakṣ-* were considered unacceptable in recitational traditions. On the contrary, he simply lists forms of this type,[18] thereby implying nothing other than that these forms are irregular in terms of the norms of his own and Śākalya's speech, that is, that they are archaisms found in the *saṃhitāpāṭha.*

2.4 We have, therefore, to seek another reason for Pāṇini's not formulating *sūtras* to account for variants of the type *dakṣ-*. Now, it is generally accepted that the *padapāṭha* of a Vedic text, although historically later than its corresponding *saṃhitāpāṭha,* is taken as the source of the *saṃhitāpāṭha* in terms of derivation. Śaunaka explicitly formulates this position, which is found stated also in the

Nirukta.[19] In accordance with this, commentators like Sāyaṇa cite forms of the type *adhukṣat* instead of *adukṣat* in the course of commenting on pertinent passages. There is no reason whatever to assume that Pāṇini's attitude should be any different. Accordingly, he would accept that Śākalya's *padapāṭha* to the *Ṛgveda* served as the basis for deriving, by rules of morphophonemic conversion, the *saṃhitāpāṭha* of this tradition. Given this, it is not unreasonable to suppose that Pāṇini did not consider it necessary to account for forms of the type *dakṣ-* through rules of his own grammar. Since the basic forms were already given in the *padapāṭha*, he did not need to formulate special rules to account for unaspirated initial consonants in the type *dakṣ-* any more than he needed to formulate rules for introducing affixes to derive bases such as *bhīma*, which Pāṇini accepts as being derived with affixes of the *uṇādi* set. Thus Pāṇini fits right in with a long tradition of considering the *padapāṭha* the source text by means of which the *saṃhitāpāṭha* and recitations such as the *kramapāṭha* are accounted for.

The conclusion I am led to also fits in with another aspect of Pāṇini's relation to the *Ṛgveda*. *Aṣṭādhyāyī* 2.4.80: मन्त्रे घसह्वरणशवृदहाद्वृच्कृगमिजनिभ्यो लेः । accounts for a series of aorist forms in *mantras* by providing that the abstract suffix *li*--that is, *cli*--is deleted after certain verbs. Among the verbs given is *dah*. According to commentators, moreover, the *sūtra* accounts for the root aorist form *dhak* (3sg. injunctive), which western exegetes derive from *dagh* 'reach'. Pāṇinīyas and others derive *dhak* from *dah*, although they give contextually appropriate glosses. For example, in his comments on RV 6.61.14b: °मा नु आ धक् ,

Sāyaṇa glosses *mā́ . . . dhak* with *nābhidaha*, then explains that this means 'do not push . . . away' (मा . . . आ धक् नाभिदह न बाधस्व). Commenting on the same passage repeated in *Taittirīya-brāhmaṇa* 2.4.3.1, Sāyaṇa glosses with *ma dhākṣīḥ*, then says that this means 'do not cause . . . to disappear, perish' (मा धक् मा धाक्षीः मा विनाशय ।). There is, indeed, no *sūtra* of the *Aṣṭādhyāyī* other than 2.4.80 that accounts for the morphological formation of *dhak*. Accordingly, it is most reasonable to accept that Pāṇini, too, considered this a derivative of *dah*. This implies that he accepted not only a received text of the *R̥gveda* but also a tradition of exegesis according to which *dhak* was considered a form of *dah*.

3 Summary. There is irrefutable evidence that Pāṇini knew Śākalya's *padapāṭha* to the *R̥gveda*. In this *padapāṭha*, Śākalya regularly gives forms of the modern type *dhakṣ-* instead of archaic forms of the type *dakṣ-*, where the *saṃhitāpāṭha* has the latter. In his *Aṣṭādhyāyī*, moreover, Pāṇini does not formulate rules especially to account for unaspirated initials in forms of the type *dakṣ-*. This is most appropriately explained on the assumption that Pāṇini took the *padapāṭha* forms as the Vedic forms to be explained directly and accepted, and that the archaic forms of the *saṃhitāpāṭha* were to be accounted for by other rules, proper to *prātiśākhya* treatises. This stand accords with what is accepted in Indian traditions of exegesis. We should consider not only that Pāṇini accepted interpretations reflected in the *padapāṭha* but also that he received texts like the *R̥gveda* together with particular exegetical traditions that he accepted.

Notes

1. The first part of this paper (**1.-1.3**) was originally submitted, on January 6, 1983, for publication in the felicitation volume for Dr. U. P. Shah. Unfortunately, this has yet to be published, at least to my knowledge. Nor has the editor of the proposed volume, Dr. S. K. Bhawmik, responded to inquiries concerning the volume's publication. I have, therefore, incorporated a revised version of my contribution in the present paper.
2. *Aṣṭādhyāyī* 6.1.125: प्लुतप्रगृह्या अचि नित्यम् (प्रकृत्या ११५).
3. *R̥gvedaprātiśākhya* 1.68: ओकारो आमन्त्रितजः प्रगृह्यः । , 2.51-52: प्रकृत्येतिकरणादौ प्रगृह्याः । स्वरेषु चाष्यर्मि् ।.
4. I leave out of consideration the arguments found in the *Mahābhāṣya* and later works concerning whether *Aṣṭādhyāyī* 1.1.17 should be split into two rules.
5. The *padapāṭha* to the *Vājasaneyisaṃhitā* also has *pragr̥hya* *ūm̐* for *u* of the *saṃhitā* text, and the *Vājasaneyiprātiśākhya* accounts for this (1.95, 4.94: उकारो ऽपृक्तः । , उकारो ऽपृक्तो दीर्घमनुनासिकम् ।), but it is known that Pāṇini was not directly acquainted with the *Vājasaneyisaṃhitā*, and if, as some scholars maintain, the author of the *Vājasaneyisaṃhitā* is the same Kātyāyana as the one who composed *vārttikas* on Pāṇinian *sūtras*, Pāṇini could not have known this work. Details concerning other *padapāṭhas* are not directly germane to my discussion.
6. See *Pāṇini, a Survey of Research* (The Hague: Mouton, 1976; reprinted Delhi, 1980: Motilal Banarsidass), page 274, for a brief survey of different views concerning this point.

7. *Ṛgvedaprātiśākhya* 1.76, 4.27: ऊष्मा रेफी पञ्चमो नामिपूर्वः ।, सर्वोपधस्तु स्वरघोषवत्परो रेफं रेफी ते पुना रेफसन्धयः ।.
8. *Ṛgvedaprātiśākhya* 1.81: प्रातः ।.
9. *Ṛgvedaprātiśākhya* 4.31-32: अघोषे रेफ्यरेफी चोष्माणं स्पर्श उत्तरे तत्सस्थानमनूष्मपरे । तमेवोष्माणमूष्मणि ।. *Ṛgvedaprātiśākhya* 4.33-34: प्रथमोत्तमवर्गीये स्पर्शे वा । ऊष्मणि चानते provide for optional assimilation of *-ḥ* before velar and labial stops--where *-ḥ* alternates with *jihvāmūlīya* and *upadhmānīya*--and spirants that are not the result of retroflexion. Although editions of the *Ṛgveda* regularly give *pada*s with *-ḥ* before *s-* in passages such as 4.35.7a and 10.128.9a, I have cited the pertinent passages with full assimilation (*-s s-*) in accordance with *Ṛgveda-prātiśākhya* 4.32.
10. In **1.3**, I have rehearsed briefly some facts I would have assumed to be well known to all informed scholars, because of what Johannes Bronkhorst has asserted on pages 184-85 of his paper, "Some Observations on the Padapāṭha of the Ṛgveda" (*Indo-Iranian Journal* 24:181-89 [1982]): "We get into difficulties if we try to further specify whether P.1.1.16 is about the Padapāṭha or about the Saṃhitāpāṭha. It cannot be about the Padapāṭha, for **there is no sandhi between words**, so that no purpose is served by saying that a final *o* is *pragṛhya*. The sūtra must, of necessity, be about the Saṃhitāpāṭha. But there is no '*iti* which is not uttered by a Ṛṣi' in the Saṃhitāpāṭha! The only way to make sense of this sūtra may be to assume that for Pāṇini the Saṃhitāpāṭha and the Padapāṭha were not two different texts but two forms of one and the same text. Pāṇini puzzles over the ques-

tion how the Mss. of the *Ṛgveda* (=Padapāṭha) must be read such that a correct recitation (=Saṃhitāpāṭha) is the result" (emphasis added). Patently, Bronkhorst's claim rests on a false appreciation of Śākalya's full procedure. Clearly, there could be pronunciation with close junction (*saṃhitāyām*) in the *padapāṭha*, so that the *Ṛgvedaprātiśākhya* quite rightly distinguishes between this and the close junction that occurs in the original Vedic text (*ārṣī saṃhitā*; see note 3).

11. See "On the Dialect Status of Vedic Forms of the Types *dakṣ-/dhakṣ-*," appearing in the felicitation volume for Bh. Krishnamurti.
12. *Aṣṭādhyāyī* 8.2.31-32: हो ढः । दादेर्धातोर्घः । , 8.2.37: एकाचो बशो भष् झषन्तस्य स्ध्वोः ।.
13. *Aṣṭādhyāyī* 7.4.65: दाधर्त्तिदर्धर्त्तिदर्धर्षिबोभूतुतेतिक्तेलर्ष्यापनीफणत्संसनिष्यदत्करिक्रत्कनिक्रदद्भरिभ्रद्दविध्वतोदविद्युतत्तरित्रतः सरीसृपतंवरीवृजन्मर्मृज्यागनीगन्तीति च । In connection with *bharibhrat*, note that this *sūtra* also accounts for *-ri-*, that is, for *bhari-* instead of *bhar-*. The rule accounts for other irregularities, which need not be considered here.
14. *Ṛgvedaprātiśākhya* 2.82: इतरा स्थितिः ।. On the pronunciations in question and their historical background, see "Some Neglected Evidence Concerning the Development of Abhinihita Sandhi," *Studien zur Indologie und Iranistik* 13-14 (1987) [= *Festschrift Wilhelm Rau*]: 59-68.
15. *Ṛgvedaprātiśākhya* 6.29: स्पर्शा यमाननुनासिकाः स्वान्परेषु स्पर्शेष्वनुनासिकेषु । It is not necessary to consider here details concerning differences among various *Prātiśākhyas*' descriptions of just what *yamas* are.

16. *Ṛgvedaprātiśākhya* 6.36-37: यमान्नासिक्या स्वरभक्तिरुत्तरा गार्ग्यस्य । ऊष्मा सोष्मणः ।

17. *Ṛgvedaprātiśākhya* 6.38: वर्जयेत्तम् .

18. *Ṛgvedaprātiśākhya* 4.98: जुगुक्षतोदुदुक्षन्गा अदुक्षद्दुक्षन्वृधे ऽस्यदुक्षतानु दक्षि । दक्षन्न पत्मन्दक्षुषो ऽभि दक्षत् कृष्णासो दक्षि हियानस्य दक्षोः ।

19. *Ṛgvedaprātiśākhya* 2.1: संहिता पदप्रकृतिः ।, *Nirukta* 1.17: पदप्रकृतिः संहिता । पदप्रकृतीनि सर्वचरणानां पार्षदानि ।. As shown, Yāska not only remarks that a *saṃhitāpāṭha* has a *padapāṭha* as its source but he also says that *prātiśākhyas* of different Vedic branches take the *padapāṭha* as their original text. As is well known, Bhartṛhari later considers another position, involving a different interpretation of the compound *padaprakṛti*, according to which the continuously recited text is the source for the divided *padapāṭha*. Durga discusses the alternatives in his comments on the *Nirukta* passage cited but this does not concern us in the present context.

THE SYNTACTIC ROLE OF ADHI- IN THE PĀṆINIAN KĀRAKA-SYSTEM*

Achyutananda Dash

The Pāṇinian *kāraka* system is the keystone of the syntactic and semantic relations in Sanskrit grammar.[1] The term *kāraka* is not defined by Pāṇini but later grammarians and logicians accept the definition of *kāraka* as *kriyānva-yitvaṃ kārakatvam*, that is, 'a *kāraka* is an item construed with an action'. The description of *kāraka* relations in Pāṇini's grammar is no doubt scientific but the hierarchy of the Pāṇinian *kāraka* system, as it is presented in the *Aṣṭādhyāyī*, sometimes remains ambiguous to modern students. However, considerable research is in progress, especially among orientalists and modern linguists in the schools of Relational Grammar (RG) and Transformational Generative Grammar (TGG), on different aspects of the concepts and theories of relations between the verb and its nominal dependents.

In this paper, an attempt is made to represent the syntactic and semantic role of *adhi-*, a pre-verb (PV)/ pre-position (PP), in the Pāṇinian *kāraka* system. According to Pāṇini's grammar, *adhi-* is both an *upasarga* and a *karmapra-vacanīya* (*kmpv*). It is necessary to provide here some explanation of the status of an *upasarga* and a *kmpv* in a sentence. According to Pāṇini, the twenty-two PVs/PPs starting with *pra-*, etc., are called *upasargas* when they have an intrinsic semantic relation with the verb (V) (see P.1.4.58-59). To clarify: when the PVs *pra-*, etc., bring some modification or extension of the meaning of a V, then they are called *upasargas*. Thus, Kātyāyana defines *upasarga* as *kriyāviśeṣaka upasargaḥ*.[2] On the other hand, they (*pra-*, etc.) are called *kmpvs* when they have the status of an independent word and are related semantically to a noun (NP). As *kmpvs*, they govern either accusative, locative, or ablative case-endings (see P.2.3.8-11).

Adhi- is called an *upasarga* if and only if it can bring some change in the sense of the verb root or if it can extend its meaning. For instance:

(1) *adhigacchati śāstrārtham*

'(He) understands the meaning of the *śāstra*'.

Here, the original meaning of the verb root *gam-* is 'to go' but when it is associated with *adhi-* the root meaning is changed to 'understanding'. Such is the magic touch of an *upasarga*, which brings a total (sometimes partial) modification in the meaning of the verbal base.

Our present problem lies with P.1.4.46 and P.1.4.48, wherein we find that, when intransitive roots like *śīṄ-* 'to sleep', *sthā-* 'to stay', *ās-* 'to sit', and *vas-* 'to reside' are associated with the PV *adhi-*, the locative item gets the *kāraka* designation *karman* and accordingly an accusative case-ending is assigned to it by P.2.3.2.

Before stepping into the real discussion on this issue, one point is worth noting. According to the *vaiyākaraṇas*, each and every *kāraka* relation is based upon the "designations" or "labels" of the respective *kārakas* given by Pāṇini but not on their semantic definitions. On the other hand, the Naiyāyikas are of the opinion that the *kāraka* relation in Pāṇini's grammar can be represented on the basis of the semantic definition of respective *kārakas* to the extent that this is possible (cf. Jha 1984). Though the Naiyāyika's view is quite logical and scientific, it is not always true to the Pāṇinian description of *kāraka* relations. To my mind, the problem of *adhi* is one of the exceptions to the above-mentioned notion of the Naiyāyikas.

To pinpoint the problem, let us consider these examples:

(2) /*adhi-śīṄ*-/ *sā vai dakṣiṇe bhāge dhīyate, tasmād dakṣiṇam bhāgam puṃsaḥ stry adhiśete* / (Sam.Ar. 2.4)

'That/She is kept on the right side, so the woman sleeps on the right side of the man'.

(3) / -*do*- / *Candrāpīḍaḥ śayanatalam adhiśiśye* / (K 19, 206)

'Candrāpīḍa [the king] slept on the [royal] bed'.

(4) /*adhi-sthā*-/ *brahmā 'dhyatiṣṭhad bhuvanāni dhārayan* / (Tai.Br. 2.8.9.7)

'Holding upon [the worlds], the Supreme Lord [*Brahman*] resides in the worlds'.

(5) / -*do*- / *adhitiṣṭhati lokam ojasā sa vivasvān iva medinīpatiḥ* / (Ki. 2.38)

'He, the lord of the earth [the king], resides upon the world by [his] vitality, just like the sun'.

(6) /*adhi-ās-*/ *darbhāṅs tu nā 'dhyāsita* / (Tai.Br. 3.7.3.3)

'But [the Hotā] should not sit upon the *darbhas*, i.e., the sacrificial grass'.

(7) / -*do*- / *aye siṃhāsanam adhyāste vr̥ṣalaḥ* / (Mu. 3)

'Hey! The *vr̥ṣala* is seated upon the [royal] throne!'

Hundreds of such examples may be found in pre-Pāṇinian and post-Pāṇinian literature. What we find interesting for our study is this. When verbal bases like *śīṄ*- 'to sleep', *sthā*- 'to stay', and *ās*- 'to sit' are preceded by the PV *adhi*-, then locative items like *dakṣiṇabhāga* and *śayanatala* in (2) and (3), *bhuvana* and *loka* in (4) and (5), *darbha* and *siṃhāsana* in (6) and (7), respectively, get accusative case-endings. According to Pāṇini, an accusative case-ending is assigned to a grammatical object by P.2.3.2 (*karmaṇi dvitī-*

yā) and a locative case-ending is assigned to a locative item by P.2.3.36 (*saptamy adhikaraṇe ca*). Strictly speaking, on the basis of the syntactic and semantic notions found in Pāṇini, the said locative items, as defined in P.1.4.45 (*ādhāro 'dhikaraṇam*), must get the locative case-ending according to P.2.3.36. Instead we find an accusative case-ending to these locative items. What, then, is the logic behind such use of a Natural Language (NL)? For the Pāṇiniyas, that is, the followers of the school of Pāṇinian grammar, there is no problem because Pāṇini's special rule P.1.4.46 (*adhiśīṅsthāsāṃ karma*) says 'the (designation) *karman* is assigned to the substratum of the action denoted by the verb roots *śīṄ-* "to sleep", *sthā-* "to stay", and *ās-* "to sit", when they are preceded by *adhi-*'. But this explanation is not adequate for the study of Sanskrit as an NL because, even after the association of the PV *adhi-* with intransitive verbs like *śīṄ-*, *sthā*, etc., they do not change their basic verbal meaning. Neither is there any indication that transitivization (of the intransitive verbs) takes place.[3] Let us look into the problem using some traditional examples:

(8) *hariḥ vaikuṇṭhe śete* / 'Hari sleeps in *vaikuṇṭha*'
NP_1 NP_{LOC} V

= (8a) $NP_1 + NP_{LOC} + V$ (---------)

(9) *hariḥ vaikuṇṭham adhi-śete* / 'Hari sleeps in *vaikuṇṭha*'
NP_1 NP_{ACC} PV V

= (9a) $NP_1 + NP_{ACC} + PV\text{-}V$ (---------)

In (8), the locative case-suffix *-Ṅi* with the NP (*vaikuṇṭha*) expresses the substratum. But in sentence (9) the locative NP occurs with an accusative case-ending *-am* and the verb is preceded by a PV *adhi-*. According to the traditional interpretation, the PV *adhi-* transitivizes the intransitive verbs, and thus the accusative case-ending is quite justifiable.

Here the main problem lies: are intransitive verbs such as *śete*, etc., really transitivized when they are associated with the PV *adhi-*? Do substrata like *vaikuṇṭha*, etc., become the object in a real sense? First let us see what traditional scholars have to say on this issue.

In the school of Navya-Nyāya, Jagadīśa, the author of *Śabdaśaktiprakāśikā*, finds in such examples the identity of the objecthood and locationhood,[4] which is difficult for us to accept.

Gadādhara, the author of *Vyutpattivāda*, remarks that in the sentence

(10) *sthalīm adhiśete* / '[He] sleeps on the ground'

the accusative case-ending with *sthalī* ('the ground') expresses the *ādhāratva* or *adhikaraṇatva* ('substratum'). He accepts that the root is initially intransitive and its intransitivity is retained even though it is seen in its transitive form. In his opinion, in order to give a formal/grammatical justification, Pāṇini has to make an exceptional rule, giving the label *karman* to the locative item.

Gadādhara also offers another explanation on the grounds that *adhiśete* means *śayanaṃ karoti*, where *śayana* is taken to be the *kriyāphalam* (that is, the result of the action) of the verb *karoti*. Thus, due to the expression of the action, which is delimited by the result (that is, *phalāvacchinna-vyāpāravācakatva*), (10) can be a transitive construction. According to this second assumption, roots such as *śīṄ*-, etc., when preceded by the PV *adhi*-, are transitivized and are used only in the conventional sense (*nirūḍhalakṣaṇā*).

Finally, Gadādhara abandons this second suggestion and reverts to the initial intransitivity of the root.[5] Here, of course, he thinks in the correct direction. As we well know, the intransitive verb does not become transitive even after its association with the PV *adhi*-. The only unconvincing thing here is that he tries to impose a new meaning (in the present case *adhikaraṇatva*) on the accusative case-ending (almost all the Naiyāyikas do the same). Moreover, he ignores the role of *adhi*- in the present context.

Grammarians say that, though *vaikuṇṭha* is not the real object, it is a grammatical object. By grammatical object, they mean any item that is given a designation of *karman* by Pāṇini.[6]

Almost all the Naiyāyikas and the Vaiyākaraṇas accept the dictum *ādhārasya ānuśāsanikakarmatvam*,[7] that is, the objecthood of the substratum is based on the instruction (given by Pāṇini). The term *ānuśāsanikakarmatva* means that, although it is not the real object, it is assumed to be so on the basis of Pāṇini's instruction. This discussion shows that almost all the Naiyāyikas tried to provide a logical explanation for such a phenomenon of an NL but they failed because, and only because, they ignored the role of the PV *adhi-* in these constructions.

Thus, in my hypothesis, the PV *adhi-* has an important role in the syntactic and semantic relations of the items in these sentences. And, I hope, there are strong grounds for my hypothesis in the traditional school of grammar as well as in modern linguistics.

The Hypothesis

In the present context, *adhi-* is not an *upasarga* as it does not show the characteristics of an *upasarga*. Therefore, I assume it to be a *karmapravacanīya* (*kmpv*) because it has an intrinsic semantic relation with the NP and expresses/implies[8] the meaning 'substratum'. Since we do not see a locative case-ending with the NP *vaikuṇṭha*, the example does not violate the general principle *ananyalabhyaś śabdārthaḥ* or *uktārthānām aprayogaḥ*. The accusative case-ending with the NP *vaikuṇṭha* is also justifiable because a *kmpv* can govern *dvitīyā* by P.2.3.8.

On this hypothesis, there may arise some major objections. The first could come from a traditional scholar, who might ask how *adhi-* can express/imply the sense *adhikaraṇa* 'substratum'. Second, how can *adhi-* be considered a *kmpv* when Pāṇini does not state so in this context? Third, if *adhi-* is considered to be a *kmpv*, how can one explain the passive constructions?

To the first objection it might be countered that in

example (8) the locative case-ending expresses the substratum but in (9), due to the "raising" of *adhi-*, the same meaning is obtained from both sentences. This shows that *adhi-* either expresses or implies the meaning *adhikaraṇa*, 'substratum'. Patañjali in his Mbh. says: *adhir uparibhāge vartate.*[9] This implies that the meaning of *adhi-* is *adhikaraṇa*. The author of *Bālamanoramā*, a commentary on SK 542 (P.14.46), says: *adhis tu saptamyarthasya ādharasya dyotakaḥ*. With all this evidence we can assume that the meaning of *adhi-* is *adhikaraṇa* 'substratum'. Therefore, the locative case-ending is not seen after the NP *vaikuṇṭha* and there is a linkage between *vaikuṇṭha* and *adhi-*. The accusative case-ending (*-am*) following the NP *vaikuṇṭha* has no meaning in the present construction and is used only for the correctness of the sentence (that is, *sādhutvārthakam*). Therefore, with this internal and external evidence, we can assume that the meaning of *adhi-* is 'substratum' without hesitation.

To the second question, the answer will be as follows. The PV *adhi-* holds true to the definition of *kmpv* because it is semantically related to the NP in this construction, but not to the VP. Here, I must make it clear that we do not see the same nature of *kmpv* in sentences such as:

(11) *anu harim surāḥ* / 'the gods are after Hari'
kmpv NP_{ACC} NP_1

Here *anu* has the status of an independent word and is semantically related to the NP. If we closely examine all the *kmpv*s in Pāṇini's *Aṣṭādhyāyī*, we will find two varieties of *kmpv*s. I will call them *kmpv*-1 and *kmpv*-2. *Kmpv*-1 is that which has the status of an independent word and is semantically related to the NP. Moreover, it is neither associated nor compounded with the VP. *Kmpv*-2 is that which is associated with the verb but has an intrinsic semantic relation with the NP. Our present example (9) is the second variety of *kmpv* (*kmpv*-2). Such *kmpv*s are also evident in traditional examples:

(12) *nadīm anvavasitā senā* / (SK 549 on P.1.4.85)
NP_{ACC} *kmpv*.PV V NP_1

'the army camped alongside the river'.

(13) *kutaḥ adhyāgacchati* / (SK 554 on P.1.4.93)
Ad.V. *kmpv*.PV V

'whence does he come'.

In these examples, the *kmpv*-2s *anu* and *adhi* are associated with the VPs.

The third question is: how can one justify the passivization of such constructions as (9), etc., in Sanskrit? This needs more clarification. Let us consider the following examples:

(14) *yad adhyāsitam arhadbhis tad dhi tīrtham pracakṣate* / (Ku. 6.56)

'that is called a "sacred place," which is inhabited by venerable persons'.

Another example is quoted by Nāgeśa in *Vaiyākaraṇa-Siddhānta-Mañjuṣā* as:

(15) *antaḥ kañcukibhir lasanmaṇidharair adhyāsitā bhūmayaḥ* /

(i) 'the interior grounds are occupied by the serpents possessing glittering jewels (on their hoods)'.

(ii) 'the harems are occupied by the chamberlains wearing glittering jewels'.

In these examples we find the root *ās*-, which is associated with *adhi*- and bears the passive mark *Kta*; thus, the NP is marked with instrumental case-ending. According to the tradition, the passive suffix *Kta* expresses *karman* by the Pāṇinian rule P.3.4.72 / SK 3086 (*gatyarthākarmaka-ślīṣaśīṅsthāsavasajanaruhajīryatibhyaś ca*). Therefore, if *adhi*- is considered to be a *kmpv*-2 and the accusative case-ending is assigned by P.2.3.8 but not by P.2.3.2, then how can one account for the passive sentences? The passive suffix *Kta* is taught in connection with a *karman* but not in connection with a *kmpv*.

To justify passivization in these constructions, I shall present two arguments. One is based on the Relational Grammar (RG) of modern linguistics and the other on the interpretation of the Pāṇinian rules P.3.4.72 / SK 3086 and P.3.4.76 / SK 3087.

Argument One

Before I begin to discuss this issue, it is necessary to explain roughly the different nature and status of passivization in Sanskrit. Generally, in Sanskrit, passive constructions can be classified into three groups:

(i) Accusative passive or personal passive
(ii) Unaccusative passive or impersonal passive
(iii) Unergative passive or pseudo-passive

To exemplify these according to the maxim of *sthālīpulākanyāya*, consider the following examples:

(16) *devadattena odanaḥ pacyate* /

'the rice is being cooked by Devadatta'

This represents passive type (i).

(17) *phalitam vr̥kṣaiḥ* / 'the trees have borne fruit'

This represents passive type (ii) (see Postal 1986).

(18) *śeṣaḥ adhiśayitaḥ hariṇā* /

'the serpent is being slept on by Hari'

This represents passive type (iii). The unergative passive is subjective and intransitive, and formally contains a

1-arc, but not a 2-arc. In RG terminology, "1" identifies the subject, "2" the direct object, and "3" the indirect object. To introduce the basic theory of passivization in RG, let us consider two simple sentences in English.

(19) John took that book.

(20) That book was taken by John. (See diagram 1.)

(21)

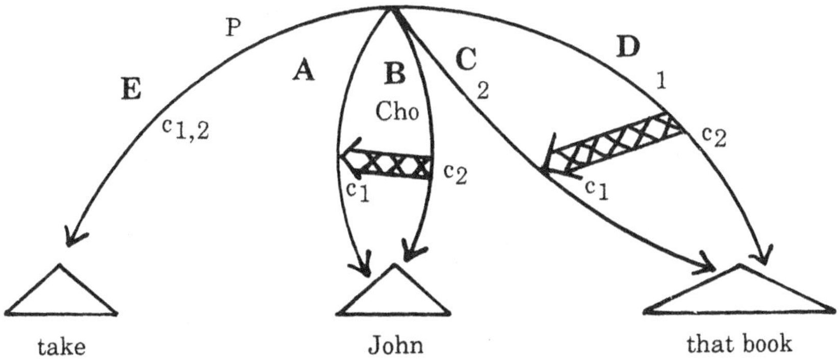

According to RG, the passive clause is characterized in terms of at least two linguistic strata or grammatical relations. In (21), "John" heads a 1-arc in the first stratum and a Cho-arc (*Chômeur* = unemployed) in the second, while "that book" heads a 2-arc in the first stratum and a 1-arc in the second. Under the interpretation of Relational Networks (RNs), (21) embodies the claim that "John" bears the 1-relation at the first linguistic level and the Cho-relation at the second, while "that book" bears the 2-relation at the first stratum (level) and the 1-relation at the second. Moreover, here A sponsors B and B erases A. So, also, C sponsors D and D erases C (see Postal 1986, 17). Thus it is claimed that the passive involves at least two strata, or levels, of structure. This is called the "bistratal" theory of passive (cf. Perlmutter 1984, 4-5). Similarly, the Sanskrit sentences

(22) *devadattaḥ odanam pacati* /

'Devadatta cooks rice'

(23) *devadattena odanaḥ pacyate* /

'The rice is being cooked by Devadatta'

can be explained by the bistratal theory of passive. In (23), *-ya-*, which is one of the morphological markers of passivization in Sanskrit, clearly represents the 2-1 Advancement Construction (cf. Rosen 1984, 55-56).

With this background of passivization in RG, let us try to explain our present problem, which is somehow complicated and has an overlapping structure. Let us consider sentence (18) in diagram 2.

(24)

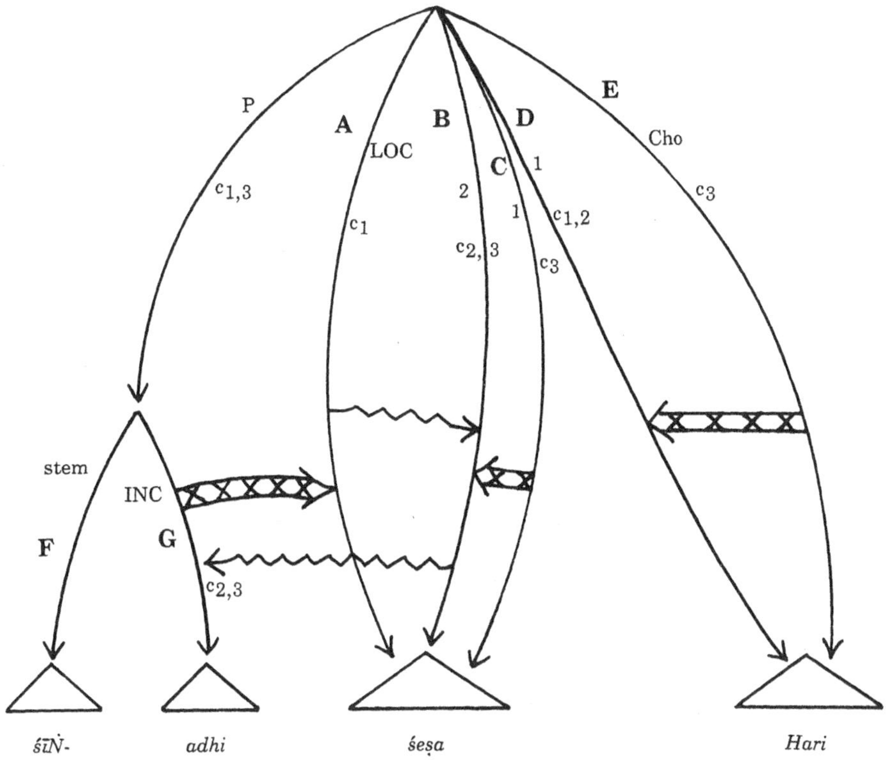

Here the passive sentence (18) presupposes two underlying constructions:

(18a) *hariḥ śeṣe śete* /

'Hari lies on *śeṣa,* the serpent'

(18b) *hariḥ śeṣam adhiśete* /

'Hari lies on the serpent'

In diagram 2, *hari* bears the 1-relation on the first and second levels and the Cho-relation on the third level. The *śeṣa* bears the LOC-relation on the first level, the 2-relation on the second and third levels, and the 1-relation on the third level. Moreover, A and B both sponsor G, and G erases only A. Also, B sponsors C, and C erases B; D sponsors E, and E erases D.

Diagram 2 is my modified version of a structure originally proposed by the relational grammarian Paul Postal in a personal communication to P. Dasgupta, who had consulted him about this type of Sanskrit sentence. Postal states: "the key thing is that, there is some element bearing a non-nuclear relation which advances to 2, leaving a copy. Suppose it is a locative. Then there will be a locative copy. In English, since locatives are in general flagged, this copy will be, yielding things like

[25] The serpent is lain on by Hari.[10]

because, the copy pronoun itself is invisible in English. It would seem that what goes on in Sanskrit involves in some way incorporation of the copy or conceivably, of the preposition which flags it, into the verb."

Perlmutter and Postal (1984) and Postal (1986) have recorded some evidence from Bantu languages that locatives and instrumentals can advance to 2-relation in an NL. Here, of course, the locative advancement to 2-relation is seen with the "raising" of a complement (*adhi-*), a PV, which takes the responsibility of the intrinsic relation of locative with the "marquee" and a grammatical adpositional linking with the intransitive verb *śīṄ-*. Thus, here the passive marker *Kta* is justifiable after the advancement of the locative to the 2-relation. Moreover, such passivization never violates the 1-Advancement Exclusiveness Law (1-AEX).

Such passive clauses are similar to "pseudo-passive" clauses in English (cf. Postal 1986). Let us examine some "pseudo-passive" constructions in English:

(26) The bed was slept in by the Shah.

(27) This hall has been played in by some of the finest orchestras in Europe.

(28) The room was exercised in by the Spider Man. (See Perlmutter and Postal 1984, 100-1)

Another significant point in this connection is that, as a scientific and logical presentation of the structures of an NL, the grammar of Sanskrit ought also to justify its "pseudo-passive" construction(s) with some morphological element(s), which bears an intrinsic semantic relation to the other regular grammatical elements in a sentence. Here the PV *adhi-* has just such an important role in these Sanskrit constructions.

Argument Two

As we have seen, according to the tradition, the rule P.3.4.72 / SK 3086 (*gatyarthākarmakaślīṣaśīṅsthāsavasa-janaruhajīryatibhyaś ca*) teaches *Kta* in the sense of *karman* (also in the sense of *kartṛ* and *bhāva*) and in the examples (14), (15), (18), etc., the *Kta* expresses the same meaning (see SK 3086 and *Kāśikā* on P.3.4.72).

In my opinion, in these sentences, the suffix *Kta* expresses *adhikaraṇa* but not *karman* by P.3.4.76 / SK 3087 (*kto 'dhikaraṇe ca dhrauvyagatipratyavasānārthebhyaḥ*). Thus, Kāśikākāra explains this aphorism as *dhrauvyārthāḥ akarmakāḥ, pratyavasānārthāḥ abhyavahārārthā iti svanikāya-prasiddhiḥ / dhrauvya-gati-pratyavasānārthebhyaḥ yaḥ kto vihitaḥ so 'dhikaraṇe bhavati / cakārād yathāprāptaṃ ca / dhrauvyārthebhyaḥ kartṛ-bhāvādhikaraṇeṣu, gatyarthebhyaḥ kartṛ-karma-bhāvādhikaraṇeṣu, pratyavaśānārthebhyaḥ karmabhāvādhikaraṇeṣu* / etc.

The *dhrauvyārtha* roots as *svanikāyaprasiddha* are *śīṄ-*, *sthā-*, *ās-*, etc., when they are preceded by *adhi-*. In support of this, an old *kārikā* is quoted by Jagadīśa as "*dhrauvyāṇām adhiśīṅāsasthānām. . . .*" (see SSP 2:173). Bhaṭṭoji Dīkṣita in SK explains *dhrauvya* as *sthairyam,* on which the author of *Bālamanoramā* writes a note as "*dhrauvyam ity asya vivaraṇam sthairyam iti / sthirībhavanam, upaveśanaśayanādikriyeti yāvat /.*"

All this evidence strongly supports our hypothesis that the *Kta* suffix in examples (14), (15), (18), etc.,[11] expresses *adhikaraṇa* (and not *karman*) by P.3.4.76, since we have seen that the suffix *Kta* is taught only in the sense of *adhikaraṇa, kartṛ*, and *bhāva* for the *dhrauvyārtha* roots.

Moreover, I did not find examples such as

(29) **vaikuṇṭhaḥ adhiśayyate hariṇā /*

(30) **anena āsanam adhyāsyate /* etc.

wherein '*-ya-*', the passive suffix, is found in the sense of *karman.*

Therefore, it can be stated that in such constructions, both passive and active, the PV *adhi-* regularly expresses or implies the sense of *adhikaraṇa* ('substratum') in pre- and post-Pāṇinian literature. Of course, a few exceptional examples occur in pre-Pāṇinian literature, for example:

(31) *bhadraiṣām lakṣmīr nihitādhivāci /* (Rg.V. 10.71.2)

(32) *yasmin idam adhitiṣṭhati /* (Tai.Br. 1.1.3.6)

These variations of Vedic language need no comment, as the Pāṇinian description *bahulam chandasi* is enough to serve the purpose. On the other hand, as far as our hypothesis is concerned, *adhi-*, being a *kmpv*, can govern accusative case-ending as well as locative case-ending by P.2.3.8 and 9, respectively. We can thus give grammatical justification to the locative phenomenon in Vedic language also.

Therefore, on the basis of the above arguments, I hope there is every possibility that my hypothesis will be well treated as a thesis.

Notes

* I am grateful to Paul M. Postal of IBM's T. J. Watson Research Center, New York, for providing an explanation of the present issue in light of RG. I express my humble regard to my teachers, Dr. (Mrs.) Saroja Bhate, Dr. V. N. Jha (C.A.S.S., University of Poona), and Dr. P. Dasgupta (Deccan College, Poona), for their valuable suggestions on this issue, each of which led to substantial revision. Above all, I express my esteem to my revered Guru and guide, Prof. S. D. Joshi, who has kindly gone through this article; thus it is dedicated to him.

1. See Joshi and Roodbergen (1975); Kiparsky and Staal (1969); Cardona (1974), and Deshpande (1990).
2. See Mbh., 1:256, cf. (दुर्गवृत्ति on निरुक्त १.१)

क्रियावाचकमाख्यातम् उपसर्गो विशेषकृत् ।
सत्त्वाभिधायकं नाम निपातः पादपूरणः ॥
निपाताश्चादयो ज्ञेया उपसर्गास्तु प्रादयः ।
द्योतकत्वात् क्रियायोगे लोकादवगता इमे ॥
धात्वर्थं बाधते कश्चित् कश्चित् तमनुवर्तते ।
तमेव विशिनष्टयन्य उपसर्गगतिस्त्रिधा ॥

3. Ostler (1979), on the example *rāmaḥ parvatam adhyāste* / 'Rama is settled on the mountain', agrees with the impossibility of interpreting the accusative semantically. He thinks that when the intransitive verb is compounded with adpositions it becomes transitive. According to him, the compounding process creates a new LE jointly from the verb's and the adposition's LEs. After the compounding takes place, "it [the verb] takes on a life of its own most particularly, it becomes independent of the continued existence of the adposition as an independent element" (p. 344).

   Simply speaking, Ostler thinks along the lines of *upasargeṇa dhātvarthaḥ balād anyatra nīyate*, which is not the case in the present problem. As a matter of fact, we see that the sense of the root is kept intact even after its association with the adposition. Only the FS is found to be different.
4. On *adhikaraṇatvam eva karmatvam,* see SSP 2:173-74.
5. See the whole discussion in *Vyutpattivāda*:

अधिशीङ्स्थासां कर्मेत्यादिना यत्राधारस्य कर्मसंज्ञा तत्राधारत्वमाधेयत्वं वा द्वितीयार्थः । स्थलीम् अधिशेत इत्यादौ तादृशार्थे द्वितीयायाः स्थल्या अधिशयितेत्यादौ कृद्योगे षष्ठ्याश्च साधुत्वार्थमेवाधारस्य कर्मसंज्ञा-विधानात् । अथ कृञर्थव्यापाररूपक्रियान्तरं धात्वर्थेऽन्तर्भाव्य शयनादि-रूपफलावच्छिन्नव्यापारार्थकसोपसर्गशीङ्प्रभृतिधात्वर्थतावच्छेदकशयनादि-रूपफलाश्रयतयाधारस्य कर्मत्वोपपादनसम्भवात् तादृशसूत्राणां वैयर्थ्यमेव । अध्याद्युपसृष्टशीङ्प्रभृतीनामेव च तादृशार्थे निरूढलक्षणा, न त्वनुपसृष्टानामतो न स्थलीं शेत इत्यादयः स्वारसिकप्रयोगा इति चेन्न । धातोर्मुख्यार्थपरत्वेऽपि दर्शितप्रयोगनिर्वाहाय भगवता पाणिनिमुनिना तादृशसूत्रप्रणयनात् ।

तदप्रणीतवतां शर्ववर्मप्रभृतीनां मुख्यार्थपराणां स्थल्यामधिशेत इत्यादिप्रयोगाणां साधुताया दुर्वारित्वाच्च ॥

6. See, *sakalasādhāraṇakarmatvam ca saṃketaviśeṣasambandhena karmaśabdavattvam eva bodhyam* (Nāgeśa in VSM, 158).
7. See VV, 144; and PVR, 607-8.
8. In this paper I am not concerned with the debate about whether the *upasargas* and *nipātas* express the meaning (*vācaka*) or imply the meaning (*dyotaka*). This issue needs separate treatment; thus I have avoided it here.
9. See Mbh., 1:256; and *Niruktam* 1.3.21.
10. Postal actually used other nouns; I have changed the example so that the discussion bears on sentence (18). It should be noted that in the same letter Postal says, "It is obviously very difficult to analyse a single sentence without knowing much about the rest of the language. My guess though is that. . . ." and he goes on to propose the above analysis.
11. One may object that, by P.2.3.68, Pāṇini teaches genitive case-ending for the *kartṛ* when *Kta* conveys *adhikaraṇa*. But how to account, then, for the instrumental case-ending in examples (14), (15), (18), etc.? To this objection my reply is: Kātyāyana and Patañjali have not commented on this rule. But, in connection with the earlier rule (P.2.3.67), to justify usages like *ahinā sṛptam* and *aheḥ sṛptam*, Kātyāyana suggests *śeṣavijñānāt siddham* (Va. 2, on P.2.3.67). I think the same explanation is applicable in this context, so there will be no problem with the instrumental case-ending here.

Abbreviations

I.	ACC	Accusative
	Cho	Chômeur
	INST	Instrumental
	kmpv	*Karmapravacanīya*
	LOC	Locative
	LE	Lexical entry
	NL	Natural language
	NOM	Nominative
	NP	Noun phrase
	P	Predicate
	PP	Pre-position
	PV	Pre-verb
	RG	Relational grammar
	TGG	Transformational generative grammar
	V	Verb
II.	K	*Kādambarī*
	Ki.	*Kīrātārjunīyam*
	Ku.	*Kumārasṃbhavam*
	Mbh.	Patañjali's *Vyākaraṇa Mahābhāṣyam*
	Mu.	*Mūdrārākṣasa*
	P	Pāṇini's *Aṣṭādhyāyī*
	PVR	*Padavākya-Ratnākara* of Gokulanātha Upādhyāya
	Rg.V.	*Ṛgveda*
	Sam.Ar.	*Sāṃkhyāyana-Āraṇyaka*
	SK	*Siddhānta-Kaumudī*
	SSP	*Śabda-śakti-prakāśikā* of Jagadīśa

Tai.Ar.	*Taittiriya-Āraṇyaka*
Tai.Br.	*Taittiriya-Brāhmaṇa*
Va.	Kātyāyana's *Vārtika* on Pāṇini's *Aṣṭādhyāyī*
VV	*Vyutpattivāda* of Gadādhara

Bibliography

Bālamanoramā, a commentary on *Vaiyākaraṇa Siddhānta Kaumudi*, by Vāsudeva Dīkṣita, pt. 1, Chaukhamba Surabhārati Prakashana, Varanasi, 1979.

Cardona, G. 1974: "Pāṇini's Kāraka: Agency, Animation and Identity," *Journal of Indian Philosophy*, Vol. 2, Nos. 3-4, pp. 231-306.

Deshpande, Madhav M. 1990: "An Exploration of Philosophical and Linguistic Issues," in *Sanskrit and Related Studies, Contemporary Researches and Reflections*, edited by Bimal K. Matilal and Purushottama Bilimoria, pp. 33-57. Sri Satguru Publications, Delhi.

Jha, V. N. 1984: "Language and Reality," *Acta Indologica*, Vol. 6, pp. 73-89.

Joshi, S. D., and Roodbergen, J. A. F. 1975: *Patañjali's Vyākaraṇa-Mahābhāṣya, Kārakāhnika*, PCASS, No. 10, Class C, University of Poona, Poona.

Kiparsky, Paul, and Staal, J. F. 1969: "Syntactic and Semantic Relations in Pāṇini," *Foundations of Languages*, Vol. 5, pp. 83-117.

Marantz, Alec. 1985: *On the Nature of Grammatical Rela tions*, MIT Press, Cambridge, Mass., and London.

Norbert, Hornstein. 1981: "Case Theory and Preposition Stranding," *Linguistic Inquiry*, Vol. 12, No. 1, pp. 55-91.

Ostler, N. D. M. 1979: "Case-Linking: A Theory of Case and Verb Diathesis Applied to Classical Sanskrit," Ph.D. diss. MIT, Cambridge, Mass.

Padavākyaratnākara (PVR) of Gokulanātha Upādhyāya, Vārāṇaseya Saṃskṛta Vishvavidyālaya, Varanasi, 1960.

Perlmutter, D. M. 1984: "The Inadequacy of Some Monostratal Theories of Passive," *Studies in Relational Grammar 2*, University of Chicago Press, Chicago.

Perlmutter, D. M., and Postal, M. P. 1984: "The 1-Advancement Exclusiveness Law," *Studies in Relational Grammar 2*, University of Chicago Press, Chicago.

Postal, M. P. 1986: *Studies of Passive Clauses*, State University of New York Press, Albany.

Rosen, C. G. 1984: "The Interface Between Semantic Roles and Initial Grammatical Relations," *Studies in Relational Grammar 2*, University of Chicago Press, Chicago.

Śabdaśaktiprakāśikā of Jagadīśa, Tara Printing Works, Benares.

Vaiyākaraṇa-Siddhānta-Mañjuṣā of Nāgeśa, Saṃpūrṇānanda Saṃskṛta Viśvavidyālaya, Varanasi, 1977.

Vyutpattivāda of Gadādhara, Chaukhamba Amarabharati Prakasana, Varanasi, 1976.

PĀṆINI 7.2.15 (YASYA VIBHĀṢĀ): A RECONSIDERATION*

Madhav M. Deshpande

1 Paul Kiparsky, in his 1979 book, *Pāṇini as a Variationist,* proposed a novel interpretation of the option terms *vā, vibhāṣā,* etc. Traditionally, Pāṇinian commentators have been unable to make significant distinctions between the import of these terms, and have not offered a satisfactory explanation of Pāṇini's definition of the term *vibhāṣā,* that is, P.1.1.44 (*na veti vibhāṣā*). According to the tradition, these terms simply mean 'optionally'. Kiparsky started with the hypothesis that these terms in Pāṇini could not simply be synonyms and must have different meanings. He proposed that *vā* meant 'preferably'; *vibhāṣā,* defined by Pāṇini as *na vā,* meant 'preferably not', or 'marginally'; and *anyatarasyām* meant 'either' or 'optionally'. He then examined this proposed interpretation by conducting a statistical study of the relative frequencies of the optional outputs of all option rules in Pāṇini. His examination of Vedic and classical usage, especially the usage of Sanskrit in the text of the *Aṣṭādhyāyī* itself, overwhelmingly supported his hypothesis. While, in terms of this outstanding statistical demonstration, Kiparsky's interpretation is decidedly preferable to the traditional view, it is still not without its problems and weak spots. Kiparsky himself is open-minded about these. Thus, even while largely agreeing with Kiparsky's new interpretation, one needs to continue to search for explanations for the remaining areas of concern.

2 P.7.2.15 (*yasya vibhāṣā*) is one such area. Though this rule is crucial to Kiparsky's thesis, he has not been able to come up with a decisively conclusive interpretation for it. According to the traditional interpretation, the rule says that, when the augment *iṬ* is prescribed optionally (*vibhāṣā*) in any context after a root, the augment does not occur before the *niṣṭhā* suffix (*-ta* or *-tavat*) after that root. Traditionally, this rule applies to all roots after which *iṬ* is optionally prescribed with any option word. This, then, brings rules with these different option words under the scope of P.7.2.15 (*yasya vibhāṣā*). For instance, P.7.2.56 (*udito vā*), in its traditional interpretation, says that the gerund suffix *-Ktvā* optionally takes the augment *iṬ* after a root with the marker *U*. Thus, for a root such as *kramU* (*Dhātupāṭha* 1.502), we get the optional gerund forms *krāntvā* and *kramitvā*. Traditionally, P.7.2.56 (*udito vā*) comes under the scope of P.7.2.15 (*yasya vibhāṣā*) because the tradition does not make a distinction between *vā* and *vibhāṣā*. By P.7.2.15 (*yasya vibhāṣā*), a root such as *kramU* can only have a past-participle form without *iṬ*, that is, *krānta*, and the rule prohibits the derivation of *kramita*.

3 Kiparsky, to be consistent in his interpretation, needs to show that only the *vibhāṣā* rules, and not the *vā* or *anyatarasyām* rules, come under the scope of P.7.2.15 (*yasya vibhāṣā*). He has given considerable thought to problems posed by this and related rules (1979, 146-59) but this long discussion is by his own admission inconclusive. He realizes (p. 158) that, in a straightforward application of his interpretation, roots with the marker *U*, which are subject to P.7.2.56 (*udito vā*), cannot be subject to P.7.2.15 (*yasya vibhāṣā*) because in his new interpretation these terms are mutually exclusive. The result would be that roots with the marker *U*, if they are *seṭ* roots, would have their past-participle forms with the augment *iṬ*. In this Kiparsky sees a problem (p. 158): "It is true that there are some verbs with diacritic *U* which do have *iṬ* in the *niṣṭhā* forms, e.g., *dhāvU* 'run' (p.p. *dhāvita*). But the great majority of them lack *iṬ* there." Thus, strict application of Kiparsky's interpretation would allow a great many past-participle forms with the augment *iṬ* and this goes against both tradition and usage as cited by Kiparsky himself.

In the traditional interpretation, there is no routine way to derive forms such as *dhāvita*. Its derivation is achieved by traditional commentators by making P.7.2.15 (*yasya vibhāṣā*) nonobligatory (*anitya*). They achieve this through a debatable *jñāpaka* "indication."[1] While such "indications" are routinely accepted in the works of traditional Sanskrit commentators, they seriously compromise our ability to test Pāṇini's grammar and tend to reduce its systemic integrity.

4 Kiparsky's discussion is complicated by the fact that he suggests two alternative readings for the term *vibhāṣā* in P.7.2.15 (*yasya vibhāṣā*). These are as follows (1979, 157):

Reading (1): "at most (only) a *vibhāṣā* 'marginal' option"
Reading (2): "at least a *vibhāṣā* 'marginal' option"

Of these two, reading (1) is more strictly in accordance with Kiparsky's general interpretation of the term *vibhāṣā* but, as he himself states (p. 158), "Reading (1) does not correspond to usage in the past participles of the verbs with diacritic *U* (P.7.2.56)." Kiparsky's reading (2), in his own words (p. 158), is "equivalent in its effect" to the traditional reading. In effect, it includes all option terms under *vibhāṣā*. Even reading (2) leaves some problems unresolved, and, more importantly, its acceptance would amount to saying that *vibhāṣā* occasionally includes *vā*. This would be damaging to Kiparsky's main thesis. He is careful not to say this openly, hence his wording "at least a marginal option." However, it is unlikely that one could read the words *at least* into the rule without any textual basis for it. Strictly, the word *vibhāṣā* stands only for *vibhāṣā* and nothing else. Then, the question of whether this notion of *vibhāṣā* is inclusive of all option terms must be kept a separate issue.

5 There are additional issues. Kiparsky (pp. 44-45) says that "*na* . . . *vā* is equivalent to *vibhāṣā*, and *na vibhāṣā*, i.e., *na na vā*, is equivalent to plain *vā*." This may be fine as regards logical equivalences but a rule containing the term *vā*, and having *na* continuing from a previous rule, would obviously be problematical. Is it a *vā* rule because it contains the term *vā*? Or is it a *vibhāṣā* rule because the cumulative logical value of *na* and *vā* is the same as that of *vibhāṣā*? The same problem would arise in rules containing the word *vibhāṣā* with a *na* continuing from a previous rule. Are logical equivalences sufficient to transfer designations if the term *vibhāṣā* in P.7.2.15 (*yasya vibhāṣā*) is taken as referring to rules with the designation *vibhāṣā*?

This is also related to problems created by using the principle of *anuvṛtti*, "continuation of words into following rules." This principle is no doubt part of Pāṇini's grammar, yet we do not fully understand its working. At the hands of commentators, it has become, like many other features of the *Aṣṭādhyāyī*, a device to generate desired outputs rather than a method to seek Pāṇini's intentionality. For instance, on P.7.2.65 (*vibhāṣā sṛji-dṛśoḥ*), Kiparsky follows tradition by continuing the words *thali*, *na*, and *iṭ* (p. 151) into this rule. With these words continued, the rule, according to Kiparsky, means "The 2pl. perfect ending *-tha* marginally fails to take *iṬ* after the roots *sṛj* 'emit' and *dṛś* 'see.'" This would mean that normally the affix *-tha* after these roots does take *iṬ*. Kiparsky, however, remarks (p. 151) that "Whitney cites only *saskartha* (classical), not *sasarjitha*, which goes against Pāṇini's preference." In continuing *na* into this rule, Kiparsky follows the tradition but there seems to be no reason to do so, and it is clearly not continued into the following rules. Thus, if the word *na* is not continued into P.7.2.65 (*vibhāṣā sṛji-dṛśoḥ*), then its interpretation *à la* Kiparsky would be that *-tha* marginally takes *iṬ* after *sṛj* and *dṛś*. This would be more in line with the attested usage. A problem in using the traditional notion of continuing words such as *na*, *vā*, or *vibhāṣā* as the basis for a modern Kiparskyan interpretation is that the tradition made no logical distinction between *vā* and *na vā*, on the one hand, and *vā* and *vibhāṣā* on the other. Thus, Kiparsky's use of the traditional *anuvr̥tti* as the basis for his interpretation raises the spectre of an anachronistic expectation that the traditional commentators implicitly believed in the distinctions discovered by Kiparsky.

6 We can illustrate another problem by using P.7.2.65 (*vibhāṣā sr̥ji-dr̥śoḥ*). If *na* is continued into this rule, then the cumulative value of *na vibhāṣā* or *na na vā* makes it a *vā* rule according to Kiparsky's interpretation; as such it cannot logically come under the scope of P.7.2.15 (*yasya vibhāṣā*). On the other hand, if *na* is not continued into this rule, as I have argued above, then it remains a *vibhāṣā* rule, which can come under the scope of P.7.2.15 (*yasya vibhāṣā*). Given the fact that the past-participles of both of these roots lack *iṬ*, that is, *sr̥ṣṭa* and *dr̥ṣṭa*, it may not be appropriate that they come under the scope of P.7.2.15 (*yasya vibhāṣā*), which is expressly designed to prevent the occurrence of *iṬ*. However, as both of these roots are inherently *aniṭ* roots (listed in the *aniṭ kārikās* in the *Siddhānta-kaumudī*, p. 177), which means they would not get *iṬ* in the past-participle anyway, one sees no purpose in bringing them under the scope of P.7.2.15 (*yasya vibhāṣā*). This raises questions not only about Kiparsky's interpretation but about our most basic understanding of the function and scope of P.7.2.15 and other related rules.

In general, the same holds true for P.7.2.68 (*vibhāṣā gama-hana-vida-viśām*), which in Kiparsky's interpretation (p. 151) means "The perfect participle suffix *-vas* can marginally get *iṬ* after *gam, han, vid* and *viś*." All of these verbs (with *vid* in the sixth conjugation according to the *Kāśikā-vṛtti* on this rule) are inherently *aniṭ* roots. P.7.2.68 contains the word *vibhāṣā* (with no continuation of *na* from previous rules claimed by anyone); hence, according to the traditional view and Kiparsky's view, this rule comes under the scope of P.7.2.15 (*yasya vibhāṣā*). Here, too, because the roots are themselves *aniṭ*, one sees no purpose in bringing this rule under the scope of P.7.2.15 to derive past-participles without *iṬ*. (There is, however, some difference of opinion concerning the *seṭ* or *aniṭ* nature of the root *vid* among commentators. See *Mādhavīyadhātuvṛttiḥ*, 492.) Interestingly, P.7.2.65 and P.7.2.68 are the only rules that could possibly come under the scope of P.7.2.15, and also contain the word *vibhāṣā*, but in both cases the purpose of bringing them under the scope of P.7.2.15 remains unclear.

7 A similar situation prevails as regards our understanding of P.7.2.56 (*udito vā*) and several related rules. On page 150 of his book, Kiparsky does not continue the word *na* into this rule. Thus, this must be a *vā* rule, not subject to P.7.2.15 (*yasya vibhāṣā*). This interpretation would then allow the derivation of past-participle forms with *iṬ* for roots marked with the diacritic *U*. According to Kiparsky (p. 158), this goes against recorded usage. On page 159, he proposes another interpretation for P.7.2.56 (*udito vā*). Here, he proposes to read this rule simply as *uditaḥ*, with *na vā* continuing from previous rules, and connect the word *vā* in the traditional reading with the following rule. In this procedure, Kiparsky is using techniques of textual alteration that remind one of Patañjali's methods. Be that as it may, this novel interpretation of P.7.2.56 would make it a *vibhāṣā* rule, because of the proposed continuation of the words *na vā*, and thus the rule would become subject to P.7.2.15. By this one can prevent the derivation of past-participle forms with *iṬ* for roots marked with the diacritic *U*, which in Kiparsky's opinion "fits the facts reasonably well" (p. 159).

8 Here I would like to raise a more basic question regarding the word *fact* as used by Kiparsky. What "*facts*" are we supposed to use to judge our interpretation of Pāṇinian rules? Recent research has shown that (1) several extremely rare euphonic and syntactic phenomena, which are clearly not statistically dominant in the classical language, are most probably normal in Pāṇini's own Sanskrit; and (2) the whole notion of "un-Pāṇinian usages" is circularly dependent upon our interpretation of Pāṇini's rules.[2] In many respects, Pāṇini's own Sanskrit was markedly different from what we now know as classical Sanskrit.

Such might be the case for rules like P.7.2.56 (*udito vā*) and P.7.2.44 (*svarati-sūti-sūyati-dhūñ-ūdito vā*). According to both Kiparsky and the tradition, these rules come under the scope of P.7.2.15, though for different sets of reasons. Both claim that this helps prevent the derivation of past-participle forms with *iṬ* for roots marked with the diacritics *U*, *Ū*, etc. According to Kiparsky, this fits the facts of usage well, at least in the case of roots marked with *U*.

Suppose one takes a more straightforward Kiparskyan view and argues that both of these are *vā* rules because they contain the word *vā*, and that therefore they are not subject to P.7.2.15 (*yasya vibhāṣā*). (Please note that this is not Kiparsky's own view.) This would allow the derivation of past-participle forms with *iṬ* for roots marked with *U*, *Ū*, and others. While, according to Kiparsky (p. 159), this would not fit the facts reasonably well, there is evidence to show that this interpretation is not without merit. The evidence is of two kinds.

[A] Attested Forms

Roots		Forms
References to *Dhātupāṭha*, Böhtlingk's edition (1887)		Whitney's *Roots* (1885), etc.
luñcU	(1.202)	*luñcita*
ṣṭhivU	(1.592)	*ṣṭhīvita*
dhāvU	(1.632)	*dhāvita*
śansU, *śāsU*	(1.660)	*śaṃsita*, *śāsita*
śasU	(1.763)	*śasita*
syandŪ	(1.798)	*syandita*
vanU	(8.8)	*vanita*
kliśŪ	(9.50)	*kliśita*
mṛjŪ	(10.304)	*mṛjita*
kṣamŪ	(4.97)	*kṣamita*
asU	(4.10)	*asita*
yasU	(4.101)	*yasita*
vañcU	(10.163)	*vañcita*

Whitney also cites many *aniṭ* forms for some of these roots but the fact remains that the past-participles with *iṬ* for roots marked with *U* are not as rare in usage as Kiparsky claims.

[B] Evidence from Kāśakr̥tsna's Grammar

Kāśakr̥tsna's grammar is not available in its entirety. Its fragments are available in a commentary in Kannada by Cannavīrakavi on a *Dhātupāṭha* ascribed to the tradition of Kāśakr̥tsna. This Kannada work has been rendered into Sanskrit and published by Yudhishthir Mimamsak (1966). The following extracts are from this Sanskrit rendering. Kāśakr̥tsna's date has been a subject of long debates and we know little about his regional base. Some claim him to be pre-Pāṇinian but most likely he is post- Pāṇinian and pre-Kātyāyana.[3] In any case, his grammar offers a unique alternative glimpse of grammatical activity close to Pāṇini's time.

Cannavīrakavi has preserved two rules of Kāśakr̥tsna.

1) *udanubandhād iḍ vā* (pp. 29-30)
2) *ūdanubandhād iḍ vā* (p. 159)

On the face of it, rule (1) seems comparable to P.7.2.56 (*udito vā*), and rule (2) seems comparable to a portion of P.7.2.44 (*svarati-sūti-sūyati-dhūñ-ūdito vā*). But, if Cannavīrakavi's interpretation of these two rules is right, they differ significantly from seemingly comparable rules in Pāṇini. Cannavīrakavi explains this as follows.

(1) *ṇamu prahvatve śabde / udanubandhād iḍ vā / ukārānubandhavato dhātor iḍ āgamo vā bhavati / namitam /* (pp. 29-30)

(2) *vraścū chedane / ūdanubandhād iḍ vā / ūkārānubandhānāṃ dhātūnām iḍ āgamo vā bhavati / vr̥ścitaḥ vr̥ścitavān /* (p. 159)

According to the traditional explanation, P.7.2.56 (*udito vā*) says that the gerund affix *-Ktvā* optionally takes *iṬ* after roots marked with *U*.[4] It does not itself apply to past participles. However, according to Cannavīrakavi's explanation, rule (1) of Kāśakr̥tsna makes the augment *iṬ* optional for the past-participle affix after roots marked with *U*. This rule may also have applications for other affixes but we have no information about them. Similarly, P.7.2.44 (*svarati-sūti-sūyati-dhūñ-ūdito vā*), according to the traditional explanation, makes *iṬ* optional for any *ārdhadhātuka* affix beginning with *vaL* (that is, consonants excluding *y*) after the listed roots and roots marked with *Ū*. But the tradition makes this rule subject to P.7.2.15 (*yasya vibhāṣā*), which prohibits *iṬ* in past-participles from these roots.[5] Kāśakr̥tsna's rule (2), according to Cannavīrakavi, makes *iṬ* optional for the past-participle affix after roots marked with *Ū*, and clearly does not seem to be subject to a rule like P.7.2.15 (*yasya vibhāṣā*). We have no idea whether Kāśakr̥tsna's grammar even had a rule comparable to P.7.2.15.

Cannavīrakavi not only interprets the two rules of Kāśakr̥tsna in this way but in his commentary on the *Kāśakr̥tsna-Dhātupāṭha* he tacitly applies these rules to derive past-participles of roots marked with *U* and *Ū*. I have examined the entire commentary and located the following examples, in addition to the two cited above.

3)	*śasU hiṃsāyām*	*śasitam*	(p. 47)
4)	*śaṃsU stutau*	*śaṃsitam*	(p. 47)
5)	*dhāvU gati-śuddhyoḥ*	*dhāvitam*	(p. 109)
6)	*śāsU icchāyām*	*śāsitam*	(p. 125)
7)	*srivU gati-śoṣaṇayoḥ*	*srevitaḥ*	(p. 134)
8)	*ṣṭivU kṣivU nirasane*	*ṣṭevitaḥ, kṣevitaḥ*	(p. 134)
9)	*ṣṇusU adane*	*snositaḥ*	(p. 135)
10)	*knusU hvaraṇa-dīptyoḥ*	*knositaḥ*	(p. 135)
11)	*śamU damU upaśame sahane*	*śamitaḥ damitaḥ*	(p. 140)
12)	*tamU kāṅkṣāyām*	*tamitaḥ*	(p. 140)

While the Pāṇinian *Dhātupāṭha* lists *ṇamA* for Kāśakr̥tsna's *ṇamU*, most of the other roots are marked with *U* in both traditions and about half of Kāśakr̥tsna's participle forms with *iṬ* are actually attested in known Sanskrit (as shown above).

9 In conclusion, the above evidence points to a strong possibility that one could accept Kiparsky's new interpretation of Pāṇini's option terms without accepting his interpretations of specific rules. A stricter interpretation of a rule like P.7.2.56 (*udito vā*), in accordance with Kiparsky's general thesis and in contrast to his specific interpretation of this rule, keeps the rule beyond the scope of

P.7.2.15 (*yasya vibhāṣā*) and yields forms that may not be statistically dominant in the known classical language but were evidently a common feature of the Sanskrit known to ancient grammarians like Pāṇini and Kāśakṛtsna. A possible dialectal character of these forms certainly needs to be further investigated by looking closely at the linguistic evidence. While the problems connected with a fuller understanding of P.7.2.15 and related rules are difficult indeed, this paper points to directions for possible solutions.

Notes

* Originally presented at the Sixth World Sanskrit Conference, Philadelphia, October 1984.

1. *dhāvu gatiśuddhyoḥ / kathaṃ gatau dhāvito dhāvitavān iti / yasya vibhāṣeti niṣedhasyānityatvād iṭo 'nityatā / bījaṃ ca kṛticṛtinṛtīnām īditkaraṇam / tad dhi śvīdito niṣṭhāyām* [7.2.14] *iti niṣedhārthaṃ kriyate / yasya vibhāṣā* [7.2.15] *iti niṣedhasya nityatve tu tenaiva siddhatvād anarthakaṃ tat syāt /* [*Dhātupradīpaḥ*, pp. 44-45]. *Īditkaraṇaṃ 'yasya vibhāṣā' ityasyānityatvajñapanārtham / tena dhāvita ityādi siddhyatīty ātreyamaitreyau / svāmikāśyapau tu avayave 'caritārthatvād yaṅluṅnivṛttyartham iti / atra 'yasya vibhāṣā' nāsti, 'se 'sici' ityatra ekāca ity anuvṛtter iḍvikalpasyaivābhāvād iti tayor abhiprāyaḥ /* [*Mādhavīyadhātuvṛttiḥ*, p. 404].

   The form *patita* presents similar problems. See *tanipatidaridrāṇām upasaṅkhyānam* [Vārttika on *sanīvantardha. . .*, etc.] *iti pater vibhāṣiteṭkasyāpi 'dvitīyā śritātītapatitagatātya' iti nipātanād iḍāgamaḥ* / [*Kāśikāvṛttiḥ* on P.7.2.15]. The *Siddhāntakaumudī* has the same argument on P.6.4.52. Nāgeśabhaṭṭa in his *Laghu-śabdenduśekhara* on this rule seems to disagree with these *jñāpakas*: *anityatvajñāpanād veti / idam bhāṣye na dṛśyate / kṛntater īditvam anārṣam iti pare* / [*Vaiyākaraṇasiddhāntakaumudī, tattvabodhinībālamanoramāśekhara-subodhinīsahitā. Rājasthānasaṃskṛtagranthamālā* 42, *dvitīyo bhāgaḥ*, p. 435]. Most commentaries discuss these and other issues.

2. See Deshpande (1982; 1983).
3. For a brief discussion of various views, see Deshpande (1974).
4. See *Kāśikāvṛtti* and *Siddhāntakaumudī* on this rule.
5. See *Kāśikāvṛtti* and *Siddhāntakaumudī* on P.7.2.15.

Bibliography

Böhtlingk, Otto. (1887). *Pāṇini's Grammatik.* Leipzig.

Deshpande, Madhav M. (1974). Review of *Karmadhārayāhnika,* translated by S. D. Joshi and J. A. F. Roodbergen. *Orientalistisches Literaturzeitung.*

-------. (1982). "Linguistic Presuppositions of Pāṇini 8.3.26-27." *Proceedings of the International Seminar on Pāṇini.* Centre of Advanced Study in Sanskrit. University of Poona. Pp. 23-42.

------. (1983). "Pāṇini as a Frontier Grammarian." *Papers from the Nineteenth Regional Meeting, Chicago Linguistic Society.* Pp. 110-16.

------. (1984). Review of Kiparsky's *Pāṇini as a Variationist. Language*, Vol. 60, No. 1, March 1984. Pp. 161-64.

Dhātupradīpaḥ. By Maitreyarakṣita. Edited by Srish Chandra Chakravarti. *Savitaray Smr̥tisaṃrakṣaṇa Granthamālā* 1. Rajshahi, 1919.

Kāśakr̥tsnadhātuvyākhyānam. By Cannavīrakavi. Translated from Kannad into Sanskrit by Yudhishthir Mimamsak. Ajmer, 1966.

Kāśikāvr̥ttiḥ. By Vāmana and Jayāditya. With the commentaries *Nyāsa* and *Padamañjarī*. 6 vols. *Pracya Bharati Series* 2. Tara Publications. Varanasi, 1965-67.

Kiparsky, Paul. (1979). *Pāṇini as a Variationist.* Poona University Press and MIT Press.

Kṣīrataraṅgiṇī. By Kṣīrasvāmin. Edited by Yudhishthir Mimamsak. *Ramlal Kapur Trust Granthamālā* 25. Ajmer, 1958.

Mādhavīyadhātuvr̥ttiḥ. By Sāyaṇa. Edited by Svami Dvarikadas Shastri. *Pracya Bharati Prakashan*, Varanasi, 1964.

Siddhāntakaumudī. By Bhaṭṭojī Dīkṣita. With the commentary *Tattvabodhinī* by Jñānendra Sarasvatī. Edited by Wasudev Laxman Sastri Panshikar. 7th edition. *Nirnaya Sagara Press*, Bombay, 1933.

Wackernagel, Jakob. (1954). *Altindische Grammatik, Band II, 2. Die Nominalsuffixe*, by Albert Debrunner. Vandenhoeck und Ruprecht. Gottingen.

Whitney, W. D. (1885). *The Roots, Verbforms, and Primary Derivatives of the Sanskrit Language.* London, Trubner.

ON IDENTIFYING THE CONCEPTUAL RESTRUCTURING OF PASSIVE AS ERGATIVE IN INDO-ARYAN*

Peter Edwin Hook

One of the outstanding problems in the typology of case and voice is devising a plausible model of the transition from ergative-absolutive to nominative-accusative and vice versa. For languages in the Indo-Aryan group of Indo-European (as well as the Polynesian group of Austronesian) scenarios have been proposed that derive the ergative construction from a passive ancestor.[1] For example, the Old Indo-Aryan passive construction represented by

a)	*bhaktam*	*devadattena*	*pakvam*
	rice-NM	devadatta-IN	cooked

'The rice (has been) cooked by Devadatta'

would have as its etymological reflex some 2,500 years later the New Indo-Aryan ergative construction represented here by Hindi:

b)	*devdatt*	*ne*	*bhāt*	*pakāyā*
	devadatta	ER	rice-NM	cooked

'Devadatta cooked the rice'

When considered in detail, this proposal entails certain difficulties. The passive construction, in languages (such as English, Latin, and Japanese) that are generally considered to have one, is a marked construction in which the patient of the action, not the agent, has many of the properties associated with the grammatical category of subject. Examples include deletability/inferability under identity with the subject noun phrase of a preceding clause in coordinate constructions (St. John went out and was slain by the dragon), a tendency to precede other noun phrases (in particular, the agent noun phrase), and control of reflexivization (John was defeated by himself). By contrast, its constructional descendant, namely, the absolutive noun phrase in ergative-absolutive constructions, has none of these properties. What is not known is the sequence of stages and syntactic reanalyses through which the agent and patient noun phrases in the original passive construction pass as they evolve into the ergative and absolutive.

When we examine the OIA passive in detail, we discover that it is syntactically quite unlike the passive in modern Indo-Aryan (or in English). Many of the subject properties that one would expect to find in the nominatively cased patient noun phrase in the Sanskrit passive seem already to have been lost by the time of Patañjali (circa the second or third century BC). For instance, the instrumental agent noun phrase is free to precede the nominative patient if the discourse structure warrants it (example from *paspaśā ad V* 13):

c) *na* *hi* *pāṇininā* *śabdāḥ* *proktāḥ*
not for Pāṇini-IN words-NM taught

'For it was not words [=language] that were taught by Pāṇini (but rather sutras [=grammar])'

Furthermore, the nominative patient noun phrase in the OIA passive is not the one inferred to be (or deleted as) the agent of a conjunctive participle:[2]

d) *tataḥ* *śabdād* *abhijñāya* *sa* *vyaghreṇa*
then voice-AB recognize-CP he-NM tiger-IN

hataḥ
killed-NM

'The tiger recognized him by his voice and killed him'

(Not 'He recognized the tiger by his voice and was then killed by him')

Contrast this example (from the *Hitopadeśa*) with the passive in NIA, in which the nominative patient in a passive may be the antecedent of the missing (or inferred) noun phrase (example from Sharma 1969, 38):[3]

e) *altūniyā* *cāhtā-thā* *ki* *bahrām* *ko* *gaddi* *se*
Altuniya wanted that Bahram DT throne AB

utār-kar *phir* *sultān* *banā* *diyā* *jā-y* . . . .
depose-CP then sultan make given go-OPT

'Altuniya wanted to be made sultan after having removed Bahram from the throne'

and where the conjunctive participle itself has developed a passive form (example from Kashmiri):

f) *su* *ratini* *yith* *sapon* *bēndy*
he-NM catch-INF come-CP became prisoner

'He was apprehended and put in prison.'[4]

g) *vo* *gaid-kiye* *jā* *kar* *murśidābād* *lāe* *gae*
he-NM arrested go CP Murshidabad brought went

'. . . having been arrested, he was brought to M. . . .'[5]

Of course, it could be the case that the NIA ergative is not the etymological outcome of the OIA passive but, if we assume as correct the suggestion that ergative systems arose in Indo-Aryan as a result of the passive's encroaching on and finally replacing the active as the unmarked voice (at least in tenses based on the past participle), then what may we consider the litmus test for identifying the "moment" at which the community of Indo-Aryan speakers reanalyzed/restructured the passive as ergative?

Linguists have not had notable success in developing tight definitions for such predicate roles[6] as *agent* and *patient* but it seems clear that, however else these categories are to be characterized, they are the least labile in case-voice systems and probably persist as invariants in the evolution of ergative from passive. Case, in the sense of a set of nominal affixes, is a highly unstable category and can appear or disappear independent of a language's typology (Magier 1983). Much the same can be said for verbal affixes of agreement, although it seems that either a system of case affixes, pre- or postpositions, or a system of verbal agreement affixes is required in order to recognize the presence of ergativity. This leaves grammatical functions such as subject and object as the diagnostic domain for identifying the conceptual restructuring of the passive as ergative. Specifically, the migration of subject properties from the patient noun phrase in the passive at an earlier stage to the agent noun phrase at a later one marks the completion of the transition to the ergative.[7] Between these two stages there must be a period in which either both the agent and the patient noun phrase have some claim to subject status or neither of them does.

If linear precedence over other noun phrases in the clause is a property of subject, then neither the agent nor the patient of the passive in Patañjali's Sanskrit has a clear claim. Hock (1982) presents statistics to show that in the Rig-Veda the patient noun phrase precedes the agent of a passive 70 percent of the time. A similar sample from Patañjali's Sanskrit shows the patient noun phrase preceding the agent no more frequently than 50 percent of the time.

If control of reference (or the power to delete a coreferent) in a conjunction (as in sentence d) is a subject property, then the agent noun phrase in Sanskrit has this, regardless of case or voice, from the earliest period onward.[8] Does the patient noun phrase in the Sanskrit passive have any syntactic properties that define subject?

One suggestion made by Keenan (1976a) as a result of his study of Malagasy is that there are languages in which relativizability is limited to subjects. That is, the relative, or "shared," noun phrase in a relative-correlative construction must be the subject in the relative clause. Assuming that this property, qua diagnostic of subjecthood, is something more than an arbitrary stipulation,[9] we can show that on this count the patient noun phrase in a Sanskrit passive has at least one property of subject.

Relative constructions in OIA include those introduced with some form of *yad* 'who, which', as in sentence (h), as well as those in which a non-finite, participial form of the predicate appears, as in sentence (i):

h)	*yo*	*māṇavako*	*vedān*	*paṭhati*	*tam*	*ānaya*
	which-NM	boy-NM	Vedas-AC	reads	him-AC	bring

'Bring the boy who is studying the Vedas'

i)	*vedān*	*paṭhantam*	*māṇavakam*	*ānaya*
	Vedas-AC	reading-AC	boy-AC	bring

'Bring the boy who is studying the Vedas'
(lit. 'Bring the "Vedas-studying" boy')

In the first type the shared noun may, in either clause, be of any predicate role and any case. In the second type the shared noun must be either the agent or the patient of the relative clause. Furthermore, in the corresponding simple finite clause (that is, the clause from which, in a transformational account, it would derive), it must appear in the nominative case. This means that, if it is the patient of its predicate, that predicate must appear in the passive voice:

j)	*māṇavakena*	*paṭhyamānān*	*granthān*	*ānaya*
	boy-IN	read-PASS-AC	books-AC	bring

	**māṇavakaḥ*	*paṭhataḥ*	*granthān*	*ānaya*
	boy-NM	reading-AC	books-AC	bring

'Bring the books being read by the boy'

In effect, the form of the participle shows the predicate role ([+agent] or [+patient]) of the missing nominative in the Sanskrit relative phrase in a manner quite similar to Malagasy and other Austronesian languages (see Manaster-Ramer, n.d.) and quite different from what is found in analogous constructions in Japanese, Korean, Marathi, Tamil, etc., wherein the predicate role of the missing noun phrase must be inferred from the context and/or by examining the case marking of the remaining noun phrases in the relative phrase. Compare the unchanging stem of the Marathi participle *kelalā* in (k) and (l):

k) *malā fon ke-lel-ā māṇus kutha gelā*
me-DT phone do-PP-ms man-NM where went

'Where did the man go who phoned me?'

l) *mi fon ke-lel-ā māṇus kutha gelā*
I-ER phone do-PP-ms man-NM where went

'Where did the man go who I phoned?'

A second subject property that appears to characterize nominative noun phrases in OIA, be they the agents of active verb forms or the patients of passives, is the power to "host" a dependent infinitival phrase. In the following example, taken from *Mahābhārata* I.3.98, the agent of the infinitive *gantum* 'to go' is coreferential with the patient *aham* 'I'[10] of *anujñā* 'permit, allow':

m) *upādhyāyenā 'smy anujñāto gr̥ham gantum*
teacher-IN am permitted home-AC go-INF

'I have been permitted by my guru to go home'

We may say, then, that the nominative patient in (m) shares with nominative agents the ability to condition (or "trigger") deletion of coreferential noun phrases. There are more controversial instances of this general kind, in which the deleted/inferred noun phrase is (or would have been) the nominative patient of the infinitive:

n) *samudram netum icchāmi bhavadbhir*
ocean-AC take-INF want-1s you-1N-p

'I want to be taken to the ocean by you'

To the extent that example (n) is admissible usage,[11] we may regard it as providing evidence of a third subject-defining property for nominative patients: the power to be the target of a deletion (or, in a nontransformational syntax, to be an "inferred" noun phrase).

When we examine reflexivization in OIA, we find the kind of confusion that is to be expected if the restructuring of passive as ergative is accomplished by a feature-by-feature transfer of subject properties from the patient noun phrase to the agent noun phrase. During the period of Patañjali (second-third centuries BC) the reflexive pronoun was controlled by the nominative noun phrase, be it agent or patient. Thus, in a syntactic discussion in Patañjali's *Mahābhāṣya*, we have the following pair of examples (as cited in Deshpande 1985, 10):

o) *hanty ātmānam*
kills self-AC

'X kills himself'

p) *hanyata ātmanā*
is-killed self-IN

'X is killed by himself'

However, the text of Kalidasa's *Mālavikāgnimitra,* written some five or six hundred years later, yields an example in which the appearance of the reflexive is controlled by the agent even when it is the instrumental noun phrase in a passive construction (example from Act 3, between verses 19 and 20):

q) *mayā* *yathākathañcid* *ātmā* *vinoditaḥ*
me-IN in-whatsoever-way self-NM amused

'I amused myself in whatever way I could'
(lit. 'Myself was amused by me somehow or other')

A similar example can be found in the *Hitopadeśa* (*suhr̥dbheda* 24):[12]

r) *abudhair* *ātmā* *paropakaraṇīkr̥taḥ*
fools-IN self-NM other's-tool-made-NM

'Fools make themselves the tools of others'

Constructions like (q) and (r)[13] are exactly what one should expect to find if one were to back-translate from descendant ergative constructions in Middle (or New) Indo-Aryan into the morphologically and syntactically ancestral constructions of Old Indo-Aryan. For instance, in Kashmiri, wherein the ergative construction is found in most past tenses, the reflexive pronoun *panun pān* 'X's self' is found in the nominative case and the controlling or antecedent noun phrase is in an oblique case:

s) *kōryav* *vuch* *panun* *pān* *ēnas* *manz*
girls-ER saw self's self-NM mirror in

'The girls saw themselves in a mirror'

cf. *kanyābhir dṛṣṭa ātmā darpaṇasya madhye*
girls-IN seen self-NM mirror-GN middle-LC

'The girls saw themselves in a mirror'

Works like *Mālavikāgnimitra* or the *Hitopadeśa*, composed in the scholastic language, were written at a time when Sanskrit had long ceased to be anyone's mother tongue. Through them, even if imperfectly, we may glimpse the evolution of the contemporary Indo-Aryan vernaculars. Constructions like those of (q) and (r), which seem so unnatural in English translation or in the context of the syntactic structure of the Sanskrit of earlier periods, must be seen as unconscious calques on syntactic patterns found in the spoken languages of the early centuries of the first millennium.[14] From the evidence that they provide we may conclude that the restructuring of the Indo-Aryan passive as ergative (at least in tenses based on the past participle in *-ta* or *-na*) had reached completion by that time.

Notes

* Earlier drafts of this paper date from 1976 (Hawaii) and 1978 (AOS Toronto). A more recent version was presented at the 1986 annual meeting of the Association for Asian Studies as part of a panel on passives in Asian languages organized by Noriko Nagai (Duke University). It

has benefitted from discussions over the years with M. H. Klaiman, Alexis Manaster-Ramer, Hans Hock, and Madhav Deshpande, none of whom is in agreement with every part of it.

1. See Régamey (1954) and Pray (1976) for Indo-Aryan, and Hohepa (1969) for Polynesian. Estival and Myhill (1988) looks at these and a number of other language groups. Klaiman (1981) argues that the relevant ancestor construction in OIA was *already* ergative and hence the attempt to explain the development of the NIA ergative from the OIA passive is misguided. She bases her argument on the use of past participles in OIA: if intransitive, these modify their agents; if transitive, their patients (*gataḥ puruṣaḥ* vs. *kr̥tam karma*, 'gone man' vs. 'done work'). However, since these participles have morphological parallels in the branches of Indo-European in which ergativity has not developed, their existence in OIA cannot in itself be considered equivalent to the ergativity that we find in the New Indo-Aryan languages. The central issue is the transfer of subject properties from the nominative patient NP in the "passive" to the oblique agent NP (see Comrie 1978).
2. An example from Patañjali (*paspaśā*):

a) *atha* *kam* *padārtham* *matvā* *eṣa* *vigrahaḥ*
so which sense inferred-CP this analysis

kriyate. . .
is-made. . .

'So having assumed which element to be the word-meaning is this analysis (of a compound) made?'

Here the nominative patient noun phrase *vigraha* (the putative "subject" of the passive *kriyate*) is not the antecedent of the missing/inferred agent noun phrase in the subjoined clause *kam padārtham matvā* 'having inferred which sense'. Of course, the example, for pragmatic reasons, hardly admits of an interpretation of *vigraha* 'analysis' as agent of *matvā* 'having considered', and thus it is less telling than the example from the *Hitopadeśa* in which either participant is endowed with the physical ability to be the agent of the conjunctive participle *abhijñāya* 'having recognized'. See Hook (1976, 309, nn. 19, 20) for a discussion of an apparent counterexample:

a) *śriśailaśikharam dr̥ṣṭvā sarvapāpaiḥ pramucyate*
(name of place)-AC see-CP all-sins-IN is-freed

'Merely seeing S. one is freed of all sins'

3. The context makes it clear that Altuniya is the agent of the conjunctive participle *utār kar* 'having deposed'. In other instances the agent of the conjunctive participle is the same as the agent (even if implicit) of the finite passive (example taken from Sharma 1969, 36):

a) *unhõ ne socā ki firoz ko gaddi se utār kar*
they ER thought that Firoz DT throne AB depose CP

kisi any yogy vyakti ko gaddi par
some other competent individual DT throne on

biṭhāyā jā-y
installed go-OPT

'They thought that, having removed Firoz from the throne, (they) should put some other competent person on it'

4. From Grierson (1911, 1:75, sentence 93). The transcription is mine. /i/ and /e/ are high central and middle high central, respectively. /y/ marks palatalization. Contrast the corresponding Hindi given in Kachru (1980, 128, sentences 661-63).
5. From *Premsāgar*, as cited in Schumacher (1977, 190). The passive conjunctive participle seems not to be universally recognized for Hindi (see Kachru et al. 1976, 93).
6. In this paper I assume for *agent* and *patient* the definitions given in the *Aṣṭādhyāyī* for *kartr̥* and *karman*. See Hook (1985, 265, 274, n. 5) for further discussion.
7. I am not considering the rare subtype of syntactically ergative languages, such as Dyirbal, in which subject properties cluster in the absolutive noun phrase and the ergative construction is the unmarked (or only) mode of expression.
8. Hock (1982, 131; 1986, 22) suggests that in the language of the Samhita the subject (rather than the agent) noun phrase of the passive is the (inferred) agent of the conjunctive participle. This is appealing in the con-

text of other evidence, which he adduces from word order and reflexivization in order to demonstrate that nominative patient noun phrases in passive sentences have more subject properties in early (as opposed to Classical) Sanskrit. However, he no longer considers the conjunctive participial data from the Samhita texts to be probative (personal communication).

9. Of course, the substantiality of a case made for some given property's power to distinguish a putative category depends on the degree to which other defining properties cluster together with it cross-linguistically.
10. The nominative form *aham*, qua patient of *anujñā*, is (like all nominative noun phrases in Sanskrit) optional in this sentence. However, qua agent of the infinitive form *gantum*, *aham* cannot appear in this sentence unless it is simultaneously the agent (or patient) of the finite verb.
11. This example, from *Rāmāyaṇa* 4.58.33, is discussed in more detail in Hook (1980, 81-82).
12. Notice that the controlling forms *mayā* 'by me' in (q) and *abudhair* 'by fools' in (r) come to the left of their anaphors.
13. The construction found in (q) and (r) is in most relevant points isomorphic with the reflexive constructions found in Tagalog and other Philippine languages (example cited in Schachter 1976, 503):

a) *iniisip*	*nila*	*ang*	*kanilang-sarili*
DT-think-about	A-they	TP	their-self

'They think about themselves'

In Tagalog the antecedent of the reflexive must be the "actor" (equivalent to "agent" in this paper). In an earlier tradition of analysis the particle *ang* was taken to mark the subject. Schachter (1976), in part on the basis of reflexivization data like those in (a), contends that, whatever the "topic" or *ang*-phrase in Tagalog is, it is not the subject. The same argument, *mutatis mutandis*, applies to the nominative noun phrases in (q) and (r). See Hook (forthcoming) for further discussion.

14. The *Uktivyaktiprakaraṇa* provides explicit confirmation of the dependency of late Classical Sanskrit syntax on that of contemporary Indo-Aryan. See also Deshpande (forthcoming).

Abbreviations

A	agentive
AB	ablative
AC	accusative
CP	conjunctive participle
DT	dative
ER	ergative
GN	genitive
IN	instrumental
INF	infinitive
LC	locative

n	neuter
NM	nominative
OPT	optative
p	plural
PASS	passive marker
PP	past participle
s	singular
TP	topic marker

References

Anderson, Stephen R. 1976. "On the notion of subject in ergative languages." In Charles N. Li, ed. Pp. 1-23.

-------. 1977. "On mechanisms by which languages become ergative." In Charles N. Li, ed. *Mechanisms of Syntactic Change*. Austin: University of Texas Press. Pp. 317-63.

Cardona, George. 1970. "The Indo-Iranian construction *mana (mama) kr̥tam*." *Language* 46:1-12.

-------. 1976. "Subject in Sanskrit." In Manindra K. Verma, ed. Pp. 1-38.

Comrie, Bernard. 1978. "Ergativity." In Winfred P. Lehmann, ed. *Syntactic Typology: Studies in the Phenomenology of Language*. Austin: University of Texas Press. Pp. 329-94.

-------. 1979. "Some remarks on ergativity in South Asian languages." *South Asian Languages Analysis* 1:211-19.

DeLancey, Scott. 1981. "An interpretation of split ergati vity and related patterns." *Language* 57:626-57.

Deshpande, Madhav M. 1985. *Ellipsis and Syntactic Overlap ping: Current Issues in Pāṇinian Syntactic Theory*. Poona: Bhandarkar Oriental Research Institute.

-------. Forthcoming. "The language of the *Girvāṇavāṅ-mañjarī*."

Estival, D., and J. Myhill. 1988. "Formal and functional aspects of the development from passive to ergative systems." In Masayoshi Shibatani, ed. *Passive and Voice*. Amsterdam: J. Benjamins.

Gonda, J. 1951. *Remarks on the Sanskrit Passive*. Leiden: E. J. Brill.

Grierson, George A. 1911. *A Standard Manual of the Kashmiri Language*. 2 vols. Oxford: Clarendon Press. (1973 reprint. Rohtak and Jammu: Light and Life Publishers.)

Hale, Kenneth L. 1970. "The passive and ergative in lan guage change: The Australian case." In S. A. Wurm and D. C. Laycock, eds. *Pacific Studies in Honour of*

Arthur Capell. Canberra: Australian National University. Pp. 757-81.

Hendriksen, Hans. 1944. *Syntax of the Infinite Verb Forms of Pali.* Copenhagen: Munksgaard.

Hock, Hans Henrich. 1982. "The Sanskrit passive: Synchro nic behavior and diachronic development." *South Asia Review* 10:127-37.

-------. 1986. "'P-oriented' constructions in Sanskrit." In Bh. Krishnamurti, ed. *Proceedings of the Second International Conference on South Asian Languages and Linguistics.* Delhi: Motilal Banarsidass.

Hohepa, J. 1969. "The accusative-to-ergative drift in Poly nesian languages." *Journal of the Polynesian Society* 78:295-329.

Hook, Peter E. 1976. "*Aṣṭādhyāyī* 3.4.21 and the role of semantics in Paninian linguistics." *CLS* 12. Chicago: Chicago Linguistic Society. Pp. 302-12.

-------. 1980. "*Aṣṭādhyāyī* 3.3.158 and the notion of subject in Panini." *Revue Roumaine de Linguistique* 25:79-87.

-------. 1985. "Coexistent analyses and participant roles in Indo-Aryan." In Arlene Zide et al., eds. *The Semantics of Participant Roles: South Asia and Adjacent*

Areas. Bloomington: Indiana University Linguistics Club. Pp. 264-85. (A later version was published in *Indian Linguistics*, vol. 45.)

-------. Forthcoming. "*Aṣṭādhyāyī* 3.4.69, 2.3.1 and 2.3.46: The first topic-and-focus analysis in history."

Kachru, Yamuna. 1980. *Aspects of Hindi Grammar*. New Delhi: Manohar.

Kachru, Yamuna, Braj Kachru, and Tej K. Bhatia. 1976. "The notion *subject*: A note on Hindi-Urdu, Kashmiri and Panjabi." In Manindra K. Verma, ed. Pp. 79-108.

Kachru, Yamuna, and Rajeshwari Pandharipande. 1979. "Ergati vity in selected South Asian languages." *South Asian Languages Analysis* 1:193-209.

Keenan, Edward L. 1976a. "Remarkable subjects in Mala gasy." In Charles N. Li, ed. Pp. 247-302.

-------. 1976b. "Towards a universal definition of 'subject.'" In Charles N. Li, ed. Pp. 303-34.

Klaiman, M. H. 1978. "Arguments against a passive origin of the IA ergative." *CLS* 14. Chicago: Chicago Linguistic Society. Pp. 204-16. A later version was published as "The diachronic relationship of the IA ergative and passive constructions." In B. Johns and D. Strong, eds. 1981. *Syntactic Change*. Natural Language Studies No. 25. Ann Arbor: Department of Linguistics, University of Michigan. Pp. 135-58.

Li, Charles N., ed. 1976. *Subject and Topic.* New York: Academic Press.

Magier, David. 1983. "Components of ergativity in Marwari." *CLS* 19. Chicago: Chicago Linguistic Society. Pp. 244-55.

Manaster-Ramer, Alexis. N.d. "Malagasy and the topic/subject issue." Unpublished.

Masica, Colin P. 1976. *Defining a Linguistic Area.* Chicago: University of Chicago Press.

-------. 1982. "Ergativity in South Asia." *South Asia Review* 6.3:1-11.

Pathak, Pandit S., and Pandit S. Chitrao. 1927. *Word Index to Patañjali's Vyākaraṇa Mahābhāṣya.* Poona: Bhandarkar Oriental Research Institute.

Pirejko, Lija A. 1979. "On the genesis of the ergative construction in Indo-Iranian." In F. Plank, ed. Pp. 481-88.

Plank, F., ed. 1979. *Ergativity: Towards a Theory of Grammatical Relations.* London: Academic Press.

Pray, Bruce. 1976. "From passive to ergative in Indo-Aryan." In Manindra K. Verma, ed. Pp. 195-211.

Régamey, Constantin. 1954. "A propos de la 'construction ergative' en indo-aryen moderne." *Sprachgeschichte und Wortbedeutung: Festschrift Albert Debrunner.* Bern: Francke Verlag. Pp. 363-81.

Schachter, Paul. 1976. "The subject in Philippine languages: Topic, actor, actor-topic, or none of the above." In Charles N. Li, ed. Pp. 491-518.

Schokker, G. H. 1969. "The *jānā*-passive in the NIA lan guages." *Indo-Iranian Journal* 12:1-23.

Schumacher, Rolf. 1977. *Untersuchungen zum Absolutiv im Modernen Hindi.* Frankfurt am Main: Peter Lang.

Sharma, Mathuralal. 1969. *Dillī Saltanat.* Gwalior: Kailash Pustak Sadan.

Shibatani, Masayoshi. 1985. "Passives and related construc tions: A prototype analysis." *Language* 61:821-48.

Smith, Richard R. 1974. "Awadhi/Kannauji Transition Phenomena and their Correlates: A Study in Dialect Geography." Ph.D. diss. Cornell University.

Speyer, J. S. 1886. *Sanskrit Syntax.* Leyden: E. J. Brill.

Stump, Gregory T. 1983. "The elimination of ergative patterns of case marking and verbal agreement in Modern Indic languages." *Ohio State Working Papers in Linguistics* 27:140-64.

Trask, R. L. 1979. "On the origins of ergativity." In F. Plank, ed. Pp. 385-404.

Uktivyaktiprakaraṇa of Damodar Pandit. 1953. Singhi Jain Series, No. 39. Bombay: Bharatiya Vidya Bhavan.

Verma, Manindra K., ed. 1976. *The Notion of Subject in South Asian Languages.* Madison: Department of South Asian Studies, University of Wisconsin.

Vyākaraṇamahābhāṣya of Patañjali. 1962. Gurukul Jhajjar (Rohatak): Haryana Sahitya Sansthanam.

Whitney, William Dwight. 1889. *Sanskrit Grammar.* London: Geoffrey Cumberlege, Oxford University Press. (1955 reprint. Harvard University Press.)

A NOTE ON PĀṆINI 3.1.26, VĀRTTIKA 8

Daniel H. H. Ingalls

In contributing to Professor Joshi's felicitation volume I wish to choose a subject that will interest him. What will be sure to interest him is Patañjali's *Mahābhāṣya*. But what can I say of the *Mahābhāṣya* that S. D. Joshi does not already know, he who is the authority of both East and West on that marvellous book? For something new I am left with only minor matters, such as the following.

Vārttika 8 on Pāṇini 3.1.26 runs as follows: *ākhyānāt kr̥tas tad ācaṣṭe, kr̥lluk, prakr̥tipratyāpattiḥ, prakr̥tivac ca kārakam.*

Patañjali repeats and comments on this *Vārttika*: *ākhyānāt kr̥dantāṇ ṇij vaktavyaḥ tad ācaṣṭa ity asminn arthe / kr̥lluk, prakr̥tipratyāpattiḥ, prakr̥tivac ca kārakaṃ bhavatīti vakta- vyam / kaṃsavadham ācaṣṭe kaṃsaṃ ghātayati / balibandham ācaṣṭe baliṃ bandhayatīti /*

In English: "[Among the uses of the causative suffix *ṆIC*] there should be added this, that *ṆIC* is suffixed to a stem ending in a *kr̥t* suffix after [the name of] a story, in the sense 'he tells this story'. One should also state that the *kr̥t* suffix then drops, the base reasserts itself, and the case relationship becomes as it would be with the base. Thus, *kaṃsavadham ācaṣṭe* 'he tells the Death of Kaṃsa' [may be rendered as] *kaṃsaṃ ghātayati* [literally,] 'he causes Kaṃsa to be killed'; *balibandham ācaṣṭe* 'he tells the Binding of Bali' [may be rendered as] *balim bandhayati* 'he causes Bali to be bound.'"

In the story title, *Kaṃsavadha* [The death of Kaṃsa], we have an objective genitive compound composed of *kaṃsa*, plus the root *han*, plus the *kr̥t* suffix *AP*, used to form an action noun (Pāṇ. 3.3.75). Before the suffix *AP*, *han* must be replaced by *vadhá* (Pāṇ. 3.3.76).[1] In the alternative form of expression prescribed in our *Vārtika* we begin by adding *ṆIC*. Thus,

kaṃsa + vadhá + AP + ṆIC

Then the *kr̥t* suffix (that is, *AP*) drops, and the base, for which *vadhá* was substituted, is restored. Thus,

kaṃsa + han + ṆIC

Finally, the case relationship becomes accusative, as it would be with the base, not genitive, as it is with the derivative in compound. Thus,

kaṃsaṃ ghātaya(ti)

The same process is followed in transforming *balibandham ācaṣṭe* into *baliṃ bandhayati.*

What lies at the base of such usage is a hyperbole (*atiśayokti*) by which a poet or storyteller is regarded as actually bringing about the events of which he speaks. This sort of hyperbole occurs in languages other than Sanskrit. It is especially common among the Classical Latin poets. Thus, Horace (*Sat.* 1.10.36-37) writes:

> *turgidus Alpinus jugulat dum Memnona, dumque*
> *defingit Rheni luteum caput. . . .*

> 'While the turgid poet Alpinus cuts the throat of King Memnon; while he disfigures the muddy headwaters of the Rhine. . . .'

Vergil (*Ecl.* 6.62-63), expressing how a pastoral poet tells the story of the metamorphosis of Phaethon's sisters into alder trees, writes:

> *tum Phaethontiadas musco circumdat amare*
> *corticis atque solo proceras erigit alnos.*

> 'Then he encloses the sisters of Phaethon with the bitter moss of bark and sets them up as tall alder trees'.

Or Horace again (*Od.* 3.25.3-6):

> *quibus*
> *antris egregii Caesaris audiar*
> *aeternum meditans decus*
> *stellis inserere et consilio Jovis?*

> 'In what groves shall I be heard singing the glory of great Caesar, to set him among the stars and in Jove's council?'

These Latin examples employ the simplex rather than the causative as prescribed by Kātyāyana's *Vārttika*. But there is no formal causative in Classical Latin. The alteration of a root by addition of a causative suffix (for example, *decet* › *docet, necat* › *nocet*) had ceased to be productive before Classical Latin times. Furthermore, in these cases the older Sanskrit language seems to have used the simplex as readily as the causative. If my interpretation is correct, a passage from the *Taittirīya Saṃhitā* exhibits both idioms.

As my interpretation of the passage (*Tait. Saṃ.* 2.5.2.4-5) differs from that of Sāyana, it will be well by way of justification to translate the whole passage, which tells of the killing of Vṛtra, from the beginning of 2.5.2. In the course of the story numerous ritual prescriptions are explained. In fact, it is for their sake that the story is told.[2]

"Tvaṣṭṛ, when his son had been killed, gave a soma offering without Indra. Indra desired an invitation but Tvaṣṭṛ did not invite him because Indra had killed his son. Indra broke into the ceremony by force and drank of the soma. Tvaṣṭṛ hurled what was left on the *āhavanīya* fire, saying, 'Svāhā! Grow to be Índraśatru'.[3] In that he hurled it [*prāvartayat*], Vṛtra was called Vṛtra. In that he said 'Svāhā! Grow to be Índraśatru', Indra therefore became the slayer of Vṛtra.

"On coming into being, Vṛtra devoured Agni and Soma. He kept growing--the length of an arrow-shot each time, on all sides--until he covered [*avṛṇot*] these worlds. That is [another reason] why Vṛtra was called Vṛtra. Indra was afraid of him. He ran to Prajāpati, saying, 'One has been born who will slay me'. Prajāpati annointed Indra's vajra for him and said, 'Strike him with this'.

"Indra advanced [against Vṛtra] with the vajra. Agni and Soma cried out, 'Do not strike. We are inside him'. 'But you are mine', [said Indra,] 'come out to me'. They asked a reward. He gave them the *agniṣomīya* offering that is placed on eleven potsherds in the full-moon sacrifice. They said, 'We have been chewed up; we cannot get out'. So Indra produced from himself hot and cold fevers. That was the origin of hot and cold fevers. Hot and cold fevers will not kill him who knows thus the origin of hot and cold fevers. Indra infected Vṛtra with them so that when his teeth chattered Agni and Soma came out. Indeed, the out-breath and the in-breath left him. The out-breath is ability [*dakṣa*] and the in-breath is will [*kratu*]. That is why a man chattering with fever speaks [the charm]: '[Stay] with me, ability and will' and his out-breath and his in-breath remain in his body and he lives many years.

"Indra, calling the gods out of Vṛtra, offered the Vṛtra-killing oblation at the full moon. Indeed, they tell of the death of Vṛtra at the full moon and they tell of his increase at the dark of the moon. That is why the two Vṛtra-killing verses [*vārtraghnī*] are recited at the full-moon ceremony and the two increase-making verses [*vṛdhanvatī*] at the dark of the moon."

The story continues, with Indra giving other ritual rewards to sky and earth, then killing Vr̥tra, and finally giving a ritual reward to cows. But we have reached the passage that I think exemplifies our *Vārttika*: *ghnánti vā́ enam pūrṇámāsa ā́, amāvasyā̂yām pyāyayanti.* I take *ghnánti vā́ enam* to mean *tadvadham* (that is, *Vr̥travadham*) *ācakṣate* and I take [*Vr̥tram*] *pyāyayanti* to mean something like *Vr̥travr̥ddhim* (or **Vr̥trapyātim*, if there were such a word) *ācakṣate.* The first of these instances exhibits the simplex, the second the causative. I fail to see what subject can be assigned to the verbs, or how they make sense, under any other interpretation.

In Classical Sanskrit literature I cannot point to any instances of either locution except in the grammarians. Patañjali himself, under the very next *Vārttika*, furnishes the example *rājānam āgamayati* as equivalent to *rājāgamanam ācaṣṭe.* In discussing the syntax of this phrase Nagoji adds a counterexample, *Devadattena pācayati*, as equivalent to *Devadattapākam ācaṣṭe.* But these examples smell of the inkhorn.

Notes

1. Such is the interpretation of the *Kāśikā*, which adds that the *ādeśa* is *antodātta*, that is, *vadhá*. When the final accented vowel of this substitute combines with the unaccented *a* of *AP* (by *ato guṇe* 6.1.97), the resultant vowel becomes accented (by *ekādeśa udāttenodāttaḥ* 8.2.5). Boehtlingk (1887) in translating 3.3.76, takes the sub-

stitute to be *vadh* expressed in the ablative case. Under the entry *vadha* in the section "Pāṇini's Wortschatz" (p. 272*), he argues that if the substitute were *vadha* there would be no need to include *vadhi* in 7.3.35. Perhaps. But to make the substitute in 3.3.76 monosyllabic is to accuse Pāṇini of a more serious fault: *vadh* plus *AP* would become **vádhaḥ*.

2. The standard translation by Keith (1914, 190) contains several errors, which make some parts of the story unintelligible. Keith mistranslates *abhí sámabhavat, abhyā̂nayat,* and *vā̂rtraghnam,* despite the commentators, who furnish the correct sense.
3. As Patañjali notes in the introduction to his work (Kielhorn 1962, 2, l. 11-12), Tvaṣṭṛ misplaced the accent. He meant to say 'Indraśátru, a slayer of Indra'. But the initial accent transforms the *tatpuruṣa* compound into a *bahuvrīhi*, meaning 'one whose slayer is Indra'. Hence the denouement of the story.

References

Boehtlingk, Otto. 1887. *Pāṇini's Grammatik.* Leipzig: Verlag von H. Haessel.

Keith, Arthur Berriedale. 1914. *The Veda of the Black Yajus School, Entitled Taittirīya Saṃhitā.* Harvard Oriental Series, vols. 18, 19. Cambridge: Harvard University Press.

Kielhorn, Franz. 1880. *The Vyākaraṇa-Mahābhāṣya of Patañjali.* Vol. 1. 3d ed., 1962. Pune: Bhandarkar Oriental Research Institute.

ON EKĀRTHĪBHĀVA AND VYAPEKṢĀ

V. N. Jha

There is an age-long debate between the Grammarians (that is, traditional Sanskrit grammarians) and the Naiyāyikas (logicians belonging to the school of Nyāya) over the meaning of compounds. Does a compound form, as a single unit, have a primary relationship with its meaning over and above the relationships of the constituents of the compound with their meanings? Is there any necessity of postulating a relationship with the compound as a single unit, such that primary relationships of the constituents of a compound, with their respective meanings, are sufficient to account for the meaning conveyed by the compound?

The Grammarians hold the view that it is necessary to postulate an additional relationship (*sāmarthya*) in the compound form as a whole, over and above the relationships of the constituents of that compound, and that this expressive capacity (or relationship) is called *ekārthībhāva-sāmarthya*.[1]

The Naiyāyikas reject this proposal, maintaining instead that the expressive powers (or relationships) of the constituents of a compound are sufficient to account for its meaning. This individual capacity of each constituent of a compound conveys the meaning--and through mutual expectancy the compound-meaning is understood. This is *vyapekṣā*.[2]

This paper is an attempt (1) to present faithfully some of the Grammarians' salient arguments in support of their stand for *ekārthībhāva-sāmarthya*, (2) to advance the Naiyāyikas' refutations of these arguments and present their own position, and (3) to evaluate the arguments of both sides in order to draw some conclusions.[3]

Part I: The Grammarians' Position

The following are the grounds of the Grammarians' stand in favor of *ekārthībhāva* in compounds.

Compound forms such as *citraguḥ*, etc., cannot generate knowledge of *citragosvāmī* 'the owner of the cows having variegated color'. The Naiyāyikas would explain the same compound as follows: the word *go* stands for *go-svāmin* 'the owner of the cows' and the meaning of the word *citra* is construed with 'cows' by the relation of identity, giving rise to an understanding of *citrābhinna-go-svāmī* 'the owner of the cows that are identical to (the cows) having variegated color'. But such an explanation is not acceptable because the relation of the meaning of a word is not allowed with a part of the meaning of another word.

To avoid this difficulty, the Naiyāyikas could let 'cows' be understood from the word *go* by primary relationship, and by the secondary relation (*lakṣaṇā*) let it convey 'the owner'. Then the meaning of the word *citra* can easily be related to the cows since 'cows' are now the *padārtha* and not a part of the *padārtha*. But this trick cannot be adopted either, since one would have to accept two relationships in the same word, which is absurd.

Naturally, the Naiyāyikas must then adopt another way, namely, to say that the word *go* would itself convey *citra-go-svāmin* by *lakṣaṇā*, and that the word *citra* would perform the function of indicating the intention of the speaker. This will save the Naiyāyikas from the earlier defect, no doubt, but it will land them in another difficulty. For, if the word *citra* is a mere indicator of the intention of the speaker, then the formation of *citraguḥ* as a *bahuvrīhi* compound itself would be impossible. This is so because the rule that allows the *bahuvrīhi* compound is *anekam anya-padārthe*, which means "when more than one word ending in a case-suffix conveying a third entity come to be compounded, that compound is a *bahuvrīhi* compound." Here, since the word *citra* does not convey any meaning, and, since it simply indicates the intention of the speaker, the *bahuvrīhi* is not possible.

Moreover, according to the Naiyāyikas, *citraguḥ* is a sentence. As such it is conceived as having the property of being the prompter of the *viṣayatā*, described by the *viṣayatā* prompted by that word. And, although the meaning of the word *citra* appears in the cognition, that cognition is not caused by the word *citra*. Hence, because the criterion that causes compounding (namely, the *ekavākyatva*) is absent, there will be no compounding at all, which is contrary to the facts of Sanskrit usage.

Furthermore, if what the Naiyāyikas say is accepted, then the Grammarians can also let the last phoneme *a* in *ghaṭa* express the meaning 'pot' and let the other phonemes be treated as mere indicators of the speaker's intention.

From what has been said above, it can be concluded that the Naiyāyikas' theory of *tātparya-grāhakatva* cannot be supported. Hence, the example of *citraguḥ* compels one to accept *samāsa-śakti* or *ekārthībhāva-sāmarthya.*

Similarly, the compound *prāptodakaḥ* (*grāmaḥ*) '(the village) that the (flood-)water has reached' cannot generate the *śābdabodha* as *udaka-kartṛka-prāpti-karma (grāmaḥ)* '(the village is) the object of the reaching of the water' if *samāsa-śakti* is not accepted.

The Naiyāyikas may let the word *udaka* stand for the entire meaning of the compound by *lakṣaṇā* and let the word *prāpta* be the indicator of the intention of the speaker. This would not be proper, however, because an indicator of the intention of the speaker can only be a word whose expressed meaning forms the part of the meaning to be indicated. Here the meaning of the word *prāpta* (namely, *prāpti-kartā*) does not form a part of the indicated sense (*udaka-kartṛka-prāpti-karma*) and so our only choice is to accept the *śakti* in the whole of the compound (that is, *samudāya-śakti*).

Likewise, if *samudāyaśakti* is not accepted, another problem will arise in the case of the compound *pañcagava-dhanaḥ* 'one who has the wealth of five cows'. The Naiyāyikas would let the word *dhana* itself convey, by *lakṣaṇā*, the meaning of the entire compound (*pañca-gavābhinna-dhana-svāmī*, that is, 'one who is the owner of wealth in the form of five cows') and let the remaining portion of the compound be an indicator of the intended meaning of the speaker. But in that case they cannot establish the identity relation between the meaning of the word *pañcan* and the meaning of *go*, since in this explanation these words are not expressive of any meaning but are merely *tātparya-grāhaka*. And, if the identity between these two meanings is not understood, it should be accepted that there is no coreferentiality (*sāmānadhikaraṇya*) between *pañcan* and *go*. As a result, the *samāsānta*-suffix *ṭac* cannot be added to it[4] and one cannot get the compound form *pañcagavadhana*. Thus, the acceptance of *ekārthībhāva* becomes imperative.

Similarly, in the compound *rājapuruṣaḥ*, the Naiyāyikas say that the constituent *rāja* stands for *rājasambandhin*, by *lakṣaṇā*, and that as a result this meaning is related to the meaning of *puruṣa* by the relation of identity. But this is not possible because the Naiyāyikas are caught by their own statements elsewhere. They make a general rule in order to deny the grammaticality of such sentences as **taṇḍulaḥ pacati*, in the sense of 'he cooks rice', as follows: *prāti-padikārtha-niṣṭha-prakāratā-nirūpita-viśeṣyatā-sambandhena śābdabodhaṃ prati viśeṣyatā-sambandhena pratyaya-janyopa-sthitiḥ kāraṇam*, that is, the remembrance of the meaning of a suffix by the relation of *viśeṣyatā* is the cause for a verbal understanding arising by the relation of *viśeṣyatā* described by the *prakāratā* existing in the meaning of a nominal stem.

Now, as this generalization does not allow the sentence **taṇḍulaḥ pacati* to become grammatically correct, it also will not allow the relation of the meaning of *rāja* with that of *puruṣa* since the meaning of *puruṣa* is not the qualificand (*viśeṣya*) remembered from any suffix.

According to the doctrine of the Grammarians, such a difficulty will not arise because, according to this doctrine, the meaning of a nominal stem is always related to that of a suffix alone and not to another stem-meaning. Even in the sentence *śubhraḥ taṇḍulaḥ*, the meaning of the base *śubhra* is related only to the meaning of the nominative singular suffix.

Moreover, if the Grammarians were to attempt, as the Naiyāyikas do, to relate the meaning of *rāja* with that of *puruṣa*, by the identity relation, the Naiyāyikas should accept *rājapuruṣa* as a *karmadhāraya samāsa* and not as a *ṣaṣṭhī-tatpuruṣa*. In that case the meaning of the *samasta-pada* and the meaning of *vigrahavākya (rājñaḥ puruṣaḥ)* will not match. Likewise, following Gaṅgeśa, if one says that the word *rāja* in this compound can stand for *rājasambandha*, then the understanding from *rājapuruṣaḥ* should be *rājasam-bandhābhinna puruṣaḥ*, which is absurd. To avoid all these unwanted consequences it is wise to accept *ekārthībhāva*.

In addition, in the compound *upakumbham*, an explanation stating that the word *kumbha* can stand for *kumbhasamīpa* 'near the jar', and that the prefix *upa* can be treated as a mere indicator of the speaker's intention, is not proper either. Only where the indicated meaning is a qualifier, the remembrance of what is indicated by the prefix *upa* is not a qualifier but a qualificand. So the desired under-standing cannot be obtained from the compound *upakumbham* if *vyapekṣā* is accepted.

Furthermore, if a *samāsa* does not have *ekārthībhāva*, then, in the sentence *citragum ānaya* 'bring the owner of the cows that have variegated color', the owner cannot be related to the meaning of the accusative case-ending. This will be the case since a suffix causes the understanding of its own meaning connected with the meaning of the base to which it is added. Thus, here the base (*prakṛti*) is *citragu*, not *go*. The meaning of *citragosvāmī* is not the meaning of the stem *go* through a *vṛtti*; hence, it is not possible to relate the meaning of the accusative case-ending with *citragosvāmin*.

Also, the *ekārthībhāva-sāmarthya* must be accepted because without it the case-ending following the stem *citragu-* cannot be justified. If the compound unit *citragu-* does not have *ekārthībhāva*, this implies that the unit does not express any sense as a whole. As a result, it cannot be designated as *prātipadika*,[5] and unless it is so designated no case-ending can be added to it.

Moreover, unless *samāsa-śakti* is accepted, even the *yogarūḍhi* word *paṅkaja* cannot express lotus in general, since the constituent words alone can express the meaning 'lotus', that is, 'a flower that grows in the mud'. So the Naiyāyikas need not accept *samudāya-śakti* here. They need not argue that, although a lotus growing in the mud can be understood by the *avayava-śakti* in each constituent of the word *paṅkaja-*, still, in order to remember the meaning as lotus (that is, as possessed of "lotusness") it is necessary to accept *samudāya-śakti* here also. Like a compound, it is possible to understand lotus possessed of lotusness from that word. Thus, as the Naiyāyikas accept *samudāya-śakti* with the word *paṅkaja*, they should accept it also in a compound form.

Similarly, unless we accept *ekārthībhāva*, the order of the constituents of a compound has no significance. For instance, there will be no difference in the understandings arising from the sentence *brāhmaṇaḥ paṇḍitaḥ* (wherein *paṇḍita* is the predicate) and the compound *paṇḍita-brāhmaṇa* (in which *brāhmaṇa* is the predicate). This can be avoided if we accept *samāsa-śakti* because in that case we accept the *śakti* in the fixed sequence of constituents.

Because of the acceptance of *samāsa-śakti*, the Mīmāṃsaka's arguments in the case of the interpretation of *prathama-bhakṣaḥ* in the sentence *vaṣaṭ-kartuḥ prathama-bhakṣaḥ* can be supported. The compound *prathama-bhakṣa* conveys a single integrated meaning, namely, 'food to be eaten first', only because there is *ekārthībhāva* in it. But, if *vyapekṣā* is accepted, then *prāthamya* 'firstness' cannot be predicated to *bhakṣa* ('eating') because this would lead to the fault of *eka-prasaratā-bhaṅga*.[6]

If someone utters the sentence *ṛddhasya rājapuruṣaḥ* with the intention of conveying 'the man of the king who is rich', this is not grammatical. But the ungrammaticalness of such expression can be maintained only if one accepts *ekārthībhāva*. According to the *vyapekṣā* theory, there is no difficulty in using the above expression in that sense.

Thus, if *rājapuruṣa* is a single unit, only then can the meaning 'king' be considered a part of the word-meaning 'king's man'. The relation of the meaning of *ṛddha* will not be possible with 'king' because of the operation of the generalization, namely, *padārthaḥ padārthena anveti na tadekadeśena* ('the meaning of a word is related to another word-meaning and not to a part of it'). This fact also prompts us to accept the *ekārthībhāva-sāmarthya.*

These, in brief, are the arguments of the Grammarians in favor of accepting the *ekārthībhāva-sāmarthya.* Let us now turn to the reaction of the Naiyāyikas.

Part II: The Naiyāyikas' Reply

The Naiyāyikas have this to say.

Since there is no means of knowing the *ekārthībhāva-sāmarthya*, it is not proper to postulate innumerable *śakti*s in innumerable compounds. The Grammarians cannot argue that *Pāṇini sūtra*s (*cārthe dvandvaḥ* P.2.2.29, etc.) will cause the knowledge of the like *śakti* of respective compounds, and that therefore the Naiyāyikas' contention is not true. If it is accepted that those *sūtra*s also express the meaning of the compound, then obviously it will be a case of *vākyabheda* since the same *sūtra* will assign designation of a compound and also express the meaning. Moreover, the Grammarians accept as their *siddhānta* that *sūtra*s such as *cārthe dvandvaḥ* (P.2.2.29) merely designate a particular compound.

Turning towards the Grammarians' arguments in part I, the Naiyāyikas have the following to submit.

The Grammarians expressed the fear that the word *go-*, in the compound *citragu*, stands for *citragosvāmin* by *lakṣaṇā*. This need not be true because, in *anyapadārthe vidyamānam anekam subantam samasyate*, the expression *anyapadārthe vidyamānam* means 'the causer of the understanding of a third entity'. This is equally applicable to the word *citra*, so there are no grounds for fear.

This contingency is applicable if the Grammarians' theory of *ekārthībhāva* is accepted because, since the whole unit *citragu-* is meaningful, and not an individual constituent, they must accept that the word *citra-* has no meaning in isolation. How, then, can they apply the designation *bahuvrīhi* to the expression *citragu-*?

It is also claimed by the Grammarians that, if the word *citra-* is treated as indicative of the intention of the speaker, there will be no compounding at all. But this is not well thought out. It is a fact that the appearance of the meaning of the word *citra* is not caused by the remembrance of that meaning from the word *citra*. Still, the understanding *citrābhinnagosvāmī* does depend upon the juxtaposition of the words *citra* and *go*. Here doubt has no base.

According to the Grammarians, the final phoneme *a* of the word *ghaṭa* will become expressive of *ghaṭa* if the *tātparyagrāhakatva*-theory is accepted. But such a situation will never arise since the primary relationship of the meaning 'pot' is established with the word *ghaṭa*, not with *a*.

Moreover, how can the Grammarians compare the cases of *citragu-* and *ghaṭa*? In the case of *citragu-*, unless *citra-* has meaning it cannot be an indicator of the indicated meaning. But such is not the case with *ghaṭa*. Here *gh*, *a*, and *ṭ* are not expressive of any meaning, so how can such a contingency arise? To the difficulty posed regarding the compound *prāptodakaḥ (grāmaḥ)*, the Naiyāyika reply would be as follows.

According to the Nyāya theory, an indicator of intended meaning is conceived as that which causes knowledge of the intended meaning. This, in turn, consists of its indicated meaning (*sva-bodhya-ghaṭakārtha-ghaṭitārthe tātparya-grāhakasya lakṣaṇā-tātparya-grāhakatva-niyamaḥ*). This principle is applicable also in the case of *prāpta*. It is not difficult to demonstrate the relation of the meaning of the root *prāp-* (namely, *prāpti*) and that of the past passive participle *-ta* ('the agent').

In the case of *pañcagavadhanaḥ*, the Grammarians contend that there can be no coreferentiality (*sāmānādhikaraṇya*) between the meaning of *pañcan* and the meaning of *go-*, and hence the suffix *ṭac* cannot be added. But this is not the case because the meaning of *sāmānādhikaraṇya* between *x* and *y* is "being the generator of the knowledge of the meaning of *x* related with the meaning of *y* through the relation of identity." "Being the meaning of *y*" means "being the locus of the *viṣayatā* prompted by the word *y*." The word *citra* does prompt the *viṣayatā* in the meaning of *pañcan* in the verbal understanding arising from the compound *pañcagavadhana*. Here, then, there is no difficulty.

The Grammarians state that, in the compound *rājapuruṣa*- the meaning of *rāja* (namely, *rājasambandhin*), by *lakṣaṇā*, cannot be related to the meaning of the word *puruṣa* by the relation of identity because, to a verbal understanding in which the meaning of the stem is the qualifier, the remembrance of the meaning of the suffix is the cause. This is not correct. The worry that, if such a *kāryakāraṇabhāva* is not accepted, the understanding *taṇḍula-karmaka-pākānukūla-kṛtimān* will arise from the sentence **taṇḍulaḥ pacati* is also baseless. Juxtaposition of the word *taṇḍulam* and the root *pac* is in fact the expectancy (*ākāṅkṣā*), so such an understanding cannot occur. Hence, the *kāryakāraṇabhāva* is unnecessary and there is no difficulty in the case of *rāja-puruṣaḥ*.

Also, if one accepts that the meaning of *rāja-* is related to the meaning of *puruṣa* by the identity relation, then the compound *rājapuruṣa-* should be designated as *karmadhāraya*. But there is no reason to think like that. The grounds for *karmadhāraya* is that (without resorting to *lakṣaṇā*) one meaning should be relatable to another by identity relation. Here the meaning *rājasambandhin* is obtained by *lakṣaṇā*, so it cannot be considered a *karmadhāraya* compound.

The Grammarians contend that, if *rāja-* stands for *rājasambandhin-*, by *lakṣaṇā*, then the meaning of the compound *rājapuruṣaḥ* and the phrase *rājñaḥ puruṣaḥ* will not be symmetrical. This is groundless. There is no invariable rule that the understandings arising from a compound form and the underlying phrase (*vigrahavākya*) of that compound form must be symmetrical. For instance, the understanding arising from *citrāḥ gāvaḥ yasya* would be *yatsambandhinayaḥ citrābhinna-gāvaḥ*. From *citraguḥ* the understanding will arise as *citrābhinnagosambandhī (yaḥ)*. This change in qualifier and qualificand is unavoidable.

Moreover, how will the Grammarians apply their rule in the case of the formation of the word *Vaiyākaraṇa*? This word is derived from the underlying sentence *vyākaraṇam adhīte*, which will result in the understanding *(caitra-) kartr̥ka-vyākaraṇa-karmaka-adhyayanam*. But, from the complex form *Vaiyākaraṇa-* the understanding will be *vyākaraṇādhyayana-kartr̥-*. Naturally, the structure of the verbal understanding arising from a complex form need not be identical with that of the phrase or sentence underlying that complex form.

The Grammarians argue that, if by *lakṣaṇā*, the element *rāja-* stands for *rājasambandha*, as Gaṅgeśa suggests, it should be related to the meaning of *puruṣa* by identity relation, and that this is absurd. Such a claim is not proper. If it were the case, the normal understanding will be *rājasambandhavān puruṣaḥ*. Of course, the general rule *nāmārthayoḥ bhedena anvaya-bodha-sthale vibhakty-arthopasthitiḥ kāraṇam* will have the same restrictions in the case of compounds.

As a matter of fact, if this restriction is accepted, there is no need to resort to *lakṣaṇā* at all in the case of *rājapuruṣa*. We can easily understand it as *rājanirūpita-svatva-vān puruṣaḥ*.

Likewise, the Grammarians think that, simply because the Naiyāyikas hold that in the compound *upakumbham* the word *kumbha* itself stands for *kumbha-samīpa*, by *lakṣaṇā*, and that *upa* is merely an indicator of the speaker's intended sense, it will violate the rule *dyotyārtha-viśeṣaṇaka-śābdabodham prati dyotyārthopasthitiḥ kāraṇam*. This is mistaken. One cannot generalize such a rule since it will not work in the case of *pratiṣṭhate*. Here the root *sthā* means 'absence of movement', the prefix *pra* indicates movement, and the indicated movement appears in the understanding as the qualificand. Similarly, there is no difficulty if *sāmīpya*, indicated by *upa*, appears as the qualificand.

The contention that, unless *samāsa-śakti* is accepted, the meaning of the accusative case-ending cannot be related to the meaning of *citragu-* in the sentence *citragum ānaya*, is not proper. The Naiyāyikas accept that a suffix causes an understanding of its own meaning as connected with the meaning of the base. In the present case, the word *go* is the base; hence, there is no difficulty in obtaining the said relationship.

The argument that, unless *ekārthībhāva* is accepted, a compound form cannot achieve the designation *prātipadika-*, and that as a result no case-ending can be added to a compound form, is also without foundation. The word *arthavat-*, in the *sūtra*: *arthavad adhātuḥ apratyayaḥ prātipadikam* P.1.2.45, is accepted to stand for *vr̥ttimad-a-viṣayaka-pratīty-aviṣaya* by *lakṣaṇā*, which means "not being an object of an understanding that does not have anything that has *vr̥tti*." Naturally, both (that which has *vr̥tti* and that which consists of that which has *vr̥tti*) are included under the domain of *prātipadika*, so there is no difficulty of justifying the designation of *prātipadika* in the case of compounds.

If this explanation is not acceptable, the Naiyāyikas suggest that the designation of *prātipadika* can be derived from the next rule of Pāṇini, namely, *kr̥t-taddhita-samāsāś ca* P.1.2.46. It should be noted that Pāṇini, after declaring the designation of *prātipadika* for a meaningful sequence that is neither a root nor a suffix, extends the designation separately to complex forms such as primary derivatives, secondary derivatives, and compounds. This in itself indicates that Pāṇini does not consider a complex form as having any *vr̥tti* over and above the *vr̥tti* for the constituents of the complex forms.

The attempt to pose a problem in the case of the word

paṅkaja (by considering it a complex form) will not be successful. For remembering the flower as a lotus, it is necessary to resort to *samudāya-śakti.* One cannot look to the *lakṣaṇā* for help here because, unless the entire expression *paṅkaja* has primary relation (*śakti*), it cannot have secondary relationship. Therefore, the suggestion that *samāsaśakti* be accepted on a par with the word *paṅkaja* is not acceptable.

Another reason proposed for the acceptance of *ekārthībhāva* is the fixed order of the members of a compound, giving rise to a fixed structure of subject and predicate, as in the case of *paṇḍita-brāhmaṇaḥ* and *brāḥmaṇaḥ paṇḍitaḥ.* This is invalid. If separately remembered meanings are grounds for the formation of a structure of the qualifier-qualificand type, then (as in the case of the word *hari-*) ten remembered meanings would all be related as the qualifier and the qualificand. This is absurd. Thus, the intention of the speaker always determines the subject and the predicate, and there is no need for *ekārthībhāva.*

Similarly, in explaining the *prāthamya-viśiṣṭa-vidhāna* in the Vedic sentence *vaṣaṭkartuḥ prathamabhakṣaḥ,* the Grammarians plead for the acceptance of *samāsaśakti.* This is not necessary. *Ekaprasaratābhaṅga* here means "not having the capacity on the part of the constituent elements of the compound to cause the understanding in a fixed order of subject and predicate." As noted above, such an understanding depends upon knowledge of *ākāṅkṣā* and *tātparya,* so there is no need to accept *samāsaśakti* at all.

Finally, the Naiyāyikas point out that, if *ekārthībhāva* is accepted in the case of compounds, compounds such as *śaśaśṛṅga* will not get the designation *prātipadika*, according to the theory of the Grammarians, since there is no meaning to that compound. No such difficulty arises in the Naiyāyika's theory since we know that, even if a compound is denied *ekārthībhāva-sāmarthya*, the *prātipadika-saṃjñā* can easily be given to it by the rule *kṛt-taddhita-samāsāś ca*.

If the Grammarians wish to justify their position by accepting a conceptual meaning (*bauddhārtha*) of *śaśaśṛṅga*, they will not succeed because the Naiyāyikas have already criticized and refuted the existence of any conceptual meaning.

From all this it is clear that the Naiyāyikas do not need *ekārthībhāva-sāmarthya* in compounds. Even without accepting this, they can explain the proper understanding arising from a particular compound form.

Part III: Analysis and Conclusions

By now we are fully acquainted with the respective positions of the Grammarians and the Naiyāyikas on the issue of *ekārthībhāva* and *vyapekṣā*. The entire issue can be reformulated as follows.

If the sequence *xy* is a compound in which *x* has a relation with its meaning (say, *x*'), and *y* also has a relation with its meaning (say, *y*'), then is it necessary to postulate another relationship for the entire sequence *xy*? "Yes" is the answer of the Grammarians and "no" is the answer of the Naiyāyikas.

Before advocating either side, let us analyze the situation further. It seems to be a general assumption on the part of the Grammarians that the meaning of the underlying phrase and the meaning of the corresponding compound form should be identical. Naturally, *rājñaḥ puruṣaḥ* and *rājapuruṣaḥ* have identical meanings but the difference between these two expressions is that, while the relation between the king and the man is expressed by the genitive ending (*-as*) in the expression *rājñaḥ puruṣaḥ*, the same relation is expressed by the compound form *rājapuruṣaḥ* even after deletion of the genitive suffix. In other words, to determine the meaning of the deleted element expressed by the compound, the Grammarians consider it necessary to postulate *ekārthībhāva-sāmarthya* in the whole sequence *rājapuruṣaḥ*. The test seems to be as follows.

If the sum of the meanings of *x* and *y* is not equal to the meaning of *xy*, then it is necessary to postulate an independent relationship between the meaning of *xy* and the compound *xy*. In other words, if *xy* expresses (*xy*)', which is not merely *x*' + *y*' (where *x*' is the meaning of *x*, and *y*' is the meaning of *y*), then there must be a separate relation between *xy* and (*xy*)'.

This is a very reasonable stand on the part of the Grammarians, and, in fact, this criterion decides and justifies a compound entry in any dictionary, too. But the real question is: if it is possible to show that *xy* expresses *x*' + *y*', is there any reason why one should attempt to postulate an extra relationship since it would be unnecessary and hence redundant? In other words, if *rāja-(x)*, in the compound *rājapuruṣa (xy)*, can express *rājasambandhin (x')*, and if *puruṣa-(y)* expresses *puruṣa* 'man' (*y*'), and if *rājapuruṣaḥ (xy)* conveys *rājasambandhi puruṣaḥ (x' + y')*, it is clear that *xy* expresses *x*' + *y*'. In that case, it is a matter of logical parsimony (*lāghava*) on the part of the Naiyāyikas, who reject the proposal of the Grammarians.

But the question still remains unanswered: How can the element *rāja-* express *rājasambandhin*? The Naiyāyikas' answer is very simple. They accept two relations between a linguistic element and its meaning, namely, *saṃketa* or *śakti* 'primary relation', and *lakṣaṇā* 'secondary relation'.[7] Thus, by *lakṣaṇā* one can obtain the meaning of *rāja-* as *rājasambandhin*. Of course, one can challenge the acceptance of *lakṣaṇā* itself. Needless to say, the Naiyāyikas have met that challenge also. But for want of space I will not go into that now. I shall present the Naiyāyikas' position on *lakṣaṇā* on another occasion.

I would like to point out in this connection that the rejection of *ekārthībhāva* by the Naiyāyikas is based on an epistemological and logical point of view. The questions of whether the paraphrasing of the expression *sāmarthya* as *ekārthībhāva* and *vyapekṣā* is right or wrong, and whether the rule *samarthaḥ padavidhiḥ* (P.2.1.1) is an *adhikāra sūtra* or a *paribhāṣā*, are not examined here.

Finally, I would like to point out that the entire dialogue between the Grammarians and the Naiyāyikas is based upon certain fixed assumptions. One is the maxim *ananya-labhyaḥ śabdārthaḥ*, which decides what could be considered as the expressed meaning of a morpheme. According to this maxim, the expressed meaning of a morpheme is 'that which is not obtained in any other way'.

Furthermore, a *padārtha* is defined by the Navya Naiyāyikas as *vṛtyā pada-pratipādya eva padārthaḥ ity abhidhīyate*, and *vṛtti* stands for *saṃketa* and *lakṣaṇā* both. Naturally, *rājasambandhin* obtained from the word *rāja-* by *lakṣaṇā* is a *padārtha*.

Another assumption is the correspondence between meanings known from compounded expressions and uncompounded ones such as *rājapuruṣa* and *rājñaḥ puruṣaḥ*. Here the Grammarians apparently have assumed that the structure of the verbal understanding arising from a compound should match that of the underlying uncompounded phrase. The Naiyāyikas point out, in rebuttal, that there are no grounds for generalizing this assumption universally. The qualifier-qualificand structure (*viśeṣya-viśeṣaṇabhāva*) may vary from case to case. Nevertheless, the total meaning intended by the speaker would remain the same.

Other, similar assumptions are made by the Grammarians, some of them technical and others analytical, for example, the *kāryakāraṇabhāva* and the theory of the root meaning being the prime qualificand in verbal understanding (*dhātv-artha-mukhya-viśeṣyaka-śābda-bodhaḥ*). Such assumptions of a particular school of thought impose restrictions on its line of argument. The Naiyāyikas, as is demonstrated in part II, have questioned some of these assumptions and have shown that they need review.[9] An impartial judgment is required to help us decide which line of thought should be pursued.[10]

Notes

1. Kaiyata defines it as *yatra padāni upasarjanībhūta-svārthāni nivṛtta-svārthāni vā pradhānārthopādānāt vyarthāni arthāntarābhidhāyīni vā sa ekārthībhāvaḥ.* In other words, *ekārthībhāva* is that (process) in which the constituent words (of a compound) have their meanings either subordinated or lost, and have either become redundant, by adopting a (different) primary sense, or convey a sense other than their own sense. For a better paraphrase, see S. D. Joshi's English translation of Patañjali's *Vyākaraṇa Mahābhāṣya (Samarthāhnika)* (Pune: University of Poona, 1968), pp. 8-9. To be precise, *ekārthībhāva* can be defined as *viśeṣya-viśeṣana-bhāvāvagāhy-ekopasthiti-janakatvam* (*Nyāyakośa*, by Bhīmācārya Jhaḷkīkar, Bombay Sanskrit Series, No. 49 [Bombay: 1893. Third ed., 1928], p. 71), that is, "being the producer of a remembrance in which the meanings of a complex formation appear as qualifier and qualified."
2. Kaiyata's definition of *vyapekṣā* is *parasparākāṅkṣā-rūpā vyapekṣā*, that is, *vyapekṣā* is of the form of mutual expectancy (between two words conveying their meaning separately). To be exact, *vyapekṣā* can be defined as *paraspara-nirūpya-nirūpaka-bhāvāpanna-viṣayatā-prayojakatve sati ekārthopasthityā janakatvam* (*Nyāyakośa*, p. 971), that is, "being the prompter of the *viṣayatā*s, which are mutual describers of each other, and at the same time not being the producer of the remembrance of a single integrated meaning."

3. I have benefitted immensely from the English translation of the *Samarthāhnika* of Patañjali's *Mahābhāṣya* (on P.2.1.1) by Professor S. D. Joshi (Pune: C.A.S.S., University of Poona, 1968).
4. Cf. Pāṇini 5.4.92 (*gor ataddhitaluki*).
5. A *prātipadika* is defined as *arthavad adhātur apratyayaḥ prātipadikam* (P.1.2.45).
6. *Ekaprasaratā-bhaṅga* is a fault. It has two meanings: (1) *vākyabheda*, and (2) change of sequence in the understanding of the predicate and the predicated. Thus, the sentence *vaṣaṭ-kartuḥ prathama-bhakṣaḥ* should be interpreted as (1) 'the *hotṛ* should eat *camasa*', and (2) 'he should eat first'. This is a fault of *vākyabheda*. According to the second interpretation of the fault, from the sequence *prathama bhakṣa*, the knowledge of the *vidheya* (namely, of *prāthamya*) arises first; that of *uddeśya* (namely, *bhakṣa*) arises later. Hence, a fault. See *Arthasaṃgraha* (Marathi translation), by S. M. Paranjape (Bombay: Nirnayasagara Press, 1927), p. 194.
7. *Saṅketo lakṣaṇā ca arthe padavṛttiḥ*, *Śaktivāda*, by Gadādhara, with commentary, *Ādarśa*, by Sudarśanācārya Śāstrī (Bombay: Śrī Veṅkaṭeśvara Press, 1923), p. 1.
8. *Śaktivāda*, p. 2.
9. The position of other types of complex formations, such as primary derivatives, secondary derivatives, denominatives, etc., has not been analyzed here.
10. I am indebted to my guru, Pandit T. S. Srinivasa Sastri, for inspiring this paper.

PARTS OF SPEECH IN PĀṆINI

Dinabandhu Kar

Parts of speech deal with the division of words into certain classes such as substantives, adjectives, pronouns, adverbs, and verbs. Works on grammar often give definitions of these classes but it is not always clear whether this division of words into various groups is based on considerations of form, meaning, or syntactic function.

Pāṇini knew this illogical nature of parts of speech, so he does not go deeply into their precise nature in his grammar. He divides words (*pada*) into two classes, *subantas*, those which end in case-inflections, and *tiṅantas*, those which end in personal endings. *Subanta* words, on formal consideration, can be further subdivided into two groups, *avyayas*, those which are indeclinables, and *an-avyayas*, those which are not indeclinables. Indeclinables are subdivided into two groups, *svarādi* and *nipātas*. *Nipāta*, in its turn, consists of *cādi*, *upasargas*, *gatis*, and *karmapravacanīyas*. Under this formal description, a particular item can belong to more than one subcategory. For instance, *anu* in *anu-gacchati* is called *pada* as it takes hypothetical case-ending *su*, which is subsequently deleted according to P.2.4.82. Thus, it is a *subanta*. Again, it is an *avyaya* as it comes under *nipātas* according to P.1.1.37.

It is an *upasarga* as it is enumerated in the *prādi gaṇa* and is connected with the verb *gacchati* according to P.1.4.59. It is also called *gati* according to P.1.4.60. Semantically, it is called *asattvavacana* as it refers to abstract meaning. Formally, it does not vary in number, gender, or case.

Tiṅanta words denote action and can be subdivided into three classes under syntactic considerations. These divisions are *kartari*, *karmaṇi*, and *bhāve* (P.3.4.69). Verbs that denote active sense belong to the first group, while those conveying passive sense belong to the second category. Intransitive verbs denote *bhāva* 'state' in impersonal passive.

All of this concerns formal classification. The reason for leaning heavily on formal considerations is that meaning, though most important, is also the most difficult category to deal with satisfactorily in any system. So Pāṇini, realizing this inherent difficulty, avoids as far as possible the grouping of words on purely semantic grounds for his grammatical theory. The classification of formal categories is theoretical in his system but the semantic categories in it are considered primitive. Hence, though these semantic categories are not defined in his grammar, they are taken as the basis on which the system of formal classification is built.

Semantic definitions of parts of speech presuppose the possibility of identifying entities, qualities, actions, states, or processes. Pāṇini took all of them into consideration while writing his grammar because he could not deal with semantic categories without the assumption of entities, qualities, etc., as they exist in the external world. The external world consists of a number of these individual objects, class entities, states, qualities, and processes, and language is meant to represent them in one way or another in communication. Language must establish ways and means to represent these various factors through its vocabulary, which is, of course, limited compared to the actual entities of the outside world. Therefore, some sort of hierarchical relationship should be assumed among these entities so that basic and secondary semantic features can be established, features that will later be expressed by the vocables of the language concerned. Consequent upon this stand, the *Aṣṭādhyāyī* provides the following classifications.

(i) Dravyavacana or Ekaśeṣa

These terms are taken to stand for such first-order entities as individualized objects, things, or persons. For instance, the word *gauḥ* 'cow' in the expression *gauḥ carati* 'the cow is grazing', or *gandhaḥ* 'smell' in the expression *tīvraḥ gandhaḥ* 'this strong smell', are *dravyavacana* terms, as they stand for individualized objects to which qualities can be ascribed. They do not refer to abstract entities. Pāṇini prescribes the *ekaśeṣa* operation in connection with these *dravyavacana* words.

(ii) Jātivacana

Jātivacana terms refer to the distinction between refer ence to individual object and class entities in general.

They are common nouns that stand for objects in general and refer to entities divested of individual characteristics. Thus *gauḥ* 'cow' will be considered a *jātivacana* word when it is applied to any cow, whether black, white, or variegated. From the grammatical point of view, Pāṇini uses the term *jāti* for specific operations that are not applicable to proper names. Words of this variety refer to first-order entities because, in this case also, they describe concrete things.

(iii) Bhāvavacana vs. Kriyāvacana

Bhāvavacana words refer to states, whereas *kriyāvacana* or *karmavacana* words refer to process or happening. This distinction is also applicable in the case of verbs. For instance, *gotvam*[1] refers to a state, whereas *brāhmaṇyam* refers to a process or happening associated with *Brāhmaṇa* 'a brahmin'. Similarly, the verb *asti* refers to a state, whereas *karoti* refers to a process. Words of these types stand for second-order entities that are slightly more abstract than first-order entities because, though they are connected with concrete objects, they are not as tangible as the objects with which they are connected.

There is no word for "noun class" in the *Aṣṭādhyāyī* but entities belonging to the first and second orders may be roughly called nouns. The term *viśeṣya*, which some think is equivalent to *noun*, is actually not equivalent.[2] Pāṇini does not take the help of this class in describing grammatical procedures.

(iv) Guṇavacana

The term *guṇavacana* stands for modifiers of the *dravya vacana* class. Patañjali calls them *guṇopasarjana dravya* 'substance to which qualities are subordinated'. They can be called, roughly, qualitative adjectives. Some can function semantically as adverbs also. For example, in *uccaiḥ paṭhati* 'reads loudly', *ucca* 'high' is an adverb, whereas in *uccaiḥ gṛhāṇi* 'high mansions', it is an adjective. These *guṇavacana* words describe qualities of nouns and when they are adverbially used they modify an action. But there is no evidence to show that Pāṇini meant the term *guṇavacana* to include adverbs.

(v) Sarvanāman

Words of this class are not semantically defined in Pāṇini's system. Scrutiny of *sarvādi gaṇa*, which is called *sarvanāman* in the *Aṣṭādhyāyī*, leads us to the conclusion that these words are either determiners or qualifiers. The demonstrative pronouns *saḥ, yaḥ, ayaṃ,* etc., determine their reference to be definite, whereas pronouns like *sarva, viśva, kati,* etc., are quantifiers as they determine the size of the reference in question. The personal pronouns *yuṣmad, asmad,* and *tad* determine the person of the verb as speaker, spoken to, or spoken about. These pronominal-class terms function either as *guṇavacana* words or as *dravyavacana* words.

(vi) Saṃkhyā

Saṃkhyā 'numerals' are regarded as classifiers and they indicate the number of entities being referred to. Words like *eka* 'one', *dvi* 'two', and *bahu* 'many' are singularizing, dualizing, and pluralizing classifiers. Pāṇini has indirectly referred to their semantic features by such rules as *saṃkhyāyāḥ guṇasya nimāne mayaṭ* (P.5.2.47).

(vii) Adverbs

Adverbs have no corresponding term in the *Aṣṭādhyāyī*. Pāṇini regards them as *avyaya*s and usually lists them in the *svarādi* class. They also include adverbial compounds treated in the *avyayībhāva* compound section. *Kr̥t* adverbs and *taddhita* adverbs are also treated as *avyaya*s (P.1.1.38-41). Not a single, specific, semantic feature can be ascribed to all of them. There are adverbs of degree such as *atyantam* and *adhikam*; adverbs of manner such as *tūṣṇīm* and *ciram*; adverbs of time such as *kadā, yadā,* and *tadā*; and adverbs of place such as *yatra, tatra,* and *kutra.* The semantic function of adverbs is evaluation of action. So, in a sense, they are *guṇavacana* words, as they describe the qualities of verbal action. They are *asattvavacana* because they do not speak about the features of an observable entity. Since *kriyā* is a process, it cannot be observed as a whole.

*Nipāta*s are also called *asattvavacana* (P.1.4.57). Meaning denoted by them cannot be said to occur as a participant in action. All the preverbs, prepositions and postpositions come under *nipāta*. *Avyaya* is a wider term, which includes all *nipātas* and items found in the *svarādi* list.

To conclude this discussion, there are basically two classes of parts of speech, the "major" and the "minor," in Pāṇini's system. The major class includes words that refer to the first- or second-order entities. The characteristic feature of the major class is that the items included under it enter into syntactical relations with verbs. This class includes substantives, adjectives, pronouns, etc. The minor class constitutes indeclinables such as adverbs mentioned in the *svarādi* list, particles (*cādi*), preverbs (*upasargas*), prepositions (*gatis*) and postpositions (*karmapravacanīyas*). The distinguishing feature of this class is that items included in it are *asattvavacanas* since they do not refer to concrete objects.

Another interesting feature of both classes is that items in the major class are always inflected words, whereas items in the minor class are not inflected forms in Pāṇini's system of description. Thus, we see a sort of correspondence between the syntactic and semantic functions of items described by Pāṇini. This correspondence is found in a majority of cases. Therefore, it will not be an exaggeration to assert that Pāṇini, in his description of parts of speech, followed a consistent plan and accordingly used these semantic classes for an adequate description of grammatical facts.

Notes

1. For a detailed discussion, see Dinabandhu Kar, "Semantic Basis of the *Aṣṭādhyāyī*," Ph.D. diss., University of Poona, 1980, 112-22.
2. Ibid., 132.

ECONOMY AND THE CONSTRUCTION OF THE ŚIVASŪTRAS

Paul Kiparsky

[1]

1.	a	i	u			Ṇ
2.				ṛ	ḷ	K
3.		e	o			Ṅ
4.		ai	au			C
5.	h	y	v	r		Ṭ
6.					l	Ṇ
7.	ñ	m	ṅ	ṇ	n	M
8.	jh	bh				Ñ
9.			gh	ḍh	dh	Ṣ
10.	j	b	g	ḍ	d	Ś
11.	kh	ph	ch	ṭh	th	
			c	ṭ	t	V
12.	k	p				Y
13.		ś	ṣ	s		R
14.	h					L

This is Pāṇini's *akṣarasamāmnāya*, the enumeration and grouping of the sounds of Sanskrit popularly called the *Śivasūtras* (or *Maheśvarasūtras*). The *Śivasūtras* form an indispensable part of the grammar, and their structure is thoroughly intertwined with, and determined by, that of the *Aṣṭādhyāyī*. Abbreviations (*pratyāhāras*) are defined on the *Śivasūtras* and other similarly organized lists by the convention that if x_q is followed in the list by the marker Q, then x_pQ denotes the set of elements x_p, x_{p+1}, . . . x_q. The phonological classes defined in this way are referred to in hundreds of rules in the *Aṣṭādhyāyī*.

Both traditional and modern discussions of the *Śivasūtras* recognize that their structure is motivated in large part by the fundamental principle of economy (simplicity, *lāghava*), which governs Pāṇini's entire grammatical system. The reasoning from economy goes like this. To be grouped together in a *pratyāhāra*, sounds must make up a continuous segment of the list. Economy requires making the list as short as possible, which means avoiding repetitions of sounds, and using as few markers as possible. Consequently, if class A properly includes class B, the elements shared with B should be listed last in A; the marker that follows can then be used to form *pratyāhāras* for both A and B. In this way the economy principle, by selecting the shortest grammar, determines both the ordering of sounds and the placement of markers among them.

For example, the order of simple vowels at the beginning of the *Śivasūtras* (see the first two rows of [1]) is constrained by the fact that the grammar must refer to the following groupings of them:

[2] 1. *a, i, u, r̥, l̥* (= *aK*)[1]
2. *i, u, r̥, l̥* (= *iK*)[2]

3. *u, r̥, (l̥)* (= *uK*)[3]
4. *a, i, u* (= *aṆ*)[4]

which, by the reasoning of the preceding paragraph, requires the partial ordering

[3] *a* < *i* < *u* < *r̥*, *l̥*

and markers after *u* and after the liquids.

Much of the structure of the *Śivasūtras* has been successfully explained by this kind of reasoning from economy (Faddegon 1929, Thieme 1935, Staal 1962, Cardona 1969). But there remains a substantial residue where economy is at first sight not at stake. For example, the order of *r̥* and *l̥* in row 2 could be reversed without complicating the grammar because every *pratyāhāra* needed in the grammar that includes one of them can also include the other. The same is true of *e* and *o* in the next row.[5] The systematic character of Pāṇini's grammar makes it likely that there is a rational basis for the order of these elements as well--but what?

Staal (1962) and Cardona (1969) have each suggested such a rational basis for the cases that are not explained by economy. Staal's idea is that among alternative, equally simple orderings, that of the previous set of homorganic elements is given preference.[6] Though Staal does not actually discuss the vowels, his proposal would readily explain the order *e*, *o* as continuing the order *i*, *u* of the first row.

Cardona argues instead that some aspects of the *Śivasūtras* reflect the strictly phonetic arrangement of the

Prātiśākhyas that served Pāṇini as a starting point. This was modified as necessary by inserting markers into it and by reordering its elements, and otherwise retained. On this view, the *Śivasūtras*' order *e, o* would simply reflect the order of the traditional listing *e, ai, o, au.* So Cardona, too, appeals to a notion of continuity, only his continuity is historical rather than structural and system-internal, as Staal's is.

However, neither of these accounts, or even the two of them together, can be the whole story. For example, the order of *r̥* and *l̥* in row 2 cannot be carried over from previous homorganic sounds in the list, for there are none. And it cannot be carried over from the *Prātiśākhyas*' sound lists, because they did not include *l̥*.[7]

In this paper I argue that the structure of the *Śivasūtras* follows entirely from the principles used in the construction of Pāṇini's grammar. This is because the principle of economy and the logic of the special case and the general case (*sāmānya / viśeṣa*) applies in the construction of the metalanguage as well as in the formulation of the grammatical rules. As we have seen, the groupings of sounds needed for the grammar induce a set of partial ordering constraints on their listing. We will now show that these ordering constraints, when formulated in accordance with Pāṇinian principles of economy and generalization, have as their unique solution the *Śivasūtras*.

In order to develop this idea, we must spell out exactly how economy figures in Pāṇini's system and how it is related to generalization.

Cardona (1969, 28, 30, 41) argues that economy for Pāṇini is "consequent on generalization": "the analysis of linguistic materials in order to formulate generalized rules is Pāṇini's way of achieving economy (*lāghava*)." I think this view--which I thoughtlessly endorsed in Kiparsky (1979, 227)--is not correct. It is certainly not true that Pāṇini avoids prolixity only where generalization is at stake.[8] The rules of the *Aṣṭādhyāyī* systematically maximize economy, whether or not this leads to generalization in any given case. *Anuvṛtti* often ranges over entirely disparate rules, in which case it achieves economy but not generalization (Staal 1970, 503). Indeed, some means of concision systematically employed in the grammar are *never* "consequent on generalization." For example, whenever Pāṇini can compress phrases into compounds, he invariably does so, even though this achieves nothing beyond the saving of syllables. This is true even for compounds that are not derived from analytic expressions but are simply alternative expressions of the same semantic content, namely *dvandva*s and *bahuvrīhi*s. The vowels of a given quality are invariably denoted by their short representative, even though by Pāṇini's *sāvarṇya* convention (1.1.69) the long one would have done as well. S. D. Joshi (*voce*) has brought to my attention the striking fact that Pāṇini even tends to order the words in a rule in such a way that the number of syllables in it will be minimized by sandhi.[9]

Still, this does not mean that Pāṇini is after economy for its own sake. The reverse of Cardona's formulation does hold: *economy is Pāṇini's way of achieving generalization.* More precisely, the maximization of economy is what ensures that the generalizations will emerge in the grammar. This can be concluded from the fact that Pāṇini introduces abbreviatory conventions into his metalanguage if, and *only* if, they make it possible to bring out significant generalizations in the grammar. So the theoretical goal of generalization is implemented by seeking the most economical description possible in the framework of an appropriately constructed metalanguage of grammatical description. The economy requirement works "blindly" in the service of this global objective, and is not expected to yield generalizations in each local instance.

In consequence of its purely formal nature, the economy principle typically leads to *vacuous overgeneralization.* Simplification is mandatory even if it means extending the conditions of a rule to cases that can never arise. But (and equally importantly) overgeneralized formulations are *only* chosen where economy requires it. Among a set of equally simple formulations covering all the cases, Pāṇini chooses the most restrictive one. There are, then, two principles at work, which, tending in opposite directions, fix the form of the grammar: the dominant principle that the most economical formulation is preferred, and the subsidiary principle that among equally simple formulations the most restrictive is preferred.

These principles govern all aspects of the system, including the use of *pratyāhāras*. Some examples follow.

Rule 8.4.53 [4] illustrates overgeneralization enforced by economy. Since *h* does not cluster with stops, the more restrictive *jhaR* (stops and fricatives) could have been used instead of *jhaL* (stops, fricatives, and *h*) in rule 8.4.53.

Economy, however, forces *jhaL* because it is carried over by *anuvṛtti* into the next rule, 8.4.54 [5], where it is absolutely necessary:

[4] 8.4.53 *jhalāṃ jaś jhaśi* 'obstruents (*jhaL*) are replaced by voiced unaspirated stops (*jaŚ*) before voiced stops (*jhaŚ*)'

[5] 8.4.54 *abhyāse car ca* (53 *jhalāṃ jaś*) 'in reduplication, (obstruents) are replaced by (voiced unaspirated stops) and by voiceless unaspirated segments (*caR*)'

Similarly, the class *yaṆ* (*y*, *v*, *r*, *l*) is specified as the prevocalic replacement of the single root *iṆ* 'go' in 6.4.81 *iṇo yaṇ*, where obviously the more specific *y* would have done equally well. The reason is that *yaṆ* is continued into the more general rules that follow (6.4.82 through 6.4.87), where its extra coverage becomes functional. Examples of this type can easily be multiplied.[10]

Among equally economical formulations, the most restrictive is chosen. For example,

[6] 7.4.61 *śarpūrvāḥ khayaḥ* (60 *śeṣaḥ*) 'unvoiced stops (*khaY*) after fricatives *śaR* remain'

which states that fricative + stop clusters are exceptions to the general rule deleting all but the first consonant in reduplication, could have been vacuously generalized to apply after the more inclusive set of sounds *śaL* (*ś*, *ṣ*, *s*, *h*) rather than after just the fricatives, for *h* never clusters with stops. Pāṇini has chosen the more specific formulation of the rule, which only extends to the actually occurring cases. Similarly,

[7] 8.3.33 *maya uño vo vā* (32 *aci*) '*uÑ* is optionally replaced by *v* between *m, ṅ, ṇ, n* (*maY*) and a vowel or diphthong (*aC*)'

specifies *maY*, which includes *m, ṅ, ṇ, n* rather than *ñaY* (*ñ, m, ṅ, ṇ, n*), even though the overgeneralization would have been harmless, as *ñ* does not occur in word-final position.[11]

All these principles hold equally well for the construction of the metalanguage. Technical terms are never introduced solely for brevity's sake. Their purpose is rather to allow the rules of the grammar to express significant generalizations. But, if Pāṇini needs to coin a new word for this purpose anyway, he makes it maximally short, usually no more than a mora (cf. such cover terms as *bha, ghu, ghi, ṭi* and abstract underlying forms of the type *yu, vu, jhi, v, l, cli*). And nothing in the metalanguage is motivated solely for the purpose of avoiding vacuous overgeneralization. Specifically, no markers in the *Śivasūtras* are introduced merely to avoid overgeneral *pratyāhāras*. For example, *uK* in 7.2.11 includes *u, r̥, l̥* but since there are no roots in *l̥* the last case never arises. A *pratyāhāra* that excludes it, however, would require a new marker and in the absence of positive motivation such a marker is not put in.

Given the subgroupings that the grammar must refer to, these considerations alone dictate the organization of the *Śivasūtras*. This will now be shown.

The complex vowels and diphthongs *e, o, ai, au* must be placed immediately after the simple vowels because of the groupings

[8] 1. *a, i, u, r̥, l̥, e, o, ai, au* (= *aC*)[12]
2. *i, u, r̥, l̥, e, o, ai, au* (= *iC*)[13]
3. *e, o, ai, au* (= *eC*)[14]
4. *ai, au* (= *aiC*)[15]
5. *e, o* (= *eṄ*)[16]

The semivowels must be grouped with the vowels into

[9] 1. *y, v, r, l* (= *yaṆ*)[17]
2. *a, i, u, r̥, l̥, e, o, ai, au, h, y, v, r, l* (= *aṆ*)[18]
3. *i, u, r̥, l̥, e, o, ai, au, h, y, v, r, l* (= *iṆ*)[19]
4. *a, i, u, r̥, l̥, e, o, ai, au, h, y, v, r* (= *aṬ*)[20]

and with the other consonants into

[10] 1. *h, y, v, r, l* plus consonants (= *haL*)[21]
2. *y, v, r, l* plus consonants (= *yaR*)[22]
3. *v, r, l* plus consonants (= *vaL*)[23]
4. *r, l* plus consonants (= *raL*)[24]

Together, [8], [9], and [10] yield, in addition to confirmation for *a* < *i* in [3], the new ordering constraints

[11] 1. *h* ‹ *y* ‹ *v* ‹ *r* ‹ *l*
2. simple vowels < complex vowels, diphthongs < semivowels

So far, this adds up to:

[12] 1. The simple vowels must be listed together.
2. The complex vowels (*e*, *o*) must be listed together.
3. The diphthongs (*ai*, *au*) must be listed together.
4. The semivowels must be listed together.
5. Simple vowels, complex vowels, diphthongs, and semivowels must be listed together.
6. The order of the series must be: simple vowels < complex vowels, diphthongs < semivowels.
7. Within the vowels, the order must be: *a* < *i* < *u* < *r̥*, *l̥*.
8. Within the semivowels, the order must be: *h* ‹ *y* ‹ *v* ‹ *r* ‹ *l*.

Note that the order within both vowels and semivowels in [12-7, 12-8] coincides almost completely with the "sonority hierarchy" assumed by modern phonologists and phoneticians. Although no such hierarchy was to my knowledge ever explicitly proposed in India, it emerges here as a by-product, as it were, of Pāṇini's purely distributional analysis of Sanskrit phonology.

An equally remarkable outcome is that, in terms of place of articulation, the ordering of vowels in [12-7] is fully consistent with the ordering of the corresponding semivowels in [12-8]. In this case, of course, Pāṇini must have been well aware of the phonetic classification behind the correspondence. However, the fact that it emerges from the distributional analysis is still significant. It shows that, even if Pāṇini had begun with altogether different assumptions, or with none at all, he would still have come up with a parallel arrangement of vowels and semivowels.

Because the ordering constraints [3, 11-1] are subjected to the same logic of generalization as everything else in the system, they are combined and generalized to:[25]

[13] velars/pharyngeals < palatals < labials < retroflexes < dentals

The generalized ordering constraint [13] fixes the so far indeterminate order of the syllabic liquids *r̥*, *l̥*, the complex vowels *e*, *o*, and the diphthongs *ai*, *au*.

The ordering of *e*, *o* before *ai*, *au* is dictated by simplicity because it allows a shorter *pratyāhāra* for the class *e*, *o*, *ai*, *au*, viz. *eC* (rather than **aiṄ*).

This establishes the first six *Śivasūtras* in full:

[14]

a	i	u			Ṇ
			ṛ	ḷ	K
	e	o			Ṅ
	ai	au			C
h	y	v	r		Ṭ
				l	Ṇ

The groupings in [15] require, by the same reasoning as above, that the nasals and voiced stops come next in that order. They are demarcated by *M*, *Ś*, respectively, giving the *pratyāhāra*s

[15]
1. vowels, diphthongs, semivowels, nasals, voiced stops *(aŚ)*[26]
2. semivowels, nasals, voiced stops *(haŚ)*[27]
3. *v*, *r*, *l*, nasals, voiced stops *(vaŚ)*[28]
4. voiced stops *jhaŚ*
5. vowels, diphthongs, semivowels, nasals *(aM)*[29]
6. *y*, *v*, *r*, *l*, nasals *(yaM)*[30]

Notice that the previously seen subdivisions of the semivowels reappear in *vaŚ* and *yaM*, reaffirming [11] and the generalized [13].

The voiceless stops and the fricatives must follow, in that order, with the marker *Y* after the former, to give the groupings

[16]
1. *y*, *v*, *r*, *l*, nasals, voiced stops, voiceless stops *(yaY)*[31]
2. nasals, voiced stops, voiceless stops *(maY)*[32]

3. voiced stops, voiceless stops *(jhaY)*[33]
4. voiceless stops *(khaY)*[34]

and with the marker *R* after the latter, to give

[17] 1. *y, v, r, l,* nasals, voiced stops, voiceless stops, fricatives *(yaR)*[35]
2. voiced stops, voiceless stops, fricatives *(jhaR)*[36]
3. voiceless stops, fricatives *(khaR)*[37]
4. fricatives *(śaR)*[38]

Within the voiceless stops, aspirated stops precede unaspirated stops in order to allow the latter to be grouped with the fricatives *(caR)*.[39] The same order is motivated in the voiced stops by the fact that *bh* patterns with the sonorants *(yaÑ)*, on which see below.

The consonant *h*, already listed as the first of the semivowels, must be listed a second time at the end of the *Śivasūtras* because it must also be included in two sets of groups: among the obstruents *(haL)* and the fricatives *(śaL)*, as well as in the classes *vaL* and *raL* mentioned above. This is the only repetition necessary in the system.

In sum, the order of the series must be

[18] nasals < voiced aspirates < voiced unaspirates < voiceless aspirates < voiceless unaspirates < fricatives < *h*

If we now arrange the series of consonants according to [18], put the consonants within each series according to place of articulation according to [13], and add *pratyāhāras* where needed, we get

[19]						
	ṅ	ñ	m	ṇ	n	M
	gh	jh	bh	ḍh	dh	Ṣ
	g	j	b	ḍ	d	Ś
	kh	ch	ph	ṭh	th	
	k	c	p	ṭ	t	V
			ś	ṣ	s	R

from which the arrangement of the actual *Śivasūtras* can be derived by the minimal local modifications needed for consonantal *pratyāhāras* as follows.

The three nasals *ṅ*, *ṇ*, *n* must be grouped together as a class, which figures in

[20] 8.3.32 *ṅamo hrasvād aci ṅamuṇ nityam* 'after a *pada* ending in *ṅam* preceded by a short vowel and followed by a vowel or diphthong *(aC)*, [the initial augment] *ṅam* is obligatorily inserted'

Theoretically, the palatal nasal *ñ* could be included in *ṅaM*, too, because palatals cannot occur at the end of a *pada*, as noted at [7]. Hence there are two possible specific (*viśeṣa*) ordering constraints for nasals that could override the general (*sāmānya*) ordering constraint [13]:

[21] 1. ñ, m < ṅ
2. m < ṅ, ñ

These alternatives can be visualized as rearrangements of [13] by moving either the velar to the right after the labial or the labial leftward to the beginning of its row. As far as the rules of the grammar are concerned, there is no difference in simplicity between the two; both differ from the general place-ordering constraint [13] in the minimal possible way.

Pāṇini's choice of [21-1] over [21-2] is justified by two independent considerations involving, respectively, the subsidiary principle and the dominant principle stated above. The first is that vacuous overgeneralization is avoided. On the second alternative, *ṅaM* would include not only *ṅ*, *ṇ*, *n* but vacuously also *ñ*. Therefore, the first, which is equally simple but allows a more restrictive formulation, is preferred.

The second reason for choosing [21-1] is that it generalizes to both the aspirated and unaspirated series of voiced stops in a desirable way. First, the order corresponding to [21-1] yields classes that exclude the palatal stops required for the "Grassmann's Law" alternations (*budh-s* --> *bhut-s*), in which *jh*, *j* do not participate (*jabh-s* --> *jap-s*) (8.2.37). If [21-1] is extended to nasals, these classes can be designated as *baś*, *bhaṣ*.[40] Doing this by [21-1] (rather than, for example, simply placing the palatals in front) has the additional advantage of restricting *yaÑ*. This *pratyāhāra*, which defines the environment for stem-final lengthening (7.3.101, 102), must cover *n, m, y, bh* but could be allowed to include vacuously *gh* (and, indeed, all the voiced aspirates except *dh*). By generalizing [21-1] from nasals to the voiced aspirates, the vacuous overgeneralization is reduced to the necessary minimum (*jh*).

So the optimal special (*viśeṣa*) ordering constraint, superseding the general [13], is

[22] palatals < labials < velars
(for voiced consonants)

Could [22] be generalized even further, to *all* the consonants? The answer is no. In the two voiceless stop series, the coronal consonants *ch, ṭh, th, c, ṭ, t* must be grouped together. This requires the special ordering

[23] kh, ph < ch, ṭh, th, c, ṭ, t < k, p

which, with the applicable cases of the general constraints [13] and [18] within each subgroup, yields Pāṇini's ordering of these series. Insertion of the marker *V* after the coronals allows them to be grouped as *chaV* (8.3.7).

Putting all this together, we get

[24]	7.	ñ	m	ṅ	ṇ	n	M
	8.	jh	bh				Ñ
	9.			gh	ḍh	dh	Ṣ
	10.	j	b	g	ḍ	d	Ś
	11.	kh	ph	ch	ṭh	th	
				c	ṭ	t	V

12.	k	p			Y
13.		ś	ṣ	s	R
14.	h				L

which completes the construction of the *Śivasūtras*.

Having seen how the *Śivasūtras*' ordering of the consonants follows from Pāṇinian principles of generalization, we can compare it to Cardona's alternative account. This involves starting with the *Prātiśākhyas*' listing of consonants by place of articulation going from the back of the mouth to the front:

[25]	ṅ	ñ	ṇ	n	m

To get from [25] to the first row in [24] we would then have to assume that two sounds, *m* and *ñ*, were moved to the left to create the actual *Śivasūtra* grouping. *But there was no need to move the latter.* Simply moving *m* to the head of the list, and leaving *ñ* in place, would have been sufficient, for the reasons explained above.

A similar problem would arise for the voiced stops if we assume, with Cardona, that the *Śivasūtras* were made by minimally reordering an original

[26]	gh	jh	ḍh	dh	bh
	g	j	ḍ	d	b

The *pratyāhāra yaÑ* must include *bh* and exclude *dh*, and *gh*, *jh*, *ḍh* may or may not be included in it because they don't begin any suffixes of the relevant class. So the minimal change was then merely to shift *bh* to the left of *dh*. Why, then, was it shifted so far to the left? (Our answer is that it is not shifted: in virtue of [13], it is already there.) And, for the voiced unaspirated stops, the question is: why move the labial at all?

I conclude that the assumption that the *Śivasūtra*s have been reordered from an earlier *Prātiśākhya*-type listing does nothing to explain their structure.

By this I do *not* mean that Pāṇini in fact started from scratch in constructing the *Śivasūtra*s. On the contrary, it is virtually certain that he was acquainted with one or more phonetically arranged listings of sounds such as those found in the *Prātiśākhya*s, and it is even quite possible that there were previous *Śivasūtra*-style arrangements that he knew. It is also quite possible that Pāṇini started with one of those earlier arrangements and reordered it. What I do claim is that such earlier works are in no way required to explain the *Śivasūtra*s, and that therefore we cannot make any inferences about Pāṇini's sources for the *Śivasūtra*s from their structure.

An analogy may help to make the point clearer. An examination of Pāṇini's phonological rules shows that many of them are similar to sound changes assumed to have taken place in earlier stages of Sanskrit, and, moreover, that the order in which the rules have to be applied is similar to the relative chronology of the corresponding sound changes. But it would be absurd to conclude from this that Pāṇini based his grammar on a historical phonology of Sanskrit, reordering its rules where necessary. A contemporary generative phonology of a language would have the same property, and if the job were done right it should make no difference whether the author knew anything about the history of the language. Rather, because of an interesting property of language, its synchronic and diachronic analyses are going to be significantly related even if they are arrived at independently. Similarly, the fact that phonetic and phonological works on Sanskrit arrived at closely related classifications of its sounds is the result of a fundamental fact about language itself--that phonetic and phonological features are drawn from the same set--and does not warrant the conclusion that one classification was historically modeled on the other.

It is said that god Śiva revealed these fourteen classes of sounds to Pāṇini to get him started on the *Aṣṭādhyāyī*. We might now want to see a deeper point in this legend. Our conclusions imply that if we did not possess the text of the *Aṣṭādhyāyī*, but merely a pretheoretical description of Sanskrit phonology, the main principles of Pāṇini's grammar could be inferred just from the way the phonemes of Sanskrit are organized in the *Śivasūtras*.

Notes

1. 6.1.101 ff., 6.1.182.
2. 1.1.3, 1.1.48, 1.2.9, 5.1.131, 6.1.77, 6.1.127, 6.3.61, 6.3.121, 6.3.123, 6.3.134, 7.1.73 ff., 8.2.76.
3. 7.2.11, 7.3.51.
4. 1.1.51, 6.3.11, 7.4.13, 8.4.57.
5. Of course, if *e* and *o* were reversed, the *pratyāhāras*

that now begin with *e* would begin with *o*. Since no *pratyāhāra* begins with either *r̥* or *l̥*, no rule would even have to be changed in any way if they were reversed.

6. Notice that unlike the economy principle, this would be specific to the construction of the *Śivasūtras*.
7. Cardona (1969, 38). More compelling examples of this point will be given below.
8. This point has been insightfully discussed by Henry Smith, of Stanford University, in a paper to appear in the *Journal of Indian Philosophy.*
9. Therefore, the maxim *Ardhamātrālāghavena putrotsavaṃ manyante vaiyākaraṇāḥ* 'grammarians value the saving of half a mora like the birth of a son' has more than a grain of truth, and Cardona (1969, 41) is wrong in ridiculing the "mania for *mātralāghava*" as "a property of lesser original Indian grammarians [*sic*]." It is quite natural to have faith in a principle, which, in concert with an appropriately designed metalanguage, reveals deep generalizations in the grammar of Sanskrit.
10. E.g., *jhaY* rather than *jhaŚ* in 8.4.62 because of 8.4.63, and *jhaL* in 8.2.26 because of 8.2.31.
11. The avoidance of vacuous overgeneralization is, however, not observed as rigorously as the economy principle. In particular, *jhaL* (e.g., 1.2.10) and *aC* (e.g., 7.2.89), which are practically synonyms of "consonant" and "vowel," are often overused. Another case is *iṆ* for *iṬ* in 8.3.57.
12. 1.1.10, 1.1.14, 1.1.47, 1.1.57, 1.1.59, 1.1.64, 1.2.27, 1.2.28, 1.3.2, 2.2.34, 2.4.66, 3.1.22, 3.1.62, 3.1.97, 4.1.56, 4.1.89, 4.1.121, 4.1.156, 4.1.170, 4.2.72 ff.,

4.2.109, 4.2.113, 4.3.67, 4.3.72, 4.3.150, 4.4.64, 5.1.39, 5.3.78, 5.4.57, 6.1.62, 6.1.77, 6.1.125, 6.1.134, 6.1.188, 6.1.205, 6.2.83, 6.2.119, 6.2.138, 6.2.190, 6.2.194, 6.3.68, 6.3.74, 6.3.101, 6.3.119, 6.3.135, 6.4.16, 6.4.62, 6.4.63, 6.4.77, 6.4.163, 7.1.61, 7.1.72, 7.1.73, 7.1.97, 7.2.3, 7.2.10, 7.2.61, 7.2.67, 7.2.89, 7.2.100, 7.2.115, 7.2.117, 7.3.72, 7.3.87, 7.4.47, 7.4.54, 8.2.21, 8.2.108, 8.3.32, 8.3.34, 8.3.89, 8.4.12, 8.4.29, 8.4.46, 8.4.49.

13. 6.1.104, 6.3.68.
14. 1.1.48, 6.1.45 ff., 6.1.78, 8.2.108.
15. 1.1.1, 7.3.3, 8.2.106.
16. 1.1.2, 6.1.69, 6.1.94, 6.1.109.
17. 1.1.45, 6.1.77, 6.4.81, 6.4.156.
18. 1.1.51, 6.3.111, 7.4.13 ff., 8.4.57.
19. 1.1.69.
20. 8.3.3, 8.3.9, 8.4.2, 8.4.63.
21. 1.1.7, 1.2.10, 1.2.26, 1.3.3, 3.1.12, 3.1.22, 3.1.83, 3.1.124, 3.2.149, 3.3.121, 6.1.68, 6.1.174, 6.1.179, 6.3.9, 6.3.10, 6.3.59, 6.4.2, 6.4.24, 6.4.49, 6.4.120, 6.4.150, 6.4.161, 7.2.3, 7.2.7, 7.2.85, 7.2.113, 7.3.89, 7.4.60, 7.4.71, 8.2.77, 8.3.3, 8.4.31, 8.4.34, 8.4.66, 8.4.100, 8.4.113.
22. 8.4.45 ff.
23. 6.1.66, 7.2.35.
24. 1.2.26 ff.
25. Within the grammar, the convention holds that vowels and consonants are not homorganic (1.1.10). But such generalizations as [13] are, of course, not part of the grammatical system, and logically prior to it, so they

naturally do not obey its rules (though they are arrived at by the same general form of reasoning as the rest of the system).

26. 8.3.17.
27. 6.1.74.
28. 7.2.8.
29. 8.3.6.
30. 8.4.64.
31. 8.4.58.
32. 8.3.33.
33. 5.4.111, 8.2.10, 8.4.62.
34. 7.4.61, 8.3.6.
35. 8.4.45 ff.
36. 8.4.65.
37. 8.3.15, 8.4.55.
38. 7.4.61, 8.3.28, 8.3.35 ff., 8.3.58, 8.4.49.
39. 1.1.58, 8.4.54 ff.
40. To be precise, *baś* requires this order by economy; *bhaṣ* could in principle include all the aspirates because 1.1.50 *sthāne 'ntaratamaḥ* 'in replacing, the closest [replacement is chosen]' would give the right results. Exclusion of *jh* from it is preferred, however, because it avoids vacuous overgeneralization.

Bibliography

Cardona, George. 1969. "Studies in Indian Grammarians I: The Method of Description Reflected in the Śiva-sūtras." *Transactions of the American Philosophical Society* 59, 1, 3-48.

Faddegon, Barent. 1929. "The Mnemotechnics of Pāṇini's Grammar I: The Śiva-sūtra." *Acta Orientalia* 7, 48-65.

Kiparsky, Paul. 1979. *Pāṇini as a Variationist.* Cambridge and Poona: MIT Press and Poona University Press.

Staal, J. F. 1962. "A Method of Linguistic Description: The Order of Consonants According to Pāṇini." *Language* 38, 1-10.

-------. 1970. Review of Cardona (1970). *Language* 46, 502-7.

Thieme, Paul. 1935. *Pāṇini and the Veda: Studies in the Early History of Linguistic Science in India.* Allahabad: Globe Press.

BHAVĀNANDA ON "WHAT IS KĀRAKA?"

Bimal Krishna Matilal

Professor Shivram Dattatray Joshi has devoted his scholarly activities to interpreting Pāṇini and the Pāṇinīyas. He has critically examined the traditional commentaries and made a significant contribution to the modern study of Sanskrit grammar, Pāṇini, and linguistics. He has also been the source of inspiration for many scholars of younger generations. I admire his critical outlook and penetrating insight into the Pāṇinian tradition and I wish to take this opportunity to add a personal note. I respect Professor Joshi as my *satīrthya.* We both studied at Harvard with Professor Daniel H. H. Ingalls, although at different times. On this occasion, I wish to honor him by contributing to his felicitation volume a brief note on the notion of *kāraka* in Nyāya and grammar, which spans the twin areas of grammar and logic. This is undoubtedly a subject that combines both his interests and mine.

There has been much discussion in recent years about the notion of *kāraka* in the Pāṇinian system of Sanskrit grammar. Modern exponents of Pāṇini's grammar (and it goes without saying that Professor Joshi holds a unique position among them) have revived the old controversy about whether the *kāraka* categories are only "a reflection of case form"

(Whitney 1893; reprinted in Staal 1972, 166) or are "logical or ideational relations between a noun and a verb" (Faddegon 1936, 18). But, in fact, these exponents have gone further in generating controversies regarding the status of *kāraka* categories: are they extralinguistic, "purely" semantic, syntactic, or syntactico-semantic? That a *kāraka* is not what we call a "case" in Latin or western grammar is fairly obvious, hence there is no need to belabor the point. This is true despite the fact that what has been described as case grammar by C. J. Fillmore (1968) is probably very similar to Pāṇini's system. This state of affairs is not surprising for the simple reason that from a distance one tree looks exactly like another but as one draws nearer the distinction becomes clearer. Hence, Cardona is right in emphasizing the need for caution and subtlety in this matter.[1]

I do not wish to repeat the arguments and counterarguments that surround the question of the actual status of the *kāraka* categories. Obviously, they are neither "purely semantic" nor "purely syntactic," as far as Pāṇini's own system of grammar is concerned. The *kāraka*s were introduced, as far as I can see, as an expedient that would facilitate Pāṇini's own description of the Sanskrit language in general, and would, in particular, mediate between the introduction of affixes in words and the representation of certain semantic relations. Cardona says that Pāṇini's *kāraka* classifications "serve as intermediaries between grammatical expressions and their semantics" (1978, 221). What I intend to do, then, is throw some light on other aspects of the problem, deriving my material, and insight, from the writings of the Nyāya system, particularly from an old exponent of the school, Vātsyāyana (350 A.D.), and a new philosopher, Bhavānanda (c. 1570 A.D.).[2] It is by no means clear whether this rather different approach to explaining Pāṇini's section on *kāraka* can in any way resolve part of the old controversy between semantic and syntactic categories. But it is also possible that the issue is entirely counterproductive, for the controversy is heavily dependent upon our ability to draw a sharply fixed and nonarbitrary line between what we call semantics and what we call syntax. Elsewhere I have expressed doubts about this matter on different grounds.[3] The point is not that such a sharp line of demarcation between grammar and syntax, on the one hand, and meaning (or semantics), on the other, cannot be drawn, but that such a line is movable by the particular theories of grammar. Therefore, in one view, we see that *kāraka* categories in general, and the *karma-kāraka* (=object) in particular, are grammatically pertinent (for they regulate particular rules of affixation, affix replacement, and so on) but the subclassification of *karma-kāraka* as 'effected' (*kārya*), 'affected' (*vikārya*), and 'reached' (*prāpya*) is a matter for the domain of semantics. In another view, even this subclassification can be considered syntactically pertinent. However, since Pāṇini's principle concern was to derive and account for grammatical forms that occur within sentences, and the relations among such forms, the former view seems to be more compatible with his system of grammar. The same fact may explain why Pāṇini does not recognize a distinction between agents (*kartṛ*) that are sentient beings and those that are not, and why he classifies both things, a man (Devadatta) and an axe, as agents receiving the same analysis and derivation. On the other hand, expediency prompted Pāṇini to recognize this distinction in rule 1.3.88, which accounts for the active endings there after a causative verb despite the fact that the "pre-causative" primitive root-verb usually has middle endings.

It is also known that Pāṇini and the Pāṇinīyas were *śabdapramāṇakāḥ*, as Patañjali truly emphasizes (and as K. A. Subramania Iyer [1948] more recently argued). This means that we should stress the point that grammar is concerned not with ontology but with what people say, how people speak of things and events. Pāṇini's *kāraka* categories fit so well with this point that we can easily account for such usages as 'the cauldron cooks' (*sthālī pacati*) or 'the sword severs' (*asiś chinatti*). For, although we know that the cauldron is not the *agent* of cooking, as the sword is not the agent of severing, people do speak in this manner. Hence, the grammatical category "agency" must be assigned to such things to account for the role of these words in certain sentences.

Having briefly outlined the Pāṇinian approach to *kāraka* categories, I wish to deal now with the comments of the Nyāya school. The Naiyāyikas, to be sure, were *artha-pramāṇakāḥ*. In other words, they were interested in things, facts, and events, and not particularly interested in how people speak about them. They were concerned with ontology and epistemic questions, although they preferred to derive their insights into such matters through analysis of how people speak about them. Vātsyāyana got involved in the question of *kāraka* while trying to answer the Mādhyamika criticism of the notion of the *pramāṇa-prameya-pramiti-*

pramātṛ distinction, which forms the basis of their *pramāṇa* epistemology. To put it simply, the Mādhyamika argued that the *pramāṇa-prameya* distinction is arbitrary since the same item, object, or thing, can be an instrument for knowledge (*pramāṇa*) on one occasion and an object of knowledge (*prameya*) on another. Vātsyāyana, in reply, takes the bull by the horns and says that designations such as "instrument" and "object" (of knowledge) follow ultimately the general pattern of designation by such *kāraka* categories as "instrument," "agent," and "object." I quote (NS 2.1.16):

> [All] *kāraka* words apply through the incidence of some grounds or other. In "The tree stands [erect]," the tree is the *agent* because it has independence[4] with regard to the matter of its own standing erect. In "[He] sees the tree," the tree is ardently desired through the action of seeing [by the agent] and hence is the *object.*[5] In "He shows the moon by the tree," the tree is the chief instrument for showing and hence is the *instrument.*[6] In "[He] sprinkles water for the tree," the tree is intended to be the beneficiary by the action of sprinkling, and hence is the *dative* or the recipient. In "The leaf falls from the tree," the tree is the *ablative* for it is unmoved when separation through movement is intended [or it is sanctioned by Pāṇini's rule: the "unmoved" in separation is the ablative, 1.4.24]. In "The crows are in the tree," the tree is the *locative* by virtue of its being the locus or substratum [or, by Pāṇini's rule: the substratum is the locative, 1.4.45]. In this way, neither the thing

> itself nor the action itself is a *kāraka*. What then? When a thing is a participant [*sādhana*] in some action, or when it is endowed with a special functional activity, it becomes a *kāraka*. That which is independent in the performing of an act is the agent; it is neither the bare thing nor the bare action. That which is most desired to be obtained [by the agent] is the object; it is neither the bare thing nor the bare action. In this way one can explain the notion of the most efficacious [in defining the instrument], and so on. Thus, the designation of the *kāraka* categories follows the same rule. The designation of a *kāraka* applies neither to the bare thing nor to the [mere] action. What then? It applies to the thing that participates in action and to that which is endowed with some special functional activity.

Vātsyāyana's treatment of *kāraka* is rather elementary. He refers to Pāṇini's six major rules, which "define" the six *kārakas* in their *initial* or *primary* meanings. He quotes the three *sūtras* in parts. He ignores the usage of *kāraka* categories in their secondary senses. But Pāṇini's assignment of the designation of the different *kāraka* categories to objects is based upon many other considerations. For example, sometimes the presence of certain prefixes in the root verb turns a locative into an object (Pāṇini 1.4.46) or the use of certain roots with specified meanings turns an object into a dative (1.4.36). Vātsyāyana's discussion ignores such secondary *kāraka* designations. Uddyotakara comments that Vātsyāyana's definition of the object (*karma*) can be so interpreted as to include the *tathāyuktaṃ cānīpsitam* rule (1.4.50).

Let us now switch to Navya-nyāya. I shall deal with Bhavānanda's definition of a *kāraka* in particular and the Navyanyāya discussion of this concept in general. Bhavānanda wrote, among other things, an excellent treatise, very concise, called *Kāraka-cakra.*[7] I shall discuss only the general definition of a *kāraka.*

In the Navyanyāya school, the authors usually deal with two principal ways of answering the question "what is *kāraka*?" (the "quiddity" of a *kāraka*). Both definitions were prevalent in the *vyākaraṇa* tradition. One is derived partly from the etymology of the word *kāraka* and partly from the initial remark of Patañjali in his *Vyākaraṇa-Mahābhāṣya* under the *sūtra* (head rule = *adhikāra sūtra*) "*kārake*" (1.4.23):

> *karoti kriyāṃ nirvartayati*
> 'That which does, performs the action'

Etymologically, *kāraka* means 'a do-er, an actor'. From this one can say that a *kāraka* is that which performs some action or that which generates or causes in some way the action in question. This definition is variously formulated: *kriyā-janakaṃ kārakam* or *kriyā-nimittaṃ kārakam.* We must note at least two pertinent points. Although I have translated *kriyā* as 'action', there is a need for subtlety here. *Kriyā* stands for the meaning of verbal roots or *dhātu.* The *dhātus* are given in the list called *dhātu-pāṭha,* which is part and parcel of the Pāṇinian system of grammar. It just happens that certain *dhātus* in the list do not mean action, but rather substance. The root *gaḍi* means 'part of the face'. Hence, to assign *kārakatva*, in fact "agency" (=*kartr̥tva*), to the word *kapolam* ('the cheek') in the sentence *gaṇḍati kapolam* ('The cheek is identical with the part of the face'), we have to take *kriyā* in the definition not simply in the sense of action but as the meaning of the root verb.

The other point is this: if *kāraka* means 'a do-er', then it will be synonymous with the agent (*kartr̥*), and the other *kārakas* must be excluded. Bhartr̥hari points out that we can avoid this difficulty in the following way. All the *kāraka*-items are in some sense doing something, or performing some function, towards completion of the main action. When Devadatta is cooking, the logs burn to allow the cooking, the pot holds the rice for cooking, the ricegrains soften to facilitate cooking, and so on. In this rather loose sense, they are all behaving as agents. But we call one the instrument, another the object, and another the locative when we wish to underline the differences in their roles and functions toward the completion of the main action. Compare:

> *niṣpattimātre kartr̥tvam sarvatraivāsti kārake*
> *vyāpārabhedāpekṣāyāṃ karaṇatvādisambhavaḥ*
> (*Vākyapadīya* III.7.18)

The second way of defining *kāraka* is to partly emphasize its syntactic role. A *kāraka* is that which is (syntactically) connected with an action-verb, or *kriyā*. The word *kriyā* is ambiguous in Sanskrit; it can be used both as a semantic entity and as a syntactic entity, that is, in one sense it belongs to the ontological category, in another sense to the grammatical category. The Sanskrit formulation of the definition is *kriyānvayitvaṃ kārakatvam.*

Both of these definitions have been faulted. As has already been noted, the causal relationship between a *kāraka* and the action must be taken in a broader sense so that it could include both the direct relationship and the indirect or "chain" relationship. Otherwise, only the agent or the instrument could be the *kāraka.* That which we call the dative or the ablative is only very indirectly connected with the action by causal relationship. Now, if we widen the notion of causal relationship in this way, we make the definition too wide or overextensive (*ativyāpta*), for it is agreed by all parties in Sanskrit grammar that the genitive is not a *kāraka.* Intuitively it is believed that the so-called genitive (Pāṇini's term for it is *śeṣa* 'the remainder') is that which expresses a relation between one thing (*dravya*) and another--such as ownership or parenthood, Caitra's rice or Caitra's son. A *kāraka* underlines the relation between a thing (*dravya*) and an action. Of course, *dravya* 'thing' in this context should be taken in a technical sense; any substantial expression denotes a *dravya* for the grammarian.[8] At the syntactic level, the so-called genitive combines one nominal or pronominal word (*nāmapada*) with another but a *kāraka* combines a nominal or pronominal word with a verb.

The overextension of this definition can be shown in the following way. Consider the example:

caitrasya taṇḍulam pacati
'(He) cooks the rice of Caitra'

Here the word *caitra* is genitive and hence has the sixth ending (sixth triplet in *sūtras* 4.1.2 and 1.4.104). It is not a *kāraka*. The sixth triplet applies when relations other than the *kāraka* relation are to be expressed (this is the import of rule 2.3.50). But our definition for *kāraka* will be unduly inclusive of this non-*kāraka*, for here, too, the indirect and "extended" causal relationship holds between the action of cooking and Caitra. The person (the cook) could not have cooked the rice in question if Caitra had not given his tacit permission (for Caitra owns the rice). Hence, the definition is faulty.

The second definition also suffers from such a plight, for we cannot assume that this (syntactic) relation with the verb must be a *direct* relation. Why not? Pāṇini has prescribed that under certain circumstances some objects (*karma*) or some instruments (*karaṇa*) will be designated as *śeṣa*, a non-*kāraka*. Specific conditions are mentioned, for example, in rules 2.3.51 through 2.3.56. Some of these are *sarpiṣo* **jānīte** ('he acts because of *butter*') and *mātuḥ* **smarati** ('he remembers *mother*').

In these cases, the nominal items in boldface are in direct syntactic connection with their respective verbs but they cannot be designated as *kāraka*s, according to the received doctrine, because the fault of overextension (*ativyāpti*) will again arise. If, in order to avoid this difficulty, we do not qualify the syntactic relation at all, either directly or indirectly, we will run into another form of overextension. Consider the example:

brāhmaṇasya putraṃ panthānaṃ pr̥cchati
'He asks the son of a *brāhmaṇa* about the way'

Here the nominal item *brāhmaṇasya* can be said to have *indirect* (syntactic) connection with the verb *pr̥cchati* through the intermediate item *putram.* The idea is that, if *a* is connected with *b*, and *b* is connected with *c*, then *a* is in some way connected with *c*.

I shall now give Bhavānanda's own treatment of the general definition of a *kāraka.* I shall divide his comments into six parts and give the translations thereof, adding explanatory notes and my comments along the way.

Part 1: Translation (*Kāraka-cakra*): deliberation on the notion of a *kāraka.* With regard to the six *kāraka*s, we cannot say that the general definition [of *kāraka*] is: a *kāraka* is that which becomes a causal factor of an action/verb.

Note. As already noted, the Sanskrit word *kriyā* is ambiguous. The commentator interprets *kriyā* as *dhātvartha* (= the meaning of the root-verb) and says that he follows the grammarians (*śābdikas*) in this matter. The meaning of a root is usually an action (*vyāpāra*), or the result (*phala*) of such an action, or both (*phalavyāpārayor dhātuḥ*). In *grāmaṃ gacchati* ('he goes to the village') the result of going is the final contact (*saṃyoga*) between the man and the village (his reaching there). A causal factor in such contact is as much the action of going as it is the village gone to. We may avoid the problem (of overextending this tentative definition of *kāraka* to include the action of going) if we rightly insist upon the dual nature of the meaning of a root: action plus the result.

Part 2: Translation. [Such a definition is not acceptable,] for it will overextend to Caitra, etc., in such examples as *caitrasya taṇḍulaṃ pacati* ['he cooks Caitra's rice']. *Caitra* here is a genitive [a non-*kāraka*]. But he can be a causal factor of the action of cooking by his function of supplying the rice to be cooked, just as a dative or a recipient *kāraka* [the *brāhmaṇa*] becomes the causal factor in the action of giving [in, for example, *brāhmaṇāya dhanaṃ dadāti* 'he gives wealth to the *brāhmaṇa*'] by permitting the agent to give.

Note. The counterexample has already been explained in my introductory comments. The point to note here is that we have to include both direct and indirect causal factors when we are defining the *kāraka*s in this way. This leads to overextension.

Part 3: Translation. But [the acceptable definition is:] a *kāraka*, both in its principal sense and in its secondary sense, is that which is "syntactically" connected [*anvayin*] with the action/verb through the intermediary of the meanings of the case-affixes [= *vibhakti*s]. A principal *kāraka* is both a causal factor of the action and connected syntactically in this way with the action/verb. In order to avoid overextension to adverbs such as *stokam* ['seldom'] in *stokaṃ pacati* ['he seldom cooks'], we have added the phrase "through the intermediary of the meanings of the case-affixes" to the definition.

Note. Bhavānanda evidently recognizes two kinds of *kārakas*, the principal as well as the secondary ones. An example of the former is *grāmaṃ gacchati* ('goes to the village'), wherein the village is a causal factor of going, as explained above. An example of the latter is *ghaṭaṃ jānāti* ('knows the pot'), wherein the pot, in a certain view, may not be strictly called a causal factor of the action of knowing. The point is that all secondary *kārakas* would be at least syntactically connected with the action/verb through the intermediary of the meanings of case-affixes. I have taken the liberty of translating *vibhakti* as 'case-affix'. These case-affixes are enumerated by Pāṇini in his rule 4.1.2.

Pāṇini did not formulate any rule to prescribe affixes for adverbs. In a way they were left dangling. Usually the singular affix of the second triplet (*dvitīyā-vibhakti*) or that of the third triplet (*tṛtīyā-vibhakti*) is used to mark adverbs. Although these endings, or affixes, are not usually regarded as expressing *kārakas*, the syntactic connection of such adverbs as *stokam* with the verb is undeniable. Hence, overextension to such adverbs is obviously possible. It is contended that the affixes in these adverbs do not mean anything, and that they are added to the nominal stems of adverbial words in order to turn them into *usable* words in a Sanskrit sentence, that is, into a *pada*. The dictum is that a (nominal) stem has to be *Sanskritized* by adding inflections (affixes). Only an affixed or inflected word is usable in a Sanskrit sentence. Bhavānanda obviously favored this interpretation of the adverbial affix in Sanskrit and cited the above as a counterexample to justify his appendage to the definition.

There is another way of interpreting the adverbial affix: stipulating that adverbs are to be treated as adjectives or qualifiers of the verbs. In this case, the affixes that we add to the adjectival stems are said to denote identity (or *abheda*). If we say that such meanings as *abheda* or *prakāra* belong to that which is denoted by a *vibhakti*, or an affix, then obviously the adverbs (as well as the adjectives) will be treated as *kārakas*. This is an acceptable solution. In fact, one can argue that adverbs are *kārakas* according to Pāṇini. That is how we can support such formulations as *mṛdunyau*, wherein *ya(Ṇ)* is added to *mṛdu-nī* in the sense *mṛdumadhuraṃ yathā syāt tathā nayate* ('takes very softly') by rule 6.4.82. There is a *vārttika* under 6.4.82, which allows *ya(Ṇ)* after roots that are preceded or prefixed by a *kāraka* or a *gati*.[9] Now, if *mṛdu* is not to be treated as a *kāraka*, we would not expect *ya(Ṇ)*. *Mṛdunyau*, however, is an acceptable form. In sum, adverbs can be treated as *kārakas*, which implies that Bhavānanda's counterexample (meant to avoid the supposed overextension) is unnecessary, as is his additional qualification of the definition.

To solve this puzzle, it has been suggested by the commentator that, without the qualification in the definition, we will have an "overextension" problem not with regard to adverbs but with regard to the effort, or *kṛti*, which is the meaning of the verbal suffix in *pacati* ('cooks').

Part 4: Translation. In *caitrasya pacati* ['he cooks Caitra's (rice understood)'] the relatedness belonging to

Caitra is not syntactically connected with the cooking [the action, for such syntactic connection requires syntactic expectancy, which is selective]. The genitive is [syntactically] selective of the meaning of a nominal stem and the verb is selective of the object, etc., and hence between the verb and the genitive there is no mutually selective expectancy. But, if we supplement the sentence with the word *taṇḍulam* ['rice'], there will arise an awareness in which the elements will be mutually syntactically connected.

Note. If we say that in *caitrasya pacati* ('he cooks Caitra's') there is no syntactic connection between *caitrasya* and *pacati*, then we find ourselves in an impossible situation when we try to explain the connected meaning arising from such expressions. For it is undeniable that an expression such as *caitrasya pacati* is well understood as a complete thought by a Sanskritist, and hence it must be treated as a complete (natural) sentence.

Part 5: Translation. Certainly the sixth ending in such expressions as *odanasya bhoktā* ['(he is) the eater of rice'] and *maitrasya pākaḥ* ['this is the cooking of Maitra'] is to be treated as a *kāraka*-affix, for it signifies either objecthood [as in the former example] or agency [as in the latter]. The rule *kartṛkarmaṇoḥ kṛti* [Pāṇini's rule 2.3.65] prescribes the sixth endings in the sense of an agent or an object when verbal nouns ending in *kṛt* suffixes follow. Therefore, the grammarians [*śābdikāḥ*] say that general [unspecified] connectedness cannot yield a *kāraka*, for there would be no verb with which to connect it.

Note. We note that not all sixth endings are to be excluded from the affixes denotative of the *kāraka* relation.

Special rules have been formulated to show that the sixth triplet can also be denotative of agency or objecthood.

Part 6: Translation. If we [syntactically] connect the meaning of the sixth ending directly with the meaning of the root, without supplementing the sentence with a nominal word to mediate between them, as we may do in the example

> *guru-vipra-tapasvi-durgatānāṃ pratikurvīta bhiṣak svabheṣajaiḥ*
> 'The physician should cure [the diseases of] the guru, the *brāhmaṇa*, the ascetic, and the distressed persons, with his own medicine'

then the correct definition will be this. A *kāraka* is that which is syntactically connected with the action-verb and is endowed with any one of the six properties: agency, objecthood, instrumentality, recipienthood [dativehood], ablativehood, and locushood.

Note. The oddity of the translation "we [syntactically] connect the meaning of the sixth ending," etc., is obvious but it is difficult to translate the rather amorphous term *anvaya* in this context. We can certainly talk about the connection between the meaning of one grammatical element (an ending) and the meaning of another but, as long as these are also syntactic elements, and have some syntactic functions to perform, their connection has a syntactic component. The use of *anvaya* seems to underline this fact.

The cited sentence is an interesting one. Here, if we do not indulge in supplementation (cf. *adhyāhāra*), we have to say, as noted above, that the word with sixth ending (or the genitive) is directly connected with the verb even without the intermediary of the supplemented word 'the disease'. In fact, if the meaning of the root verb is simply 'curing of the diseases of', then undoubtedly the genitive would be directly connected with the action-verb. Hence, the over-extension of the given definition to the genitive, a non-*kāraka*, would be unavoidable in certain cases. The final definition given above avoids this problem by enumerating the individual properties of each of the six *kāraka*s.

We may also note that certain affixes are *upapada*-affixes, which are distinguished from *kāraka*-affixes. If the affixes are assigned under certain special conditions, that is, in connection with certain words and other items (and if such words are not directly regarded as causal factors [*sādhana*] of the action), they would be called *upapada*-affixes. An example is:

> *haraye namaḥ*
> 'Salutations to Hari'

The fourth triplet is assigned by rule 2.3.16. There may be a dual possibility in some cases, viz., the word may take a *kāraka*-affix and an *upapada*-affix when conditions for both are met. In the case of such conflict, the usual dictum is to let the *kāraka*-affix take priority over the *upapada*-affix. This exegetical rule is suggested by Patañjali under *sūtra* 2.3.4. Hence, we have the following example:

> *namaskaroti devān*
> 'He makes *namas* to the *deva*s'

Here the object-affix, second triplet, takes precedence over the fourth triplet (*caturthī*). Now, if we believe in supplementation, we can even claim that in the previous example the word *haraye* could be a *kāraka*, for certainly it would be syntactically connected with the supplemented verb through the intermediary of some affix or *vibhakti*, that is, *caturthī*.

In conclusion, we may add that, although the concept of *kāraka* was presumably clear (at least intuitively) to Pāṇini and the Pāṇinīyas, it was almost impossible to define it, or find a *lakṣaṇa* or a uniquely distinguishing feature, that would belong to all and only the six well-known *kāraka*s. Various alternative suggested definitions try to capture this intuition but fail to do so completely. In any case, the discussion of these definitions brings us closer to grasping this intuition. Hence, we can understand what Pāṇini meant by *kāraka* even though we cannot fully articulate it. Bhavānanda was well aware of this problem. His final definition takes the bull by the horns and provides a practical guide to correct usage (*vyavahāra*) of the word *kāraka*. Udayana long ago said that the purpose of a definition (or *lakṣaṇa*) is *vyavahāra-siddhi*, guidance to the correct usage of the term.

Notes

1. Cardona (1978, 233-34).
2. For Bhavānanda's date, see Matilal (1977, 109-10).

3. See Matilal (1985, 416-30).
4. P.1.4.54.
5. P.1.4.49.
6. P.1.4.42.
7. Published in *Haridas Sanskrit Granthamala*, No. 154, ed. Brahmaśaṃkara Śāstri, 1942.
8. See Matilal (1971, 110-11).
9. Patañjali under P.6.4.82.

References

Bhartṛhari, *Vākyapadīya*. Abhyankar and Limaye (eds.). Poona, 1965.

Bhavānanda, *Kārakacakra*. Brahmaśaṃkara Śāstri (ed.). Benares, 1942.

Cardona, G. *Pāṇini: A Survey of Research*. The Hague and Paris, 1978.

Faddegon, B. *Studies on Pāṇini's Grammar*. Amsterdam, 1936.

Fillmore, C. J. "The Case for Case." In *Universals in Linguistic Theory*, edited by E. Bach and R. Harms. New York, 1968.

Iyer, K. A. Subramania. "The Point of View of the Vaiyākaraṇas." *Journal of Oriental Research* 18 (1948): 84-96. Reprinted in Staal (1972, 393-400).

Matilal, B. K. *Epistemology, Logic and Grammar in Indian Philosophical Analysis.* The Hague and Paris, 1971.

-------. *Nyāya-Vaiśeṣika.* Wiesbaden, 1977. Volume 6 of *A History of Indian Literature,* edited by Jan Gonda.

-------. *Logic, Language and Reality: An Introduction to Indian Philosophical Studies.* Delhi, 1985.

Staal, J. F. (ed.). *A Reader on the Sanskrit Grammarians.* Cambridge, Mass., 1972.

Whitney, D. "On recent studies in Hindu Grammar" (1893). Reprinted in Staal (1972, 165-84).

A GLIMPSE INTO A PRE-PĀṆINIAN VIEW ABOUT VIKARAṆAS

G. B. Palsule

Pāṇini's description of the Sanskrit language is regarded as a model one. It was accepted even by the later schools of Sanskrit grammar. Although they may have introduced minor changes in it, such as replacing old code-letters (*anubandhas*) with new ones, breaking a rule in two, joining two rules into one, shifting the place of a rule in the interest of *anuvṛtti* (so as to effect economy), and so on, the main grammatical theory remained the same. But what was the position before Pāṇini? About this we know very little because Pāṇini's outstanding grammar eclipsed the older ones, which gradually were lost in the course of time. Still, one comes across a clue here and a trace there, which gives us an inkling of the older state of affairs. The position of the *vikaraṇas* is a case in point.

In Sanskrit, a verbal form, say of the present system, normally contains three elements: the verbal root; the suffix that forms the stem[1] (the *vikaraṇa* of the Sanskrit grammarians), *śap* / *śyan*, etc. / *zero* in active, *yak* in passive; and the personal ending[2] (*tiṅ* of the Pāṇiniya school). Whereas the verbal root denotes the verbal meaning in general, everything else is supposed (in the Pāṇinian system) to be conveyed by the personal ending. Thus, the tense, the person and the number of the agent (in the active voice), or the object (in the passive voice) are believed to be conveyed by the personal ending. In other words, the personal ending conveys the voice also.

What is the function of the *vikaraṇa* in all this? Apparently nil. In the active there is no uniformity of *vikaraṇas*. It is sometimes *śap*, sometimes its replacements, and sometimes its absence (as in the case of the *ad-* and the *hu-* classes). So here the *vikaraṇa* may not have a role in the expression of voice. But what about the passive? The *vikaraṇa ya(k)* is indispensable in the passive voice (and in the *bhāve* construction) in a *sārvadhātuka* construction. And, it is not found anywhere else. Why is it that the function of expressing the object, etc. (that is, the voice) is denied to it? The question seems to be legitimate but here Pāṇini's position is clear. According to P.3.4.69,[3] the personal endings (substitutes of *l*) are expressive of the agent, the object, or the verbal abstract. When it expresses the agent, *śap* (or its substitutes or its absence) is to come in;[4] when it expresses an object or the verbal abstract, the *vikaraṇa* is to be *ya(k)*.[5] The *vikaraṇas* are what are called "empty morphs" in modern linguistics. According to ancient Indian terminology, they may at best be called *dyotakas*.

But it seems that other grammarians held a different opinion before Pāṇini. A clue supporting this belief is found in the *Mahābhāṣya* of Patañjali, in which there is a discussion of whether P.2.3.1 (*anabhihite*) is necessary. Kātyāyana first takes the prima facie view that the rule is superfluous.[6] Its purpose is already served by the maxim *uktārthānām aprayogaḥ*. Patañjali, explaining this view, gives, among others, the example of the *vikaraṇa śnam*. Now, although *śap* is to be set aside by *śnam*, still *śap* could also come in side-by-side with *śnam* since they occupy different places (*śap* follows a root while *śnam* occurs as an infix).[7] Still *śap* does not come in. Why? Because, Patañjali says, its office of expressing the agent is already fulfilled. Read, for example, *śnam-bahuj-akakṣu tarhi. śnam. bhinatti, chinatti, śnamoktatvāt kartr̥tvasya kartari śap na bhavati.* Patañjali's statement that *śap* does not come in because its office of expressing the agent is fulfilled by *śnam* is somewhat surprising since in the Pāṇinian system, as we saw above, that office belongs to the personal ending and not to the *vikaraṇa*. Here Kaiyaṭa comes to our aid. He says that Patañjali's statement is based on the view held by Pāṇini's predecessors: *bhāva-karma-kartāro vikaraṇārthā iti pūrvācārya-darśanam āśrityaivam uktam.* It is questionable whether Patañjali can legitimately quote a view of some predecessors of Pāṇini (which Pāṇini definitely did not accept) while discussing some other procedure of Pāṇini. I personally do not think it reasonable. Yet the fact remains that some grammarians before Pāṇini held the view that the *vikaraṇas* were expressive of voice.

Recently I came across additional evidence, even older, concerning this view of Pāṇini's *pūrvācāryas*. Bhartr̥hari, commenting in his *Dīpikā* on the *Mbh* on P.1.1.14 (*nipāta ekāj anāṅ*), states that grammarians did not hold identical views. Among the examples given to substantiate his statement occurs the case of *vikaraṇas* also. He says that, according to some, the *vikaraṇas* (evidently *śap* and its substitutes) first come in to denote the agent. To the root, which is thus strengthened with the *vikaraṇa*, is added subsequently the personal ending, which does not add anything to the meaning. Read, for example, *tathā keṣāṃcid vikaraṇāḥ prāk kartary utpadyante / vikaraṇāntāt svārthe sārvadhātuka-pratyayo bhavati.*[8] Here Bhartṛhari expressly says that the personal endings are *svārthe*, that is, they have no meanings of their own.

An interesting point to note here is the particular sequence of additions of grammatical elements adopted by those other grammarians mentioned by Bhartṛhari. The *vikaraṇa*, according to this view, was to be added first (*prāk*), the personal ending coming afterwards. This is the opposite of the procedure followed in Pāṇini's system wherein after the verbal root P.3.1.22 (*dhātoḥ*) first comes the personal ending P.3.4.77,78 (*lasya, tip-tas-jhi*, etc.). Depending upon whether this personal ending denotes the agent or the object/verbal abstract, we get the *vikaraṇas* *śap / śyan / zero* or *yak*, respectively.

I think that this view of Pāṇini's predecessors appears to be reasonable in a way. Since *śap / śyan / zero*, etc., are invariably connected with the present active and *yak* with the present passive it is reasonable to regard these *vikaraṇas* as the markers of voice in general. The endings serve to give further particulars of the agent or the object/verbal abstract such as the person and the number. This also agrees with the views of modern grammarians according to whom the tense- and mood-stem is formed first (for example, *bhava-*, *ad-*, *juhu-*, etc., in active, and *bhūya-*, *adya-*, *hūya-* in passive). The personal ending comes afterwards.

Pāṇini's procedure, centered around the personal ending, which is made to come first, results in a major defect: his system cannot account for modal forms based on nonpresent systems (that is, based on perfect and aorist stems such as *jagamyāt*, *rurucyāḥ*, *ānaśyām;* and *kr̥dhi*, *gahi*, *badhi*, *dhātu*, *bhūtu*). Since I have dealt with this subject elsewhere,[9] I will not go into it here.

NOTES

1. This may sometimes be absent, as in the case of the roots of the *ad*-class.
2. There may sometimes be additional elements, such as the causative sign *i* (*ṇic*) or the desiderative suffix *sa(n)* suffixed, and a preverb or past augment (*aṭ*) prefixed to a root.
3. P.3.4.69: लः कर्मणि च भावे चाकर्मकेभ्यः ।
   'लकाराः सकर्मकेभ्यः कर्मणि कर्तरि च स्युः, अकर्मकेभ्यो भावे कर्तरि च स्युः ।' (सि. कौ.)
4. P.3.1.68: कर्तरि शप् : कर्त्रर्थे सार्वधातुके परे धातोः शप् स्यात् । (सि. कौ.)
5. P.3.1.67: सार्वधातुके यक् : 'धातोर्यक् प्रत्ययः स्यात् भावकर्मवाचिनि सार्वधातुके परे ।' (सि. कौ.)
6. P.2.3.1, Vār. 1: अनभिहितवचनमनर्थकमन्यत्रापि विहितस्याभावादभिहिते
7. Vār. 2: श्नम्बहुजकक्षु नानादेशत्वादुत्सर्गाप्रतिषेधः ।
8. The Bhandarkar Oriental Research Institute's new critical edition, Āhnika V, pp. 9-10, 11, 12.

9. *Verbal Forms in the Ṛgveda* (Maṇḍala VI), publication of the Centre of Advanced Study in Sanskrit, class B, no. 4 (Pune: University of Poona, 1978).

ON THE INTERPRETATION OF VĀ PADĀNTASYA (8.4.57)

K. Kunjunni Raja

There is no unanimity among scholars regarding the use of *anusvāra* and homorganic nasals (*parasavarṇa*) in Sanskrit. Pāṇini's rule prescribing homorganic nasal (*anusvārasya yayi parasavarṇaḥ*, 8.4.56) is immediately followed by the optional rule *vā padāntasya* (8.4.57). It is clear that *parasavarṇa* is compulsory only within a *pada* and is optional at the end of a *pada* or between *padas* in a sentence. *Parasavarṇa* is resorted to in the publications of the Bhandarkar Research Institute, while *anusvāra* is consistently used in the Adyar Library publications, wherever it is grammatically possible.

The late Venkatesh Shastri Joshi (1922-1979), a well-known authority on Sanskrit grammar, stated that this option in *vā padāntasya* should be applied in the case of real words and not to *upasargas* (prepositions) and to the first member of a compound, even though they are called *pada* technically by Pāṇini (Venkatesh Shastri Joshi, *Problems in Sanskrit Grammar* [Poona: Dastane Ram Chandra, 1980]). He says that "in the case of compound words as well as between the prepositions and verbal forms *parasavarṇa* sandhi should be observed necessarily (compulsorily)" (p. 28). He continues

(p. 128),

> In the previous paper "Pāṇini and the Pāṇinīyas on Saṃhitā" I had pointed out that the external Sandhi rules should not be observed as compulsory rules in a sentence. But as an exception to this system of writing I am going to suggest here in this paper that *parasavarṇa* sandhi rules should be observed necessarily in the case of compound words as well as the prepositions and verbal forms even though each member of the compound words as well as the prepositions and verbal forms could be technically treated as different padas in a sentence.

He repeats the same idea in another paper (in the same volume) written in Sanskrit:

> एवं च लेखनसमये उच्चारणानुसारिलेखनदृष्टया पाणिनीयव्याकरणानुसारं च सामासिकपदेषु तथा सोपसर्गधातुरूपेषु च परसवर्णविधिरेव युक्ततरो मन्तव्यः । "वा पदान्तस्य" इत्यस्मिन् सूत्रे पदग्रहणेन, पदमेव यत् सर्वथा लौकिकं नाम लोके पृथक् प्रयोगार्हं पदम्, न तु शास्त्रीयम्, इति तादृशं सुबन्तं तिङन्तं च पदमत्र गृह्यते । अतः अलौकिकशास्त्रीयपदत्वप्रयुक्तं यत्र पदान्तत्वम्, तादृशस्थलेषु नाम सोपसर्गतिङन्तरूपेषु समासेषु च 'वा पदान्तस्य' इति विकल्पस्य न प्रसक्तिः इत्यपि केचन मन्यन्ते ।

The hasty statements of recognized scholars are likely to mislead the unwary. Thus, probably on the basis of Pandit V. S. Joshi's theory, a scholar who reviewed Professor S. D. Joshi's edition of the ***Mahābhāṣya*** (*samarthāhnika*) in the ***Journal of the Asiatic Society, Bombay*** (vol. 43-44, p. 296) made the following remark: "One cannot help saying, however, that a critical edition of a work like the *Vyākaraṇa Mahābhāṣya* is naturally expected to print the text with *Parasavarṇa* where necessary. किञ्चिदेत्येषोऽर्थो and not किंचिदेत्येषोऽर्थो (p. 7, l. 9)."

The option sanctioned by the *sūtra vā padāntasya* applies to all *padāntas* as conceived by Pāṇini, and not merely to the final of the free words. The aim of the present paper is to show that Pāṇini's views on the interpretation of *padāntasya* are definitely against the view given by Pandit Joshi.

In the *sūtra* मो राजि समः क्वौ (P.8.3.25), the form *samrāṭ* is ordained, rejecting the form *saṃrāṭ*, which might have come optionally by the *sūtra vā padāntasya.*

Kāśikā says मकारस्य मकारवचनमनुस्वारनिवृत्त्यर्थम् ।

Nyāsa adds संपूर्वाद् राजतेः 'सत्सूद्विष..' इत्यादिना क्विप् । व्रश्चादिना षत्वम् । षकारस्य जश्त्वं डकारः । तस्य चर्त्वं टकारः । किमर्थं पुनर्मकार उच्चार्यते इत्याह मकारस्य मकारवचनमित्यादि । 'मोऽनुस्वारः' इत्यनुस्वारः प्राप्नोति । स मा भूदित्येवमर्थं मकारस्य मकारो विधीयते ।

Nāgeśa says in the *Śabdenduśekhara* निषेधस्त्वनुस्वारस्यैव स्यात् । ध्वनितं चेदम् 'एतदोऽन्' 'अमो मश्' इति सूत्रयोर्भाष्ये । 'मकारस्य मकारविधानादनुस्वारादयो बाध्यन्ते' इति तत्रोक्तेः ।

Anusvāra can come optionally here only by the *sūtra* वा पदान्तस्य. If सम् is not a *pada*, there is no possibility of the *anusvāra* by वा पदान्तस्य . Whence it shows that *padānta* in this *sūtra* is to be taken in the technical sense, which includes the *upasarga sam* also. Otherwise there was no need for the *sūtra* मो राजि समः क्वौ (P.8.3.25).

TIME FOR A LITTLE SOMETHING

J. A. F. Roodbergen

1. Two rather recent publications of the Centre of Advanced Study in Sanskrit (*VIBHA*, Introduction, vi-viii; and *Proceedings*, 59-62) have dwelt, in more or less detail, on the structure (that is, the organization of rules) of the *Aṣṭādhyāyī*. The aim has been twofold: to show that this structure reflects derivational procedure, and to show that the *Aṣṭādhyāyī* as we know it cannot reasonably be considered the work of one author, having undergone changes at the hands of later redactors, like other Vedic and Sanskrit texts. This discussion is continued, from a different angle, in the present article, written in honor of Dr. S. D. Joshi, *il maestro di color che sanno* in the field of Sanskrit grammar.

2. In the derivation of finite verb forms it is practically taken for granted that first the finite verb endings are introduced, then the *vikaraṇas*.[1] But, as will be shown, tradition has hesitated. Pāṇini himself makes a distinction, or so it is assumed:[2] the *ārdhadhātuka vikaraṇas* (except *yaK*, P.3.1.67) are introduced before the addition of the finite verb endings but the *sārvadhātuka vikaraṇas* and *yaK* come after because they are conditioned by the presence of finite, *sārvadhātuka* verb endings. Why this distinction;

what about the interpretation of the *Pāṇinisūtras* involved? The points raised here do not imply any significant change regarding the form ultimately derived. But they do have some implications for a more remote plan, which it seems worthwhile to explicate, regarding the phrasing of word-building rules and their application in a particular order.

3. We start from P.1.3.12. The rule says *anudāttaṅita ātmanepadam*. It is usually explained as "[the endings called] *ātmanepada* [are added] after [a verbal base[3] whose vowel is marked as] *anudātta*, or which [verbal base] is marked with *Ṅ*." The word *anudāttaṅitaḥ* is taken as a technical ablative. Accordingly, the endings mentioned should come immediately after the specified bases.

Vt. I on this rule (*Mbh.* 1:274, l. 13) says *ātmanepadaṃ niyamārtham*, or "[the word] *ātmanepada* [is used here] for the sake of a restriction." The restriction meant is explained by the *KV* in the sense that the *ātmanepada* endings are retained only after verbal bases that have been marked with *anudātta* or *Ṅ*, not after others.

Vt. II (*Mbh.* 1:274, l. 15) says *lavidhānād vihitam* "[the endings called *parasmaipada* and *ātmanepada*] have been prescribed after the prescription of [the section heading] *lasya*."[4] The idea is that the eighteen finite verb endings have already been prescribed by P.3.4.78. So what is the point in prescribing *ātmanepada* again in P.1.3.12? To render this statement meaningful, it is assumed that P.1.3.12 is a restrictive rule, as explained by *Vt.* I. But Patañjali's comment points elsewhere. He says (*Mbh.* 1:274, l. 16-19):

> The *niyama* [endings prescribed by the] restrictive rule [P.1.3.12] would have a chance of not applying because the *vikaraṇas* intervene.[5] The following is to be decided here: [whether] the *vikaraṇas* should be introduced [first], [or whether the endings prescribed by] the restrictive rule [should be added first]. What to do here? [The answer is that] the *vikaraṇas* [are introduced first], because [they have been prescribed by] the later rules.[6] Certainly also, the *vikaraṇas* are *nitya* 'obligatory'.[7] They have a chance of applying whether [the endings prescribed by] the restrictive rule are applied or not.

From this *Bhāṣya* we conclude that the *vikaraṇas* are introduced first, then the finite verb endings.

But there is a different opinion also. Patañjali, in his comment on the same *Vt.* (*Mbh.* 1:275, l. 11-12) says "The procedure of the Teacher offers us the clue that [the finite verb endings prescribed by] the restrictive rule [are] stronger than the *vikaraṇas* because in rules dealing with *vikaraṇas* he mentions[8] [the conditions] *ātmanepada* and *parasmaipada*."[9] This means that, unless the *ātmanepada* or *parasmaipada* endings have been added, we cannot introduce the *vikaraṇas*. From this *Bhāṣya* we conclude that the finite verb endings are added first, then the *vikaraṇas*. Tradition is ambiguous. So much for P.1.3.12.

4. The rules considered next are P.1.4.99-100. The first rule says *laḥ parasmaipadam*. The *KV* explains that here the word *laḥ* is a genitive requiring (as its correlate) the word *ādeśa* 'substitute'. In other words, *laḥ* stands for *lādeśāḥ* 'the substitutes of *l*'. Therefore, the rule is interpreted to mean that the substitutes of *l* receive the designation *parasmaipada*. The *KV* then enumerates the first nine endings stated in P.3.4.78 and adds the participle morphemes *ŚatṚ* (P.3.2.124) and *KvasU* (P.3.2.107).[10] By way of *vidhi*-rule, in which the designation *parasmaipada* is used, the *KV* mentions P.7.2.1.[11]

The Nyāsa on the *KV* contains some interesting comments. The first part of the commentary is translated as follows.

> Does [the word] *laḥ* represent a nominative or a genitive? Of these two, if [we take it that] it represents a nominative, then [by P.1.4.99] the designation *parasmaipada* would apply to *l* only, not to its substitutes *tiP*, etc. Certainly, these would also have [the designation *parasmaipada*] by *sthānivadbhāva* 'treatment like the original'.[12] But [the difficulty in this view is that the word] *laḥ* [continued] in P.1.4.100 cannot be connected with [the word] *taṅānau* [in this rule] because [the endings included in] *taṄ*[13] and [the participle morpheme] *āna*[14] are not *l*. Here [we may try to find a way out by assuming that] *taṅānau* is that *l* which is subsequently to become *taṄ* and *āna* [by replacement]. Or we have to explain that, since *laḥ* is mentioned,[15] [and since *laḥ* stands for *lādeśāḥ* 'the substitutes of *l*'] the substitutes of *l* are nothing but *taṆ* and *āna* because of *sāhacarya* '[the fact of] occurring together [in one and the same rule]'.[16] But, in that way, if the understanding of a desired meaning is to be established through *vyākhyāna* 'reasoned explanation',[17] [the result] would

be *gaurava* 'complication'. But in the view that [*laḥ* represents] a genitive this difficulty does not arise. That is why [the author of the *KV*] says *laḥ iti ṣaṣṭhī* '[the word] *laḥ* is a genitive', etc.

Then the author of the Nyāsa, after noting that this view is not without difficulties either, goes on to refer to Patañjali's *Bhāṣya* on *Vt.* II on P.1.4.99.

Kaiyaṭa agrees with the *KV*. Nāgeśa, on the same rule (P.1.4.99), observes that, if we can take *laḥ* as a nominative, the designation *parasmaipada* would be applied to the *lakāras* (*lAṬ*, etc.) only. Consequently, these *lakāras* could not be added after verbal bases marked with *anudātta* or *Ṅ*.[18] Moreover, the nominative word *laḥ*, when continued in P.1.4.100, cannot be connected with the word *taṅānau* in that rule. Therefore, Nāgeśa agrees with Kaiyaṭa.

As regards the earlier tradition, Kātyāyana and Patañjali, in their comments on P.1.4.99, keep silent on the interpretation of the word *laḥ*.[19]

In conclusion, we may say that, although the question of whether *laḥ* in P.1.4.99 is a nominative or a genitive was raised by tradition, the unanimous verdict is that *laḥ* here represents a genitive.

5. But why a genitive? Apart from P.1.4.99, the independent word *laḥ* appears only in P.3.4.69 (*laḥ karmaṇi ca. . .*), where it undoubtedly represents a nominative. The genitive form used by Pāṇini is *lasya*, which also occurs only once (P.3.4.77).

Suppose that tradition is wrong once again, and that *laḥ* in P.1.4.99 is a nominative. In that case, as stated by the

Nyāsa commentary, the rule means that *l* is called *parasmaipada*. Then what about P.1.4.100? This rule says that the finite verb endings called *taṄ* and the participle morpheme *āna* are called *ātmanepada*. Apparently, in the domain stated, P.1.4.100 overrules P.1.4.99. So what is the difficulty?

As correctly viewed by tradition (see section 4), the difficulty is that the nominative word *laḥ*, when continued in P.1.4.100, cannot be construed with *taṅānau*. The reason for the discontinuation of the nominative word *laḥ* in P.1.4.100 may, in fact, be stated as *sāmarthya* (or, rather, the lack of it).[20] But the reason tradition does not take *laḥ* as a nominative in P.1.4.100 is that it requires *laḥ* as a genitive in this rule. Here, the traditional argument begins: since we need *laḥ* as a genitive in P.1.4.100, why not take it as a genitive in P.1.4.99 also? But the question is really whether *laḥ* should be continued in P.1.4.100 at all, regardless of whether it is thought to be a genitive or a nominative. Without *laḥ*, the rule still makes sense.

6. What would be the consequences if *laḥ* in P.1.4.99 is taken as a nominative and if this term is not continued in P.1.4.100? Let us first see whether and how these suppositions would affect the interpretation and application of P.1.3.12.

In the new interpretation of *laḥ* assumed here, technically all *lakāras* will be called *parasmaipada*. These *lakāras* are subsequently replaced by the eighteen finite verb endings called *tiṄ* (and *parasmaipada*, by *sthānivadbhāva*). By way of exception to this designation, *parasmaipada*, the endings included in *taṄ* are called *ātmanepada* by

P.1.4.100. These latter endings also are substitutes of *l* (P.3.4.77). One immediate benefit of this new interpretation is that the problem stated under section 3, namely, the issue of the immediate sequence of the *ātmanepada* endings after a verbal base, does not arise. The reason is that the *lakāra* itself has been introduced immediately after the verbal base.

Now, P.1.3.12 tells us after which verbal bases these *ātmanepada* endings are to be retained, and not the other endings. They are to be retained only after verbal bases marked with *anudātta* or with *Ṅ*. Here the *parasmaipada* endings are disallowed.

Consider two arbitrary examples.

(A)	(1)	*śīṄ*					*Dhātupāṭha* 2.22
	(2)	*śī*	+	*lR̥Ṭ*			P.3.3.113
	(3)	*śī*	+	*sya*	+	*lR̥Ṭ*	P.3.1.33
	(4)	*śī*	+	*sya*	+	*ta*	P.3.4.78; 1.3.12
	(5)	*śī*	+	*sya*	+	*te*	P.3.4.79
	(6)	*śe*	+	*sya*	+	*te*	P.7.3.84
	(7)	*śe*	+	*ṣya*	+	*te*	P.8.3.59
		śeṣyate					

The rule concerned is P.3.1.33. It is conditioned by the term *lṛluṭoḥ*. The rule says that the *pratyayas sya* and *tāsI* are added after a verbal base (P.3.1.91, *dhātoḥ*) when the *lakāras lR̥* (that is, *lR̥Ṅ* and *lR̥Ṭ*) and *lUṬ* follow. Here it is clear that the *ārdhadhātuka* suffix *sya* is added at the *lakāra*-stage. At stage (4) we retain the *ātmanepada* ending because *śī*- is *Ṅit*.

(B)	(1)			*gamL̥*					*Dhātupāṭha* 1.1031
	(2)			*gam*			+	*lUṄ*	P.3.2.110
	(3)	*a*	+	*gam*			+	*lUṄ*	P.6.4.71
	(4)	*a*	+	*gam*	+	*cli*	+	*lUṄ*	P.3.1.43
	(5)	*a*	+	*gam*	+	*aṄ*	+	*lUṄ*	P.3.1.55
	(6)	*a*	+	*gam*	+	*a*	+	*ti*	P.3.4.78
	(7)	*a*	+	*gam*	+	*a*	+	*t*	P.3.4.100
		agamat							

Here the rule concerned is P.3.1.55. It is conditioned by the term *parasmaipadeṣu.* Does this mean that the aorist *vikaraṇa aṄ* is to be applied after *lUṄ* has been replaced by a finite verb ending? Tradition says yes. But in the new interpretation of P.1.4.99 the element *aṄ* is already introduced at the *lakāra*-stage because *l* is called *parasmaipada.* In the traditional interpretation of P.1.4.99 the derivation does not give rise to a problem. Rather, the difference with the derivation proposed above is one of symmetry and consistency, which is lacking in the traditional method of derivation. But here another problem arises: are the rules to be phrased with the help of elements that are already introduced at the *lakāra*-stage or with the help of elements that are introduced later on, after the finite verb endings have been added?

7. Let us now have a look at P.3.4.103, *parasmaipadeṣūdātto ṅic ca.* The *KV* explains: *parasmaipadaviṣayasya liṅo yāsuḍ āgamo bhavati sa codātto bhavati ṅic ca*, translated as "the *lIṄ*, which is to be subsequently replaced by [the endings called] *parasmaipada*, takes the augment *yāsUṬ*, and that [augment] has the *udātta* accent, and it is marked with *Ṅ*."

The Nyāsa commentary clarifies this, stating that the word *parasmaipadeṣu* in the *sūtra* should be taken as a *viṣayasaptamī*, not as a *parasaptamī*.[21] That is to say, we should not assume that the addition of *yāsUṬ* is conditioned by the presence of following *parasmaipada* endings but only that the augment is added in what is regarded as the domain in which these endings are added later.

Why this interpretation? The Nyāsa says *liṅaḥ parasmaipadānāṃ asaṃbhavāt*, "because [*lIṄ*] is incompatible with [the endings called] *parasmaipada*." Why incompatible? Because, if *parasmaipadeṣu* is taken as a *parasaptamī*, then *yāsUṬ* can only be inserted after the *lakāra lIṄ* has been replaced by the *parasmaipada* endings. But how, then, can *yāsUṬ* be said to be an augment of *lIṄ*?

Kaiyaṭa has not commented on P.3.4.103. Nāgeśa's comment does not touch upon the point under discussion. The earlier tradition, Kātyāyana and Patañjali, has nothing to say on this point either.[22]

Suppose, however, that *l* is called *parasmaipada*. In that case, we can introduce *yāsUṬ* earlier, at the stage of *lIṄ*, because *lIṄ*, being a *lakāra*, is called *parasmaipada*. As a result, we need not assume that *parasmaipadeṣu* in P.3.4.103 is a *viṣayasaptamī* but we can retain the technical grammatical value of *parasaptamī*. Then, after the introduction of *yāsUṬ*, the *lakāra lIṄ* is replaced by a finite verb ending. In this case the difficulty raised by tradition regarding the interpretation of the word *parasmaipadeṣu* does not arise. For example, consider:

(1)	*bhū*					*Dhātupāṭha* 1.1
(2)	*bhū*				+ *lIṄ*	P.3.3.161
(3)	*bhū*		+ *yāsUṬ*		+ *lIṄ*	P.3.4.103
(4)	*bhū*		+ *yās*		+ *tiP*	P.3.4.78
(5)	*bhū*	+ *ŚaP*	+ *yās*		+ *ti*	P.3.1.68
(6)	*bhū*	+ *a*	+ *yās*	+ *sUṬ*	+ *ti*	P.3.4.107
(7)	*bhū*	+ *a*	+ *yā°*	+ *s*	+ *ti*	P.7.2.79
(8)	*bhū*	+ *a*	+ *yā*	+ °	+ *ti*	P.7.2.79
(9)	*bhū*	+ *a*	+ *yā*		+ *t°*	P.3.4.100
(10)	*bhū*	+ *a*	+ *iy*		+ *t*	P.7.2.80
(11)	*bhū*	+ *a*	+ *i*		+ *t*	P.6.1.66
(12)	*bho*	+ *a*	+ *i*		+ *t*	P.7.3.84
(13)	*bhav*	+ *a*	+ *i*		+ *t*	P.6.1.78
(14)	*bhav* +	*e*			+ *t*	P.6.1.87
	bhavet					

Here the augment *yāsUṬ* is regarded as a part of *lIṄ*, and *lIṄ* is replaced by *tiP*. As a result, *yāsUṬ* becomes a part of *ti*. The suffix *ti* is *sārvadhātuka*. The addition of *ŚaP* is conditioned by the term *sārvadhātuke* 'when a *sārvadhātuka* [suffix] follows' (P.3.1.67). Therefore, *ŚaP* is added after the finite verb ending has been introduced and before *yāsUṬ* + *tiP* as a whole.

8. Another, related problem is solved at the same time, that of the relation between P.3.4.102-3 (*sīyUṬ* and *yāsUṬ*) and P.3.4.107 (*sUṬ*). The problem is that *sUṬ*, which is only applicable before finite verb endings of *lIṄ* beginning with *t/th*, is prescribed by a special rule. As such it would set aside the augments *sīyUṬ* and *yāsUṬ*, which are general augments of *lIṄ*. The traditional solution is explained in the *KV* on P.3.4.107, wherein it is assumed that between P.3.4.102-3 and P.3.4.107 no *utsarga-apavāda* relation holds because *sUṬ* is the augment not of *lIṄ* (like *sīyUṬ/yāsUṬ*) but of *t/th*. Therefore, the *KV* says, *sīyUṬ/ yāsUṬ* and *sUṬ* have different domains of application.

But this solution cannot be correct for it does not apply when both *sīyUṬ/ yāsUṬ* and *sUṬ* are introduced after the finite verb ending has been added. The reason is that *sīyUṬ/yāsUṬ* are applicable before all finite verb endings of *lIṄ*, whereas *sUṬ* becomes applicable only before verb endings that begin with *t/th*. So there must be an *utsarga-apavāda* relation between *sīyUṬ/yāsUṬ* and *sUṬ*.

In the new interpretation of P.1.4.99 the augments *sīyUṬ* and *yāsUṬ* are introduced earlier, at the *lakāra*-stage, because *l* is called *parasmaipada*. The augment *sUṬ*, on the other hand, comes after the finite verb endings have been introduced. Therefore, in this interpretation, *sīyUṬ/ yāsUṬ* do have domains different from that of *sUṬ*. Consequently, the difficulty raised by tradition does not arise here.

9. Two more examples in which the traditional *prakriyā* presents difficulties deriving from the prior introduction of the finite verb endings are *babhūva* 'he has become' and *bhavitā* 'he shall become'.

(A) The augment *vUK*

(1)		*bhū*				*Dhātupāṭha* 1.1
(2)		*bhū*		+	*lIṬ*	P.3.2.115
(3)		*bhū* +	*vUK*	+	*lIṬ*	P.6.4.88
(4)	*bhūv* +	*bhūv*		+	*lIṬ*	P.6.1.8

(5)	*bhūv* + *bhūv*		+ *tiP*	P.3.4.78
(6)	*bhūv* + *bhūv*		+ *ṆaL*	P.3.4.82
(7)	*bhū* + *bhūv*		+ *a*	P.7.4.60
(8)	*bhu* + *bhūv*		+ *a*	P.7.4.59
(9)	*bha* + *bhūv*		+ *a*	P.7.4.73
(10)	*ba* + *bhūv*		+ *a*	P.8.4.54
	babhūva			

The augment *vUK* is regarded as part of *bhū* by P.1.1.46 and P.6.4.88. Therefore, at stage (4), *bhūv* is reduplicated as a whole.

In *babhūva* the finite verb ending is *anudātta* by *sthānivadbhāva* (*tiP*, P.3.1.4). The verbal base has the *udātta* accent by P.6.1.162. In addition, we have P.6.1.195, which says that before a suffix marked with *l* the immediately preceding element takes the *udātta* accent. Therefore, we finally derive *babhū́va*.

According to tradition, just as the *ārdhadhātuka vikaraṇas* are introduced after the finite verb ending has been added, the augment is introduced only after a finite verb ending has been added, although, in fact, the augment is conditioned by *l*. This gives rise to a problem. The first stages of the traditional *prakriyā* are as follows.

(1)		*bhū*		+ *lIṬ*	P.3.2.115
(2)	*bhū* +	*bhū*		+ *lIṬ*	P.6.1.8
(3)	*bhū* +	*bhū*		+ *tiP*	P.3.4.78
(4)	*bhū* +	*bhū*		+ *ṆaL*	P.3.4.82
(5)	*bhū* +	*bhū*	+ *vUK*	+ *a*	P.5.4.82

At stage (4) two rules become applicable, namely, P.7.2.115, which prescribes *vṛddhi* for the verbal base vowel, and P.6.4.88, which prescribes the augment *vUK*. The conflict is traditionally solved by assuming that P.6.4.88 is a *nitya* rule so that (by *pb.* 38) the *vUK*-rule prevails.[23] But, actually, there should be no conflict because augment rules are word-building rules.[24] Since they are conditioned by *l*, they are applied before the endings are introduced which cause morphophonemic changes.

(B) The suffix *tāsI*

(1)	*bhū*							
(2)	*bhū*				+	*lUṬ*	P.3.3.15
(3)	*bhū*		+	*tāsI*	+	*lUṬ*	P.3.1.33
(4)	*bhū*	+ *iṬ*	+	*tās*	+	*lUṬ*	P.3.4.114; 7.2.35
(5)	*bhū*	+ *i*	+	*tās*	+	*tiP*	P.3.4.78
(6)	*bhū*	+ *i*	+	*tās*	+	*Ḍā*	P.2.4.85
(7)	*bhū*	+ *i*	+	*t°*	+	*ā*	P.6.4.143
(8)	*bho*	+ *i*	+	*t*	+	*ā*	P.7.2.84
(9)	*bhav*	+ *i*	+	*t*	+	*ā*	P.6.1.78
	bhavitā						

In *bhavitā* the ending is *anudātta* by *sthānivadbhāva* (and by P.6.1.181). The *pratyaya tāsI* has the *udātta* accent by P.3.1.3 but the accent-bearing vowel is deleted. Then, by P.6.1.161, the accent is shifted to the ending. The augment *iṬ* is *anudātta* by a statement of Kātyāyana.[25] The verbal base is accented by P.6.1.162. Here the accent of the ending prevails (see note 28). Therefore, the form should read *bhavitā́*, which is not attested as a tense-formation in the Veda.[26] This form is to be distinguished grammatically from the homophonous form *bhavitā́*, which is a *tṛC* derivation (P.3.1.133, *antodātta* by P.6.1.163). One form of *bhavitā́* is a verb, the other is a noun.

In the traditional *prakriyā* the suffix *tāsI* is added after the introduction of the finite verb ending. But *tāsI* (like *sya*) is conditioned by *l*. Therefore, it should be introduced at the *lakāra*-stage.

10. The examples cited above are of *ārdhadhātuka vikaraṇas* conditioned by a *lakāra*, and they are to be introduced at the *lakāra*-stage before a finite verb ending has been introduced in the *prakriyā*. But, as stated in section 2, Pāṇini's procedure is different in the case of *vikaraṇas* conditioned by a *sārvadhātuka* suffix.[27] *Sārvadhātuka* suffixes are always elements added later. They do not belong to the earlier stages of the *prakriyā*. The question is, why has Pāṇini adopted a different procedure here?

According to P.3.4.113, finite verb endings and suffixes marked with *Ś* are called *sārvadhātuka*. As regards the verb endings, two exceptions are made: those of the perfect (*lIṬ*) and those of the precative (*āśirliṅ*) are called *ārdhadhātuka* (P.3.4.115-16). The suffixes marked with *Ś* are mainly those mentioned in the section dealing with *vikaraṇas* (P.3.1.68-81). The point to be kept in mind here is that these *vikaraṇas* are not conditioned by *l* but by a following *sārvadhātuka* suffix.

Two examples may suffice.

(A) The *sārvadhātuka* suffix *ŚaP*

(1)	*bhū*					
(2)	*bhū*			+	*lAṬ*	P.3.2.123
(3)	*bhū*			+	*tiP*	P.3.4.78
(4)	*bhū*	+	*ŚaP*	+	*ti*	P.3.1.68
(5)	*bho*	+	*a*	+	*ti*	P.7.3.84
(6)	*bhav*	+	*a*	+	*ti*	P.6.1.78
	bhavati					

Both *tiP* and *ŚaP* are *sārvadhātuka* suffixes. They are also both *anudātta* by P.3.1.4. The verbal base takes the *udātta* accent by P.6.1.162. Thus the finished form reads *bhávati.*

(B) The *ārdhadhātuka* suffix *yaK*

(1)	*bhū*					
(2)	*bhū*			+	*lAṬ*	P.3.2.123
(3)	*bhū*	+	*yaK*	+	*lAṬ*	P.3.1.67
(4)	*bhū*	+	*ya*	+	*ta*	P.3.4.78; 1.3.13; 1.4.100
(5)	*bhū*	+	*ya*	+	*te*	P.3.4.79
(6)	*bhū*	+	*ya*	+	*te*	P.7.3.25
	bhūyate					

YaK is an *ārdhadhātuka* suffix. *Ta* is a *sārvadhātuka* suffix. The verb ending is *anudātta* by P.6.1.186 (*ad-upadeśa*). *YaK* takes the *udātta* accent. Here the accent of the *vikaraṇa yaK*, being *sati śiṣṭa*,[28] prevails over that of the verbal base. Thus the finished form reads *bhūyáte*.

11. Why this difference in treatment between *vikaraṇas* conditioned by *l* and *vikaraṇas* conditioned by a *sārvadhātuka* suffix? Could Pāṇini not have phrased a rule like *laṭ-loṭ-laṅ-liṅ-kṣu śap* '*ŚaP* [is added to a verbal base, *dhātoḥ*, P.3.1.91] when [the *lakāras*] *lAṬ*, etc., follow'?[29] Why not introduce all *vikaraṇas* at the *lakāra*-stage and establish a common pattern?

The answer is that the *sārvadhātuka vikaraṇas*, apart from playing a role in the derivation of verb forms, also serve to derive nominal forms. They are also applicable before *kr̥t*-suffixes that are *sārvadhātuka* (*Śit*). Therefore, obviously, Pāṇini could not condition their introduction in the *prakriyā* uniformly by a *lakāra* by phrasing a rule like the one mentioned above.

Consider some examples based on the sequence P.3.1.137-39. These rules prescribe the suffix *Śa*, which is *sārvadhātuka*, and also a *kr̥t*-suffix. It is added, in the sense of *kartr̥*, by P.3.4.67.

(A)	(1)	*ut*	+	*pā*			+	*Śa*	P.3.1.137
	(2)	*ut*	+	*pā*	+	*ŚaP*	+	*a*	P.3.1.68
	(3)	*ut*	+	*pib*	+	*a*	+	*a*	P.7.3.78
	(4)	*ut*	+	*pib*	+			*a*	P.6.1.97
		utpiba							

(B)	(1)	*lip*			+	*Śa*	P.3.1.138
	(2)	*lip*	+	*ŚaP*	+	*a*	P.3.1.68
	(3)	*li-nUM-p*	+	*a*	+	*a*	P.7.1.57

	(4)	*linp*			+			*a*	P.6.1.97
	(5)	*liṃp*			+			*a*	P.8.3.24
	(6)	*limp*			+			*a*	P.8.4.58
		limpa							

(C)	(1)	*vid*							*Dhātupāṭha* 2.55
	(2)	*vid*	+	*ṆiC*					P.3.1.26
	(3)	*vid*	+	*i*			+	*Śa*	P.3.1.138
	(4)	*vid*	+	*i*	+	*ŚaP*	+	*a*	P.3.1.68
	(5)	*ved*	+	*i*	+	*a*	+	*a*	P.7.3.86
	(6)	*ved*	+	*e*	+	*a*	+	*a*	P.7.3.84
	(7)	*ved*	+	*ay*	+	*a*	+	*a*	P.6.1.78
	(8)	*ved*	+	*ay*	+			*a*	P.6.1.97
		vedaya							

(D)	(1)			*dā*			+	*Śa*	P.3.1.139
	(2)			*dā*	+	*ŚaP*	+	*a*	P.3.1.68
	(3)			*dā*	+	*ślu*	+	*a*	P.2.4.75
	(4)	*dā*	+	*dā*	+	°	+	*a*	P.6.1.10
	(5)	*da*	+	*dā*			+	*a*	P.7.4.59
	(6)	*da*	+	*d°*			+	*a*	P.6.4.64
		dada							

Examples (A) and (B) can technically be derived without the addition of a *vikaraṇa* because the substitute *pib* and the augment *nUM* are conditioned by the *kr̥t*-suffix *Śa* only. In (C) the *vikaraṇa ŚaP* is needed to have *guṇa* of the immediately preceding vowel. Since the suffix *Śa* is *Ṅit* by P.1.2.4, it will prohibit *guṇa* by P.1.1.5. But *ŚaP* is *Pit*. Therefore, it allows *guṇa*. In (D) *ŚaP* is required for the application of P.2.4.75 and the subsequent reduplication.

One more example, an *upapada* compound:

(E)	(1)	((*jana* + *am*) + (*ej* + *ṆiC*)) + *KHaŚ*	P.3.2.28
	(2)	((*jana* + °) + (*ej* + *i*)) + *a*	P.2.4.71
	(3)	((*jana*) + (*ej* + *i*)) + *ŚaP* + *a*	P.3.1.68
	(4)	((*jana* + *mUM*) + (*ej* + *i*)) + *a* + *a*	P.6.3.67
	(5)	((*janam*) + (*ej* + *e*)) + *a* + *a*	P.7.3.84
	(6)	((*janam*) + (*ej* + *ay*)) + *a* + *a*	P.6.1.78
	(7)	(*janam* + *ejay*) + *a*	P.6.1.97
		janamejaya	

Here *ŚaP* is needed to have *guṇa* of the immediately preceding vowel. Like *Śa*, *KHaŚ* is *Ṅit*. See the argument above with regard to example (C).

If Pāṇini had prescribed *Śa* and *KHaŚ* as substitutes of *l*, these elements would technically be *vikaraṇas* conveying the senses of tense and mood also. As this is clearly not desirable, a distinction is required: some *sārvadhātuka vikaraṇas* are dependent on *lakāras*, others are not. Now the other question arises, namely, why are traditionally the *lakāra*-dependent *sārvadhātuka vikaraṇas* introduced after the *lakāras* have been replaced by wordform-elements? A possible answer is: in order to ensure some semblance of uniform treatment for all *sārvadhātuka vikaraṇas*. Just as in the *kr̥danta* derivations *ŚaP* comes after a wordform-element [*Śa*/*KHaŚ*] has been introduced, so also in the *tiṅanta* derivations, where *tiP*, etc., function as the wordform-elements.

12. So far, the process of establishing a reason for Pāṇini's different treatment of *ārdhadhātuka* and *sārvadhā*-

tuka vikaraṇas in the derivation of finite verbs has proceeded on the basis of the assumption that *sārvadhātuke* in P.3.1.67 represents a *parasaptamī*. As stated in note 2, a *parasaptamī* requires the presence of a following grammatical element in a particular stage of the derivation.

But what if *sārvadhātuke* in P.3.1.67 is taken as a *viṣayasaptamī*? In that case, the formal presence of a finite verb ending is no longer required for introducing the *sārvadhātuka vikaraṇas*. We could add them at the *lakāra*-stage.

Can we muster philological support from the *Aṣṭādhyāyī* for this hypothesis? There the term *ārdhadhātuke* is used twice in the sense of a *viṣayasaptamī*.[30] The only possible use of *sārvadhātuke* in the same sense is precisely P.1.3.67.[31] Thus we can only say that the use of a *viṣayasaptamī* in a closely related term is known here.

But there is at least one argument in favor of the hypothesis. In the case of the *ārdhadhātuka vikaraṇas* the *sati śiṣṭa* accent principle[32] works very well because these *vikaraṇas* are introduced in one of the early stages of the *prakriyā*. It does not work as well in the case of *Śit vikaraṇas* because, on the traditional assumption just mentioned, these *vikaraṇas* are added in the finite verb derivation after the endings have been formally introduced. But, if these *vikaraṇas* are also introduced at an early stage in the *prakriyā*, the *sati śiṣṭa* principle will work very well and we can justify the *udātta* accent of finite verb endings when required.

13. The occurrences of the *viṣayasaptamī* are restricted to the second and third *adhyāyas*. To be more precise, we may say that they occur before P.3.1.91 (*dhātoḥ*). Here the treatment of morphology begins: first that of morphemes added to a verbal base (*kr̥t* and *tiṄ*), then that of morphemes added to a nominal stem (*suP* and *taddhita*). Thus P.3.1.91 marks the boundary between base/stem-forming rules and rules dealing with suffixation.

This division in the *Aṣṭādhyāyī* corresponds with the order of the word-building process. We proceed from the left to the right--from the base, to the *vikaraṇas*, to the endings. The augments occupy a position between any two of these three. On this basis the order of application of rules may be stated as follows.

1. Base/stem-forming rules. These include rules dealing with verbal base substitutes (P.2.4.36ff.) and *vikaraṇas* (and their deletion). They also include rules dealing with compound formation.

2. Suffixation rules (*kr̥t*, *tiṄ*, *suP*, *taddhita*).

3. Morphologically and phonologically conditioned rules.

The corresponding divisions of the *Aṣṭādhyāyī*, according to the rule categories, are as follows.

1. Category 1: up to P.3.1.91.

2. Category 2: from P.3.1.91 to the end of the fifth *adhyāya*.

3. Category 3: the *adhyāyas* 6-8.

Here the rule categories 1 and 2 represent the word-building rules. They provide the analytical wordform-elements out of which a usable word (*pada*) is forged by applying the rules belonging to category 3.

14. From what has been stated above one conclusion may finally be drawn regarding the order of the word-building process and the structure of the *Aṣṭādhyāyī*. The word-building process proceeds in what is visually a left-to-right direction. This direction corresponds to what (in the order of application of rules) is a time sequence, earlier-later. This correspondence lies at the base of the *sati śiṣṭa* accent principle. But, stripped of its accent connotation, it can be said to be the governing principle of both the word-building process and of the organization of the *Aṣṭādhyāyī*. That is to say, Pāṇini's derivational procedure as reflected in the organization of the *Aṣṭādhyāyī* is dependent on one principle, namely, that of the left-to-right processing order. Rules dealing with left-side elements are introduced earlier than rules dealing with right-side elements.

This ordering principle has nothing to do with a feeding relation between rules in which the application of one rule is made dependent on the effect of the application of another rule. It has nothing to do, either, with the question of conflict of rules. To solve a conflict, other principles apply: *paratva, siddha/asiddha,* and *utsarga-apavāda.*

It is this left-to-right processing order that is violated by the position of the *taddhita* and *samāsa* sections in the present edition of the *Aṣṭādhyāyī*. The structural reason is that the rules belonging to these sections presuppose the existence of a fully derived *pada*. Therefore, in order to make the *Aṣṭādhyāyī* a more perfect processing machine, a ***word-processor*** in the literary sense of the word, these sections should be lifted from their present position and placed after the *asiddha* section.

Notes

1. *Vikaraṇa* literally means 'a change-producer'. Pāṇini does not recognize a separate class of suffixes called *vikaraṇa*. The term is used once in a *Vārttika* (*Vt.* VIII on P.6.1.186) and a number of times in the *Mbh.* In Pāṇini's grammar *vikaraṇa*s correspond to wordform-elements that occur between the verbal base and the finite verb ending or a *kr̥t*-suffix.

   As regards the derivation of finite verbs, *vikaraṇa*s may be divided into three groups: conjugation markers, tense/mood markers such as *cli* (P.3.1.43) and *yāsUṬ* (P.3.4.103), and the passive voice marker *yaK* (P.3.1.67). For a detailed enumeration, see V. S. Apte, *The Practical Sanskrit-English Dictionary*, rev. ed. (Poona, 1957). The list occurs in vol. 3, appendix F, "Grammatical Concordance" (by S. D. Joshi), 104-5, s.v.
2. The assumption is that *sārvadhātuke* in P.3.1.67 represents a *parasaptamī* not a *viṣayasaptamī*. This assumption is traditional. The difference between a *parasaptamī* and a *viṣayasaptamī* is that the first requires

the presence of the element named by the term in the locative, whereas the second does not. See also *KA*, note 1.

3. P.3.1.91 (*dhātoḥ*).
4. In P.3.4.77. *Laḥ* (that is, *l*) is the common element in the symbols *lAṬ*, etc., for tense, mood, and voice (P.3.4. 69) in the *Aṣṭādhyāyī*. For the role of *l* in the derivation of finite verbs, see *VIBHA*, "Introduction," sect. 3. The formal substitutes of *l* are enumerated in P.3.4.78.
5. The result is that the endings can no longer be added immediately after the verbal base.
6. After P.1.3.12, namely, in P.3.1.33-86.
7. Reference is to *pb*. 38, for which see *PN*, 185.
8. *Āśrayati.*
9. Reference is to P.3.1.54-55, wherein the locative terms *ātmanepadeṣu* and *parasmaipadeṣu* serve as a condition for the operations prescribed.
10. Although P.3.4.78 mentions eighteen finite verb endings, the *KV* mentions the first nine only because elsewhere the designation *ātmanepada* prevails, by P.1.4.100, which is an *apavāda* 'exception' to P.1.4.99.
11. The rule says that before the aorist marker *sIC*, followed by *parasmaipada* endings, the final vowel *i*, *u*, or *r̥* of the verbal base takes *vr̥ddhi*.
12. Reference is to P.1.1.56. Thus the real designee of the designation *parasmaipada* is *l*. The endings *tiP*, etc., are called *parasmaipada* by *sthānivadbhāva* only.
13. This *pratyāhāra* includes the second series of nine finite verb endings mentioned in P.3.4.78.

14. Mentioned in P.3.2.124 as a substitute of *lAṬ*.
15. By way of *anuvṛtti* in P.1.4.100.
16. *Sāhacaryād vā . . . iti vyākhyeyam* is to be read as one sentence.
17. Reference is to *pb*. 1, for which see *PN*, 2.
18. Nāgeśa is wrong. He should say that after verbal bases marked with *anudātta* or *Ṅ* the symbol *l* will always be called *parasmaipada*. But this is not a difficulty because at a later stage in the *prakriyā* this symbol will be replaced by *taṄ* or *āna*, and these are called *ātmanepada*.
19. We have three *Vārttika*s on this rule, all dealing with the question of how to achieve coapplication of the designation *parasmaipada* (or *ātmanepada*) with the *puruṣa*-designations prescribed by P.1.4.101. In the *ekasaṃjñā* section, in which P.1.4.99 has been put, only one designation can be applied at a time, namely, the one prescribed by the later rule. Therefore, how to ensure that the designation *parasmaipada* (or *ātmanepada*) is not set aside by the other designations? This problem is solved by Kātyāyana by means of the *jñāpaka*-procedure (*Vt.* III on P.1.4.99). The rule that offers the desired clue is P.7.2.1 (see note 11). If the *puruṣa*-designations had set aside the designations *parasmaipada* and *ātmanepada*, then P.7.2.1, which prescribes the *vikaraṇa sIC* before *parasmaipada* endings, becomes meaningless. The reason is that the finite verb endings cannot be called *parasmaipada* but only *prathama-* , *madhyama-*, or *uttamapuruṣa*.

The clue may be had from P.1.4.99-100, also, because we must give scope (*avakāśa*) to the designations mentioned here in order to prevent their being stalemated. Then why does Kātyāyana refer to P.7.2.1? His reason must be that the designation *parasmaipada* has scope, namely, with reference to the participle ending *ŚatR̥*. Therefore, he refers to a rule that deals with finite verb endings, namely, P.7.2.1.

20. See S. D. Joshi and Saroja Bhate, *The Fundamentals of Anuvr̥tti*, Publications of the Centre of Advanced Study in Sanskrit, class B, no. 9 (Pune: University of Poona, 1984), 45-47. The examples given in this book are all of the discontinuation of items on the grounds of (lack of) syntactic compatibility. One more possibility may be considered here, namely, that the nominative word *laḥ* is continued as a genitive word in P.1.4.100 by *vibhaktivipariṇāma*. But one of the findings of Joshi and Bhate's *anuvr̥tti* book (see also p. 241) is that this goes against Pāṇinian procedure. If a genitive word is needed, it must be expressly stated. See, for example, the sequence P.1.2.45-48 (wherein the genitive *prātipadikasya* is expressly mentioned) and the sequence P.3.1.43-44 (wherein the genitive *cleḥ* is expressly stated).
21. See note 2.
22. The three *Vārttikas* on P.3.4.103 are concerned only with the questions of why *yāsUṬ* should be *Ṅit* and why it should be described as having the *udātta* accent.
23. See Bhaṭṭojī Dīkṣita, *Siddhānta-kaumudī* (Bombay: Nirnaya Sagara Press, 1915), No. 2174 on P.6.4.88.

24. That is, rules providing the elements that together constitute the raw material of the wordform.

25. *Vārttika* VI on P.3.1.3. Patañjali explains the relevant part of the *Vārttika* as *āgamā anudāttā bhavantīti vakṣyāmi* 'I [Kātyāyana] am going to state that augments are accentless'.

26. W. D. Whitney, *Sanskrit Grammar*, 2d ed. (Cambridge: Harvard University Press, 1889), § 946, "the tense-use begins, but rather sparingly, in the Brāhmaṇas. . . ." J. L. Brockington, in *Righteous Rama: The Evolution of an Epic* (London: Oxford University Press 1984), notes that in the core books of the *Rāmāyaṇa*, with the exception of the first twenty-seven *sargas* of the *Ayodhyākāṇḍa*, the use of the periphrastic future is extremely rare (p. 19). It seems doubtful that the rules dealing with the periphrastic future formed part of the original *Aṣṭādhyāyī*. The following points may be noted.

    1. The suffix *Ḍā* is introduced at the end of the second *adhyāya* (P.2.4.85) as a loose appendix, and the rule concerned shows no connection with the preceding rules. The substitutes of verb-ending suffixes are not introduced in the *Aṣṭādhyāyī* until the beginning of the third *adhyāya*.

    2. P.3.3.15, which prescribes this future, is a kind of replica of P.3.2.111 (*anadyatane laṅ*). It has no intrinsic connection with either the preceding or

the following rule. If it is dropped, the continuity of rules does not suffer.

3. Finite verbs are usually unaccented in the utterance (by P.8.1.28). But P.8.1.29 makes an exception for the periphrastic future. The reason these forms are excluded from the usual verb treatment must be that they were not originally verb forms (Whitney, *Sanskrit Grammar*, § 942b).

If it is assumed that the rules dealing with these future forms are a later addition to the *Aṣṭādhyāyī*, we have another clue for Pāṇini's rather early date, presumably that of the early Brāhmaṇa period.

27. On the assumption that *sārvadhātuke* in P.3.1.67 (continued to P.3.1.86) represents a *parasaptamī* (see note 2).

28. *Vt.* IX on P.6.1.158. The idea is that a *pada* can have only one (*udātta*) accent. But, while deriving the *pada*, we may have to introduce elements that have an *udātta* accent of their own. So how to retain one accent and eliminate the rest? The answer to this question is provided by the *sati śiṣṭa* accent principle, which states that the accent that is taught, when another accent-bearing element has already been introduced, prevails. That is to say, the accent of the element added last in the *prakriyā* prevails, at least if it has an *udātta* accent of its own.

29. Here *lIṬ*, *lR̥Ṭ*, *lR̥Ṅ*, *lUṬ*, *lUṄ*, and *āśirliṅ* are excluded because in connection with these *lakāras* the suffix *ŚaP* has not been prescribed.

30. In P.2.4.35 and P.3.1.31. This is admitted by tradition; see the *KV* on these rules. Elsewhere the term *ārdhadhātuke* occurs in rules dealing with morphological and phonological operations, where it has the sense of a *parasaptamī* (P.1.1.4, 6.4.4, 7.3.84, 7.4.49).
31. The other occurrences are in P.6.4.87, 6.4.110, 7.2.76, 7.3.84, 7.3.95, and 7.4.21. Here *sārvadhātuke* represents a *parasaptamī*.
32. See note 28.

References

KV	*The Kāśikāvṛtti with the Nyāsa or Pañcikā Commentary and Padamañjarī.* Critically edited by Swami Dwarikadas Shastri and Pandit Kalikaprasad Shukla. Vols. 1-6. Varanasi, 1965-67.
Mbh.	*The Vyākaraṇa-Mahābhāṣya of Patañjali.* Edited by F. Kielhorn. Reprint of the edition of 1880-1885. Osnabrück, 1970.
PN	*The Paribhāṣenduśekhara of Nāgojibhaṭṭa.* Edited by F. Kielhorn. Second edition, edited by K. V. Abhyankar. Part II, "Translation and Notes." Pune, 1960.
Proceedings	*Proceedings of the International Seminar on Studies in the Aṣṭādhyāyī of Pāṇini.* Edited

by S. D. Joshi and S. D. Laddu. Publications of the Centre of Advanced Study in Sanskrit, class E, no. 9. Pune, 1983.

VIBHA *Patañjali's Vyākaraṇa-Mahābhāṣya: Vibhaktyāhnika* (P.2.3.18-2.3.45). Introduction, Text, Translation, and Notes by S. D. Joshi and J. A. F. Roodbergen. Publications of the Centre of Advanced Study in Sanskrit, class C, no. 12. Pune, 1980.

BIBLIOGRAPHY

Shivram Dattatray Joshi

1959 "Grammatical Concordance" (Appendix F). In V. S. Apte, *A Practical Sanskrit-English Dictionary*, volume 3. Pune, pp. 77-112.

1960 "Kauṇḍabhaṭṭa on the Meaning of Sanskrit Verbs." Harvard University dissertation, unpublished.

1962 "Verbs and Nouns in Sanskrit." *Indian Linguistics*, Vol. 23, pp. 60-63.

1964 "Upamāyāḥ Śrautyārthītvam" (in Sanskrit). *Śāradāpākṣika* (July), pp. 37-42.

1965a "The Nyāya Theory of the Denotation of the Root and Verb Ending Suffixes." In *S. Ware Commemoration Volume*. Wai, pp. 300-12.

1965b "Two Methods of Interpreting Pāṇini." *Journal of the University of Poona*, Vol. 23, pp. 53-61.

1966a "Patañjali's Definition of a Word--an Interpretation." *Bulletin of the Deccan College Research Institute*, Vol. 25, pp. 65-70.

1966b "Adjectives and Substantives as a Single Class in the 'Parts of Speech.'" *Journal of the University of Poona*, Vol. 25, pp. 19-30.

1967 *The Sphoṭanirṇaya of Kauṇḍa Bhaṭṭa.* Edited, with Translation, Explanatory Notes, and Introduction. Publications of the CASS, Class C, No. 2. Pune, pp. 1-243.

1968a *Patañjali's Vyākaraṇa-Mahābhāṣya, Samarthāhnika.* Edited, with Translation and Explanatory Notes. Publications of the CASS, Class C, No. 3. Pune, pp. i-xix, 1-32, 1-123.

1968b "Word-integrity and Syntactic Analysis." *Journal of the University of Poona* (Humanities Section), No. 27, pp. 165-73.

1969a *Patañjali's Vyākaraṇa-Mahābhāṣya, Avyayībhātatpuruṣāhnika.* Edited, with Translation and Explanatory Notes (in collaboration with J. A. F. Roodbergen). Publications of the CASS, Class C, No. 5. Pune, pp. i-xxvii, 1-71, 1-256.

1969b "Sentence Structure According to Pāṇini." In *Professor R. N. Dandekar Felicitation Volume. Indian Antiquary*, 3d Series, Nos. 1-4, pp. 14-26.

1970a "Dhātusambandhe pratyayāh." In *Ṛṣikalpanyāsa, Rajeshwarshastri Dravid Felicitation Volume.* Allahabad, pp. 48-50.

1970b "Language Study in Ancient India." *Souvenir, First All India Conference of Linguistics.* Pune, pp. 15-23.

1970c "Vākya āni Vākyārtha." In *Saṃskṛti-Sugandha (Shetye Felicitation Volume).* Pune, pp. 185-90.

1971 *Patañjali's Vyākaraṇa-Mahābhāṣya, Karmadhārayāhnika.* Edited, with Translation and Notes (in collaboration with J. A. F. Roodbergen). Publications of the CASS, Class C, No. 6. Pune, pp. i-xxviii, 1-58, 1-275.

1973a *Patañjali's Vyākaraṇa-Mahābhāṣya, Tatpuruṣāhnika.* Edited, with Translation and Notes (in collaboration with J. A. F. Roodbergen). Publications of the CASS, Class C, No. 7. Pune, pp. i-xxiv, 1-52, 1-268.

1973b "Treatment of Compounds in Sanskrit Grammar--A Survey." In *Studies in Historical Sanskrit Lexicography.* Pune, pp. 55-66.

1974a “The Mīmāṃsā Theories of Verbal Denotation.” In *Viśva-Bandhu Commemoration Volume. Vishveshvaranand Indological Journal*, Vol. 21, Nos. I-II. Hoshiarpur, pp. 139-44.

1974b “Pāṇini's Treatment of Kāraka-relations.” In *Charu Deva Shastri Felicitation Volume* (Linguistics Section). Delhi, pp. 258-70.

1974c *Patañjali's Vyākaraṇa-Mahābhāṣya, Bahuvrīhidvandvāhnika.* Edited, with Translation and Notes (written by J. A. F. Roodbergen). Publications of the CASS, Class C, No. 9. Pune, pp. i-lxiv, 1-72, 1-248.

1974d A Review of the *Śābdataraṅgiṇī* by Subrahmanya Śāstri. In *Annals of the Bhandarkar Oriental Research Institute*, Vol. 55, pp. 305-8.

1974e “Samāsa āṇi vigrahavākya.” In *Marathawada Saṃśodhana Maṇḍala Vārṣika.* Aurangabad, pp. 121-26.

1975 *Patañjali's Vyākaraṇa-Mahābhāṣya, Kārakāhnika.* Edited, with Translation and Notes (in collaboration with J. A. F. Roodbergen). Publications of the CASS, Class C, No. 10. Pune, pp. i-xiv, 1-73, 1-302.

1976a “Pāṇini's Rules 1.4.49, 1.4.50 and 1.4.51.” In *CASS Studies, No. 3.* Publications of the CASS, Class E, No. 4. Pune, pp. 59-70.

1976b *Patañjali's Vyākaraṇa-Mahābhāṣya, Anabhihitāhnika.* Edited, with Translation and Notes (in collaboration with J. A. F. Roodbergen). Publications of the CASS, Class C, No. 11. Pune, pp. i-xlxii, 1-45, 1-41.

1976c "Sanskrit Grammar." In *Ramakrishna Gopal Bhandarkar as an Indologist, A Symposium.* Pune, pp. 113-42.

1977 "Bhartṛhari's Concept of Pratibhā: A Theory on the Nature of Language Acquisition." In *Shri Ghanashyam Birla Volume.* Delhi, pp. 828-34.

1978 "The Ordering of the Rules in Pāṇini's Grammar." *Annals of the B.O.R.I.*, Vols. 58-59, pp. 667-74.

1979a "The Contribution of R.G. Bhandarkar to the Study of Sanskrit Grammar." In *Sanskrit and Indian Studies (Daniel H. H. Ingalls Felicitation Volume).* Cambridge, Mass., pp. 33-60.

1979b "Siddha and Asiddha in Pāṇinian Phonology" (in collaboration with P. Kiparsky). In *Current Approaches to Phonological Theory*. Bloomington, Ind., pp. 223-50.

1980a *Candrasenaḥ Durgadeśasya Yuvarājaḥ.* (Sanskrit Adaptation of Shakespeare's *Hamlet, The Prince of Denmark,* in collaboration with Vighnahari Deo). Publications of the CASS, Class G, No. 1. Pune, pp. 1-80.

1980b "Kauṇḍa Bhaṭṭa on the Meanings of Case-endings." In *Bhāratībhānam (Dr. K. V. Sarma Felicitation Volume).* Hoshiarpur, pp. 88-95.

1980c "Kauṇḍa Bhaṭṭa on Sphoṭa." In *A Corpus of Indian Studies (Essays in Honour of Professor Gaurinath Śāstri).* Calcutta, pp. 221-35.

1980d *Patañjali's Vyākaraṇa-Mahābhāṣya, Vibhaktyāhnika.* Edited, with Translation and Notes (in collaboration with J. A. F. Roodbergen). Publications of the CASS, Class C, No. 12. Pune, pp. l-xxxiii, 1-26, 1-114.

1981a "Kauṇḍa Bhaṭṭa on the Meaning of the Negative Particle." In *Studies in Indian Philosophy (A Memorial Volume in Honour of Pundit Sukhalalji Sanghvi).* Ahmedabad.

1981b *Patañjali's Vyākaraṇa-Mahābhāṣya, Prātipadikārtha-śeṣāhnika.* Edited, with Translation and Notes (in collaboration with J. A. F. Roodbergen). Publications of the CASS, Class C, No. 14. Pune, pp. i-xxx, 1-48, 1-175.

1981c "Siddhāntakaumudī." In *Marāthwāda Saṃśodhana Maṇḍala Vārṣika.* Aurangabad, pp. 13-34.

1982a "The Functions of Asiddhatva and Sthānivadbhāva in Pāṇini's Aṣṭādhyāyī." In *CASS Studies, No. 6.* Pune, pp. 153-68.

1982b "Kauṇḍa Bhaṭṭa on the Meaning of Compounds." In *K. K. Raja Felicitation Volume.* Madras, pp. 369-89.

1982c "Pāṇini's Rules: 2.2.11 and 2.4.2." In *Golden Jubilee Volume.* Pune, pp. 123-28.

1982d Presidential Address. In *Proceedings*, Indian Linguistics Section of the 30th Session of the All-India Oriental Conference (1980). Pune, pp. 91-111.

1982e "The Reflexive Constructions in Pāṇini." In *CASS Studies, No. 6.* Pune, pp. 199-217.

1982f "Siddhāntakaumudī." *Vidyā (Journal of the Gujarath University).* Vol. 35, Nos. 1-2, pp. 1-18.

1983a "Pāṇini's Rule 1.3.67." In *Surabhi* (*Sreekrishna Sarma Felicitation Volume*). Tirupati, pp. 63-74.

1983b "The Structure of the Aṣṭādhyāyī in Historical Perspective" (in collaboration with J. A. F. Roodbergen). In *Proceedings of the International Seminar on Pāṇini, 1983.* Pune, pp. 59-95.

1984a *The Fundamentals of Anuvṛtti* (in collaboration with Saroja Bhate). Pune, pp. 1-305.

1984b "Pāṇini." *Itihāspatrikā*, Vol. 4, No. 3, pp. 79-90.

1984c "The Role of Boundaries in the Aṣṭādhyāyī." In *Amr̥tadhārā (Professor R. N. Dandekar Felicitation Volume)*. Delhi, pp. 181-86.

1985a "On P.1.1.56" (in collaboration with J. A. F. Roodbergen). *Journal of the American Oriental Society*, Vol. 105, pp. 469-77.

1985b "The Role of the Particle *ca* in the Interpretation of the Aṣṭādhyāyī" (in collaboration with Saroja Bhate). In *Proceedings of the International Seminar on Pāṇini, 1985*. Pune, pp. 167-227.

1986 *Patañjali's Vyākaraṇa-Mahābhāṣya, Paspaśāhnika*. Edited, with Translation and Notes (in collaboration with J. A. F. Roodbergen). Publications of the CASS, Class C, No. 15. Pune, pp. i-xxiv, 1-14, 1-217.

1987a *Lokaprajñā: Pundit T. S. Srinivasa Shastri Felicitation Volume*. Chief Editor. Puri.

1987b "On Siddha, Asiddha and Sthānivat" (in collaboration with J. A. F. Roodbergen). *Annals of B.O.R.I.* (special issue, Ramakrishna Gopal Bhandarkar 150th Birth-Anniversary Volume), Vol. 68, pp. 541-49.

1987c "Traditional and Modern Linguistic Approach to Pāṇini." In *Select Papers from SALA-7*. Bloomington, Ind., pp. 220-35.

1988a *An Encyclopaedic Sanskrit Dictionary on Historical Principles*, Vol. 3, Pt. 2. General Editor. Pune.

1988b "The Rejection of P.1.1.58: A Conformation of the Exclusively Positive Aspect of Sthānivadbhāva" (in collaboration with J. A. F. Roodbergen). *Annals of B.O.R.I.*, Vol. 69, pp. 217-28.

1989 *Patañjali's Vyākaraṇa-Mahābhāṣya, Sthānivadbhāvāhnika*, Part 1. Edited, with Translation and Notes (in collaboration with J. A. F. Roodbergen). Publications of the Bhandarkar Oriental Research Institute. Pune.

1989a "Patañjali's Views on *Apaśabdas*." In *Dialectes dans les Littératures Indo-Aryennes*. Edited by Colette Caillat. Paris, pp. 267-274.

www.ingramcontent.com/pod-product-compliance
Lightning Source LLC
Chambersburg PA
CBHW031133160426
43193CB00008B/121
9780891480655